POLITICS and GEOPOLITICS

Praise for the Book

Most of the countries of South Asia—from Pakistan to Sri Lanka, and from Nepal to the Maldives—having secured independence only after the Second World War, nevertheless have a long history of close but vexed relations amongst them, with each of them nurturing a range of grievances. The shadow of China to the North of the whole region falls increasingly strongly across its countries, not just from the North but also due to its ambitious and constantly growing maritime activities, and the attractions of the Belt and Road Initiative.

For these reasons, and also due to the expertise of this volume's authors, *Politics and Geopolitics* offers a valuable contribution to the fast-growing field of scholarship on South Asia's international relevance and profile, the drivers of national and regional decision-making in each of its countries, their various relationships with China, and the geo-strategic implications thereof.

—**David M. Malone**, Rector of the United Nations University and Under-Secretary-General of the United Nations

As China 'moves closer to the centre of the world stage' and America makes a 'comeback', India faces a very different world at the beginning of the third decade of this century. The pandemic of 2020 has exposed the fragility of world order, while the developments in our periphery have brought into clearer focus the necessity of quickening the pace of the strategic re-adjustment of Indian foreign policy. China's rise is complicating the situation and the shrinking strategic space is not exclusive to our neighbourhood; there is no 'backyard' in a globalized world for any nation. There are only shared spaces, and what is important, therefore, is our capacity and the will to protect critical national interests in this space.

It is this challenge that *Politics and Geopolitics* seeks to address. It explores the possibilities for forward bilateral engagement in the strategic neighbourhood with the hindsight of challenges, and suggests workable options for policy-makers in what might well turn out to be the defining decade for Indian foreign policy in a re-defined neighbourhood.

—**Vijay Gokhale**, Former Foreign Secretary of India

POLITICS and GEOPOLITICS

DECODING INDIA'S NEIGHBOURHOOD CHALLENGE

Edited by

HARSH V. PANT

RUPA

Published by
Rupa Publications India Pvt. Ltd 2021
7/16, Ansari Road, Daryaganj
New Delhi 110002

Sales centres:
Allahabad Bengaluru Chennai
Hyderabad Jaipur Kathmandu
Kolkata Mumbai

Anthology copyright © Rupa Publications India Pvt. Ltd
Introduction copyright © Harsh V. Pant
Copyright for individual pieces vests with the respective authors

All rights reserved.
No part of this publication may be reproduced, transmitted,
or stored in a retrieval system, in any form or by any means,
electronic, mechanical, photocopying, recording or otherwise,
without the prior permission of the publisher.

The views and opinions expressed in this book are
the author's own and the facts are as reported by her
which have been verified to the extent possible,
and the publishers are not in any way liable for the same.

ISBN: 978-93-90918-57-7

Eighth impression 2022

15 14 13 12 11 10 9 8

The moral right of the author has been asserted.

Printed in India

This book is sold subject to the condition that it shall not, by way
of trade or otherwise, be lent, resold, hired out, or otherwise circulated,
without the publisher's prior consent, in any form of binding or cover
other than that in which it is published.

CONTENTS

Preface *vii*

Introduction *ix*

1. Afghanistan: Ancient Ties, New-Age Partnership　1
   Jayant Prasad

2. Pakistan: Inimical Neighbour　21
   Aparna Pande

3. China: End of the Era of Expansionism　38
   Gautam Bambawale

4. Nepal: Old Friendship, New Freeze　56
   Manjeev Singh Puri

5. Bhutan: Druk Bond　79
   V.P. Haran

6. Bangladesh: A Golden Chapter in Bilateral Ties　101
   Pinak Ranjan Chakravarty

7. Myanmar: Time to Act East Harder　126
   Gautam Mukhopadhaya

8. Sri Lanka: Towards New Turbulence 151
   Indrani Bagchi

9. The Maldives: The Island of Hope 168
   N. Sathiya Moorthy and Vinitha Revi

Notes 189
List of contributors 207
Index 209

PREFACE

Debates about India's role in South Asia have been a constant feature of India's strategic milieu. Over the last seven decades, India's role in its neighbourhood has evolved in line with the wider regional and global environment. Even as New Delhi's global footprint has expanded in accordance with its rising ambitions, doubts have continued to persist about its ability to lead in its immediate neighbourhood. At the same time, the larger picture of South Asia has also been transformed with the entry of China into the region, much like in other parts of the world.

Like its predecessors, the Modi government has also tried to prioritize South Asia in its foreign policy matrix with its 'Neighbourhood First' approach and has tried to be more proactive in dealing with its neighbours. Yet, challenges have been many as new geopolitical and geoeconomic realities have been confronted by Indian policymakers. The very idea of 'South Asia' has undergone a transformation in more ways than one.

This book is an attempt to examine and analyse some of the recent changes and challenges in India's neighbourhood. I would like to thank all the distinguished contributors, who so readily agreed to write despite their busy schedules. Each one of them deserves a special mention for agreeing to the timeline and sticking to it. It is their hard work that shines through in the pages of this book. Of course, the whole project would not have happened without the support of Yamini Chowdhury and her excellent team at Rupa Publications. From convincing me to take on this project to delivering the final published version, Yamini was instrumental in making this volume possible. My gratitude to her, Manali Das and the entire team at Rupa. I am also thankful to Observer Research Foundation and all my colleagues there who have given me a place where one can work quietly and focus on the world of ideas. Finally, my family has been supporting me for all these years and without them, nothing would have been possible.

Harsh V. Pant,
New Delhi

INTRODUCTION

HARSH V. PANT

In May 2014, shortly after being elected to office, Prime Minister Narendra Modi invited his counterparts from Afghanistan, Bangladesh, Bhutan, the Maldives, Nepal, Pakistan and Sri Lanka—members of the South Asian Association for Regional Cooperation (SAARC)—to his inauguration.[1] It was a deft exercise in public diplomacy, as no previous prime minister had made such a grand gesture, with the swearing-in ceremony being seen as an essentially 'domestic event'. It was also in keeping with his Bharatiya Janata Party's campaign manifesto, which had promised to improve India's ties with its neighbours.

Modi used the occasion to announce his 'Neighbourhood First' initiative, a new focus on prioritizing relations with SAARC member states.[2] The project was intended to give a much-needed boost to regional trade and investments and lead the way in addressing geopolitical tensions. It was also aimed at providing a natural—and lasting—bulwark against China's relentless attempts to expand its footprint across the region, especially with its Belt and Road Initiative (BRI).

Soon after coming to power, the Modi government promised

to give priority to our country's relationship with its immediate neighbours. Relations with Sri Lanka and Bangladesh saw a dramatic improvement, while Nepal was given due attention too. With Afghanistan, ties were galvanized, with security cooperation taking centre stage. Except for the Maldives, Modi visited all of India's neighbours and tried to reassure them of New Delhi's promise to deliver on its commitments.[3]

However, a few years down the line, there is a refrain that India has lost the plot in its immediate vicinity with mixed results across its neighbours. In Sri Lanka, domestic political developments continue to shape bilateral engagement with India, while in Nepal, a vocal critic of India has assumed power with a significant political mandate.[4] Pakistan continues to be a problem even as China's clout has grown markedly around India's periphery, further constraining New Delhi's ability to push its regional agenda. Ties with Bangladesh and Afghanistan seemingly hinge on the continuation of the present political dispensation in office.

In many ways, there is nothing new in the lament today about India's declining regional clout. This is a part of the Indian discourse and comes to the fore every few years with singular constancy. Contrary to what many suggest, there was never a golden age of Indian predominance in South Asia and the Indian Ocean Region (IOR). Smaller states in the region have always had enough agency to chart out their own foreign policy pathways: sometimes, they converged with those of India, and at other times, they varied significantly. There have always been 'extra regional' powers, which have come to the aid of India's neighbours, often to New Delhi's discomfiture. Yet, the challenge that China poses to India today in South Asia and beyond is of a different order.

The Sino-Indian Contestation

The year 2020 saw Sino-Indian ties plummeting to new depths with the crisis on the Himalayan frontier.[5] In June that year, there was a deadly clash between troops on the two sides, resulting in the death of 20 Indian soldiers and an unspecified number of Chinese soldiers. Since then, there have been sporadic incidents of firing across the Line of Actual Control (LAC), which the two nations have blamed on the other. This is the first time in 45 years that shots have been fired along this border, breaking the 1996 pact between both countries that barred the use of guns and explosives along the LAC.[6] After nine rounds of high-level military talks, a disengagement process began in February 2021 in the Pangong Tso lake region, which witnessed the return of Chinese and Indian troops and armour to their permanent bases. While the Indian troops still continue to lock horns with the Chinese at multiple sites along the LAC, this move is being widely viewed as the beginning of a long-drawn-out de-escalation process between the two Asian giants. As the two nations brace for a protracted stand-off with substantial force deployments, the LAC is likely to continue to remain 'hot', with military activity in the form of occasional violent clashes mirroring the Line of Control, which is the de facto boundary dividing Kashmir between India and Pakistan.

The year 2020 was when the romanticism around the Sino-Indian ties finally collapsed for good. There was a naïve belief in New Delhi, despite all the evidence to the contrary, that India will be able to manage China diplomatically and that it was possible to keep the shadow of the border dispute away from the larger trajectory of bilateral engagement. Even after the 2017 Doklam crisis at the India–Bhutan–China trijunction, Modi tried to use his personal charm to reach out to the Chinese president Xi Jinping directly.[7] This was as much about the practical necessity of dealing with a much stronger neighbour as it was about shaping the bilateral engagement. It worked out for a while, but Beijing clearly had other plans.

In its attempt to unilaterally define the LAC, Beijing ended up disregarding the central tenets of all the pacts it has signed with India since 1993 to keep the border peaceful. And inevitably, this will significantly alter the trajectory of the Sino-Indian relationship, which has been premised on an understanding that even as the boundary question remains unresolved, the two nations can move forward on other areas of engagement—global, regional and bilateral. That fundamental assumption today stands seriously undermined.

In some ways, China's assertiveness today is understandable. As long as it was the dominant party along the border, China could continue with the facade of upholding peace and tranquillity. After all, that was on its terms. It is India's assertion of its interests in the last few years that has emerged as the sticking point. The militarization of the LAC is taking place at an unprecedented pace today, partly because Indian infrastructure is in much better shape and Indian patrolling is far more effective. A more heated LAC is a result of the Indian military's presence in areas where the Chinese military is not used to seeing it.[8] That India is ready to take on Chinese aggression head-on is also reflected in the scale of casualties that both sides suffered in the Galwan Valley. The Indian military is operationally more nimble and better prepared than ever before. Therefore, if a lasting solution to the border problem is not found, we should be prepared for more such action along the LAC.

China remains a significantly more powerful entity and its infrastructure is still in a much better shape. But Indian infrastructure development has reached a critical point. And it is not without reason that the Chinese opposition to the

255 km-long strategic Darbuk–Shyok–Daulat Beg Oldie Road has been so vehement.[9] Connecting Leh to the Karakoram Pass, this all-weather road is India's frontal challenge to China's expansionist designs in the region. Despite Chinese objections, India has continued to pursue this project, given its strategic importance. China raising the temperature on the border is a pre-emptive move to dissuade India from moving ahead.

Indian foreign policy has been at the front and centre of challenging China's global designs. New Delhi was the first country to warn the world of the perils of BRI at a time when almost every other country was willing to buy into Beijing's narrative. Today, India's framing of the BRI problems is widely accepted by most major global powers. Given that BRI is Xi's key vanity project, India's role in shaping the global opposition must be particularly jarring. India has also managed to shape the global discourse on the Indo-Pacific and is now working closely with like-minded regional players into giving it operational heft.[10] Despite China's continued objections to the term, Indo-Pacific maritime geography is now widely accepted. And at a time when the United States (US) is seriously beginning the process of trade and technology 'decoupling' with China, Washington and New Delhi are closer today than ever before. Chinese attempts to marginalize India on the global stage have not worked and New Delhi's cache has only increased.

And so in its wisdom, China decided to wield the blunt instrumentality of force, hoping that this would 'teach India a lesson'. The reality is, Chinese actions have ended up triggering exactly the opposite effect of what they probably intended to do. Indian public opinion, which was already negative about China, has now become all the more anti-Chinese. Those who have been talking about maintaining an equidistance from China and the US today find it hard to sustain that position. And New Delhi has become even freer to make policy choices, both strategic and economic, which have a strong anti-China orientation. From reducing trade dependence on China in key strategic sectors to walling off critical sectors from Chinese entry, from galvanizing global support for the Indo-Pacific to the strengthening of the Quadrilateral Security Dialogue (QSD, also known as the Quad)—India's response has been across domains.

None of these options are cost-free for India, but China's actions have ensured that today India is ready to bear those costs. India's military and diplomatic responses to Chinese aggression have made it clear that neither is India without options nor is it reticent in choosing them. It is now for China to make up its mind about whether it wants a permanent foe in India or a neighbouring country with whom it can do business. Whatever the choice Beijing decides to make, it will irrevocably change the strategic landscape of the Indo-Pacific. And the impact of this contestation is being most visibly felt in South Asia.

Little Room to Manoeuvre

The truth is that post-Independence, India has never encountered anything like China in its vicinity, whose intent and capabilities are posing the kind of challenge to Indian interests that New Delhi is finding hard to manage. China's entry into the South Asian region has opened up new avenues for smaller neighbours, which can be leveraged in their dealings with India. As a result, the very idea of what South Asian geography has traditionally meant is also undergoing a paradigm shift.

Yet, the underlying factors that have traditionally framed India's difficulties in getting its neighbourhood policy right remain as potent as ever. India's structural dominance of South

Asia makes it a natural target of resentment and suspicion, which New Delhi has often found difficult to overcome. India is also part of the domestic politics of most regional states where anti-India sentiment is often used to bolster the nationalist credentials of various political formations.[11] State identity in South Asia often gets linked to oppositional politics vis-à-vis India. South Asian countries remain politically fragile, and the economic projects in the region have failed to take off. This means that the room available for India to manoeuvre in the region is severely limited despite what many in New Delhi and outside would like to believe.

There can be no doubt about China's growing clout in South Asia. When governments are being made and unmade by a not-so-invisible hand in Beijing, it should be clear that China's footprint is at an all-time high. It has been evident for some time now that countries in South Asia and the wider IOR cannot remain immune to the lure of Chinese political and economic muscle, much like the rest of the world. If India can try to get the best bargain out of China by engaging in trade and other sorts of cooperation, so can its neighbours. It's infantile to cry hoarse about smaller countries trying to make the best of their regional environment.

Yet, strategic evolution is a constant and as 2020 came to end, China seemed to be facing an interesting scrutiny about its role in South Asia from various quarters. In an embarrassing exposé in December 2020, Afghanistan's National Directorate of Security arrested Chinese intelligence agents engaged with Pakistani agents and members of the Taliban as well as the Haqqani Network in order to promote 'Beijing's geopolitical influence in the region'.[12] They were later allowed to leave Kabul but only after China was reportedly asked to apologize for sending in these agents. That China and Pakistan would collude in Afghanistan is not news, but what is important to underline is the new reality that as China becomes more proactive in shaping its regional environment, the facade of promoting peace and prosperity will quickly wear off.

Given China's widening interests across South Asia, it was inevitable that it would like to be more involved in shaping the domestic politics and preferences of the regional nations. And as China has become more involved in the domestic politics of its neighbours, it is becoming increasingly aware that it is not easy to practise what you preach. In most of India's neighbours, China has a seeming advantage that, unlike India, it is not part of the domestic political calculus. But, unlike India, it also does not have a long-term stake in the South Asian region.

China can afford to ignore the region, which it does, when its interests are not served. New Delhi doesn't have that luxury. For good or bad, India's future and that of its neighbours remain intertwined. So, while China's financial commitments to various countries in the region are much talked about, given their size, they are largely declaratory. Even in the China–Pakistan Economic Corridor (CPEC), China's actual spending has been quite limited, compared to the $62 billion amount which is often advertised.[13] India's declared loan commitments might be small, but when it comes to actual delivery, India is not far behind. Its loan terms and payment conditionalities are much better too.

To view India's neighbourhood policy through the lens of 'wins' and 'losses' is to miss the structural imperatives that shape the outcome. A region shaped by two major powers will never have a linear trajectory. And such a narrative also does a great disservice to smaller nations in the region, which have their own agency in shaping their engagements with these powers. Finally, there has never been a golden period of foreign policy when New Delhi's ties with its neighbours were seamless.

China's political, economic and military engagement in

South Asia and the IOR will continue to grow, as regional nations would want to leverage Beijing's growing heft to their advantage. But the constant lament in New Delhi that 'China is winning in South Asia' neither does justice to India's own regional profile nor does it give its due to the agency of smaller nations in the region to pursue their vital national interests in a pragmatic manner. It is easy to forget that even till the first decade of this century, the main narrative about South Asia was one of India–Pakistan dyad. For a long time, the dominant narrative with regard to South Asia has been how the India–Pakistan rivalry has constrained Indian foreign policy options in the region and prevented the region as a whole from attaining its full potential. That is now rapidly losing its salience, with the growing dominance of the South Asian landscape by the People's Republic of China. The country's rising profile in South Asia has been evident for some time now. It entered SAARC as an observer in 2005,[14] supported by most member states. India could do little about it and so acquiesced. Now, much to India's consternation, Pakistan, Bangladesh, the Maldives, Sri Lanka and Nepal are supporting China's full membership of SAARC.

China's strategy towards South Asia is premised on encircling and confining India within the geographical co-ordinates of the region. This approach of using proxies started with Pakistan and has gradually evolved to include other nations in the region, including Bangladesh, Sri Lanka and Nepal. China is entering markets in South Asia more aggressively through both trade and investment, and improving linkages with South Asian nations through treaties and bilateral co-operation. Following this up by building a ring of road and port connections in India's neighbourhood and deepening military engagements with countries on India's periphery, China has firmly entrenched itself in our backyard. China's

BRI and its approval by India's neighbours such as Nepal, despite strenuous opposition from India, is the latest example of inroads made by China in the region, with the stated aim of promoting connectivity and growth. This gradual Chinese assertion has enabled various smaller South Asian countries to exploit Indo-Chinese competition in the region for their own benefit. Most countries in the region now use the 'China card' to counterbalance the traditional predominance of India in South Asia. Forced to exist between their two giant neighbours, the smaller nations have responded with a careful balancing act.

With the rise in the economic and military capabilities of both China and India, there has been increasing friction between the two powers as China expands its presence in South Asia and the IOR and India makes its presence felt in East and South East Asia. India's long-term challenge in South Asia is to respond effectively to the impact of a rising China on the geopolitics of the subcontinent. At the same time, China's growing profile in India's neighbourhood has given greater strategic space to smaller countries in the region for diplomatic manoeuvring between the two regional giants, whereby they promote their national interests by not explicitly aligning with any one major power, but pursue policies that preserve their independent existence. This is a standard strategy adopted by small nations in regional systems that are dominated by two or more major powers.

Reimagining South Asia

New Delhi's growing capabilities and an aspirational foreign policy outlook have ensured that as we enter the third decade of the twenty-first century, South Asia is being viewed today as the pivotal theatre of the wider Indo-Pacific, where the key fault line of this phase of global politics will be played out.[15] And it is not without reason that the idea of the Bay of Bengal Initiative for Multi-Sectoral Technical and Economic Cooperation (BIMSTEC) has gained currency in India's policy-making circles. It can potentially allow India to break through the straightjacket of South Asia's traditional confines and leverage its Bay of Bengal identity to link up with the wider South East Asia. In that sense, it is about reimagining India's strategic geography altogether. But few had heard of BIMSTEC before Modi made it central to his government's regional outreach. Back in 2014, at a SAARC summit in Kathmandu, Modi suggested that opportunities for regional cooperation would be realized 'through SAARC or outside it'.[16] When his initial outreach to Pakistan failed to yield any substantive change in Pakistan's policy, his government began to emphasize the importance of BIMSTEC. Indeed, BIMSTEC has largely replaced SAARC, whose representatives were the guests of honour at Modi's last inauguration. The shift signalled that Modi may have given up on his initial desire to engage Pakistan.

Channelling India's regional foreign policy through BIMSTEC underlines New Delhi's desire to focus on the country's eastern frontier. The Bay of Bengal connects India to its eastern neighbours, not only to its traditional South Asian partners such as Bangladesh, Bhutan, Nepal and Sri Lanka, but also to South East Asia via Myanmar and Thailand. By doing this, India has tried to redefine India's strategic periphery, reimagining the country's neighbourhood on more favourable terms. As India focuses on the Indo-Pacific, BIMSTEC, if creatively engaged, can be an important platform for India to enhance its profile in East and South East Asia. As the Sino-Indian relationship becomes more turbulent, New Delhi would like to expand India's profile in the wider Indo-Pacific and carve out a stable balance of power in the region. Doing so will be important if India wants recognition as a major power in its own right, and not merely as a balancer.

The central story of our times is an ever more dynamic interaction between the two major powers of the Indo-Pacific: India and China. Despite being the weaker of the two players, it is India that is not only challenging China when it comes to major ideas of our times, but it is also standing up and confronting China to preserve its vital interests. Whether it is the narrative surrounding the BRI, or it is the discourse on the Indo-Pacific, which China tried its best to discredit, it is India's leadership that was key to make them possible. By standing up militarily to China in the Himalayan borders, India also made it possible for smaller nations at the receiving end of Chinese aggression to envision the fact that subservience to China is not the only option.

The single most important geopolitical development of the last few months has been India standing up to China post the Galwan valley incident of June 2020 and making it clear to Beijing and to the world that it is possible to successfully resist Chinese aggression. Even as Indian forces challenged their much more resource-rich Chinese counterparts along the LAC, Indian diplomacy ensured that New Delhi retained a central role in the global health crisis, emerging as net provider of a security in the realm of public health. While for most countries, challenging China at a time of turbulent domestic and global environment would have been impossible, New Delhi made it seem rather prosaic. India's message to the world was: if this is the new normal, then we are prepared.

And not only did the world notice, Beijing did too. If the Chinese Communist Party has been talking about 'the need to create enabling condition to settle border dispute',[17] it is no small measure due to a consistent message from India that the Sino-Indian relationship cannot be divorced from the border challenge. The larger strategic fabric of the bilateral ties between

India and China remains as fragile as ever and China is not going to mend its ways just because it has moved back from a part of the LAC. However, it can no longer be ignored that the ability of India to shape the terms of its engagement with China is growing.

And as the competition for influence intensifies in South Asia and the IOR, New Delhi is making it clear that not only will it fight hard to push against the Chinese Communist Party's malevolent agenda in its neighbourhood but will also ensure that its preferred model of working in partnership with its neighbours to develop a long-term, sustainable political and economic agenda continues to retain its centrality. The constant lament in India about China's rising profile in its vicinity should give place to a new awareness that this is just a beginning of a long-drawn-out struggle between two regional players which is yet to acquire its full potency. And New Delhi should be fully prepared for it.

Successive Indian governments have struggled to get a grip on the neighbourhood. Initially, the struggle with Pakistan engaged a large part of India's diplomatic capital. Today, there seems to be a clear recognition that India's Pakistan policy is merely a subset of India's China policy. And as Beijing's economic and political engagement in India's periphery has grown, New Delhi is coming to terms with the reality of a 'new' South Asia. India will not only have to more creatively reimagine its strategic geography but also evolve new terms of engagement with its neighbours: terms that reflect the reality of our times in which both India and its neighbours can have a stake in each other's success.

It is against this backdrop that this book seeks to bring together some of the finest thinkers in the country to deliberate on the gamut of political issues that India is facing in its neighbourhood beyond Chinese hostilities and the perennial lack of trust with Pakistan. Each chapter provides an overview of the last few years under the Modi government and evaluates the state of relationship as it exists today. It explicates the main areas of disputes and charts out a way forward for the bilateral engagement. The aim here is to provide a kaleidoscopic view of India's neighbourhood challenge at a time when Sino-Indian contestation is sharpening by the day and South Asia is emerging as the central node in the wider Indo-Pacific.

1

AFGHANISTAN

Ancient Ties, New-Age Partnership

JAYANT PRASAD

Prime Minister Narendra Modi's initiative to improve India's relations with its South Asian neighbours, unveiled at the time of his inaugural in May 2014, has ground to a standstill—with the notable exception of Afghanistan. He was perhaps more convinced than his predecessors that India would find it difficult to bestride the global arena without connecting constructively with its neighbours.

Modi had to face the challenge of dealing with regime change in Afghanistan and the presidential transition there from Hamid Karzai to Ashraf Ghani, almost in conjunction with the victory of the Bharatiya Janata Party in the general elections of 2014. President Karzai had prioritized Afghanistan's relations with India by deciding to conclude the 2011 Strategic Partnership Agreement between Afghanistan and India before forging similar agreements with other partners.

President Ghani decided to begin his presidency by

bringing about a paradigm shift in Afghan policy. He began by conciliating Pakistan and forging stronger relations with China, perceived to have more influence in Islamabad than the United States (US). He believes that without Pakistan's fullest cooperation, it will be impossible to ensure peace and stability in Afghanistan. Through the 1980s, Pakistan became the fulcrum of the US-, Saudi- and China-led effort to oust the former Soviet Union from Afghanistan. After the Soviets left, Pakistan helped establish the post-People's Democratic Party of Afghanistan seven-party alliance government in Kabul in 1992. It then helped install the Taliban government in 1996. Post 2001, as it assisted the US in its global war against terrorism, it behaved simultaneously as a firefighter and an incendiarist. It provided shelter to the Al-Qaeda (AQ) and Taliban leadership—its Shura, or leadership council, was Quetta-based—and equipped and nurtured the bruised Afghan Taliban back into a formidable fighting force. Over the past five years, Pakistan has brokered peace between the US and the Taliban, and is now pushing the Afghan government to share power with the Taliban.

India showed remarkable steadfastness and patience in staying the course with Afghanistan, even while New Delhi was conscious that Ghani had pursued fundamentally different foreign and security policies from his predecessor. Notwithstanding the shift in Kabul's preferences, Modi remained steady in his responses. All of the Indian commitments made to Afghanistan were kept, and even added to, in step with Afghanistan's preferences and requirements. The vicissitudes of internal political change, which tend to skew relations particularly among neighbours, were not allowed to adversely affect India–Afghanistan relations.

In an unusual gambit to script a new narrative between Afghanistan and Pakistan, Ghani visited Pakistan soon after assuming presidency, calling on the Chief of Army Staff at the Pakistani Army's general headquarters in Rawalpindi even before meeting either Pakistan's prime minister or president. He told his interlocutors in Rawalpindi and Islamabad that the two countries had been in an undeclared state of war and they had to begin by normalizing relations and building mutual trust, and thereupon move towards cooperation in a time-bound manner. Ghani exulted at the end of his visit that he had overcome with his hosts obstacles of the past 13 years.

Moreover, Ghani spelt out in his inaugural address that Afghanistan's external relations were set within five concentric circles, with India featuring in the second-last circle. In his first meeting with Modi, Ghani said that India and Afghanistan should maintain economic relations, implying that their strategic ties be kept in abeyance.[1]

Ghani based his Pakistan gambit on the understanding that Pakistan's help was critical in ensuring peace and stability in Afghanistan because the Taliban received shelter, sanctuary and support from Pakistan. In a well-reported conversation at the United States Institute of Peace, in early 2015, he said:

> The problem fundamentally is not about peace with the Taliban, the problem is fundamentally about peace between Pakistan and Afghanistan. For 13 years, we have been in [an] undeclared state of hostilities and this is the definition that we offered to our Pakistani counterparts, they have accepted this definition of the problem. That is the breakthrough.[2]

Given Pakistan's actions in the past four decades, this was perhaps too much to hope for, but there was no harm in trying.

The Pakistani Army and civilian leadership made three initial promises to Ghani: first, that they would prevent the Taliban from launching an offensive in Afghanistan; second, that they would take action against the Haqqani Network; and third, that they would persuade the Taliban to initiate peace talks with the Afghan government. On the basis of these assurances, and that Pakistan shall not thenceforth make any distinction between 'good' and 'bad', the Taliban and the Pakistani Army would take action against all terrorists, without discrimination. Ghani felt optimistic about the prospects of peace. He began his presidency by taking active steps against members and leaders of the Tehreek-e-Taliban Pakistan sheltered in Afghanistan. He agreed to exchange databases on terrorists available with the Afghan National Directorate of Security (NDS) with the Inter-Services Intelligence (ISI) of the Pakistani Army, without the guarantee of similar access to inputs on the Quetta Shura or the Haqqani Network of the Taliban. This provoked the head of the NDS, Rahmatullah Nabil, to protest, and eventually, to resign.

Instead of ceasing their military campaign, the Taliban commenced the most virulent attacks ever within Afghanistan since their defeat in 2001, and the Haqqani Network continued to enjoy impunity and support from the ISI. A promise kept by the Pakistani Army was in getting the Quetta Shura to agree to come to the negotiating table, having claimed for months that the Taliban leader Mullah Omar was fully backing the process. Within days of the 7 July 2015 peace talks in Murree, it became known that Omar had been dead for 27 months. His endorsement of the peace talks was clearly a hoax. The rejigged Shura, backed by the Pakistani Army, was never committed to reconciliation. This was a fact soon established and reconfirmed by Taliban actions on the ground, including attacks on the electoral processes of Afghanistan.

The Taliban's offensive actions in Afghanistan multiplied instead of ceasing. Their 2015 summer offensive, Operation Azm, began even as Pakistan publicly dissociated with them.

The Haqqani Network, described in testimony to the US Congress by Admiral Mike Mullen, then Chief of the US Joint Chiefs of Staff, as a 'veritable arm' of the ISI,[3] instead of being quietened, extended its control over the Taliban, with its leader Sirajuddin Haqqani becoming the new deputy leader of the group. To gain deniability, its operatives began to operate tactically in association with the Da'esh (Islamic State of Iraq and the Levant–ISIL, also known as ISIS). The Taliban's ties with the ISI have been well-documented. Steve Coll writes that the Haqqani Network has been the lynchpin of ISI's covert policy since the 1970s.[4] As Taliban's most effective armed component, the Haqqani Network had targeted American forces and even the American Embassy in Afghanistan. It has also been the prime agency targeting India's diplomats, military officers and cooperation workers in Afghanistan.

Notwithstanding a greater understanding of the double-game played by the Pakistani Army, the US, while remaining distrustful of Pakistan, decided to confront the situation and cut its losses instead. Former US president Barack Obama had promised to withdraw all American combat troops before the end of his presidency. The International Security Assistance Force (ISAF) ended its combat operations at the end of 2014. Since then, the North Atlantic Treaty Organization forces have continued to serve in advisory and training roles as part of its Resolute Support Mission. Meanwhile, the Afghan National Defense and Security Forces (ANDSF) have conducted 95 per cent of the missions against the Taliban. As of end March 2021, only 2,500 American soldiers are expected to remain in Afghanistan, the lowest number of American troops deployed in Afghanistan since the fall of the Taliban regime.

The ANDSF, though bereft of aircraft and enablers such as protected surface mobility, medical evacuation, intelligence, night vision goggles, laser sights and heavy weapons, took charge of the country's security from ISAF without losing further ground. This has, however, come at a significant human cost. In 2015 alone, ANDSF losses were higher than the total US and ISAF casualties since the beginning of the war in 2001. Such attrition would be difficult to sustain in the future. In order to bolster the morale of the Afghan forces and under the terms of the India–Afghanistan Agreement on Strategic Partnership,[5] India provided the ANDSF three attack helicopters—and might be prepared to do more, if the situation so requires. India remains the country from where the most Afghan Army officers are commissioned, over 100 a year, many times more than from Afghanistan's closest military allies.

The Pakistan Factor

Afghanistan and Pakistan are conjoined twins, with intertwined destinies. Afghanistan cannot be redeemed without Pakistan, even if doing so will be very difficult, whether by threats or cajoling. Pakistan's professed interest in peace and stabilization of Afghanistan is at odds with its continued harbouring of the Taliban, especially the Haqqani Network. If Afghanistan unravels, so inevitably will Pakistan. The Pakistani Army, unfortunately, believes that the Taliban can be controlled and managed by them even after it comes to power in Afghanistan.

Pakistan has been a spoiler for Afghanistan. There is a paranoia promoted in Pakistan by its politico-military elite that India seeks a privileged position in Afghanistan to trap Pakistan as a nut between two halves of a nutcracker. India has never sought a military role in Afghanistan. Yet, Pakistan is affronted by India's development role in Afghanistan, simply because the Afghan people like it.

Pakistan's leaders have held that given the traditional

friendship between Afghanistan and India, a well-armed and trained Afghan Army would be dangerous for Pakistan—if either Afghanistan or India began hostilities, Pakistan would be trapped.

What Afghanistan seeks from Pakistan is not assistance or investments, but the cessation of support to terrorists and insurgents. Modi continued the tried-and-tested policy of responding to Afghanistan's requirements, as desired by the Afghan people and government. India remained restrained in providing Afghanistan military hardware—lest it be misunderstood by Pakistan—and concentrated instead on development cooperation. Modi even stopped over in Pakistan in December 2015 as a goodwill gesture, the first visit by an Indian prime minister to Pakistan since 2004, on the way back from an official visit to Afghanistan.

The US policy was one of appeasement towards Pakistan, with Afghanistan encouraged to acquiesce in it. Instead of treating Pakistan as a source of terrorism and destruction against Afghanistan, Pakistan was treated as a respected strategic ally. In place of sanctioning Pakistan, the US funded and armed it. India was kept out by Pakistan on any material discussion about Afghanistan's future, as the US accepted the Pakistan red-line. India's former external affairs minister, Sushma Swaraj, told President Ghani's Special Envoy for Regional Consensus Building on Peace, Umer Daudzai, that while India backed the peace process, it would not sign on the dotted line.[6]

The security of Pakistan's western frontiers is irrevocably tied to Afghanistan. For its own future stability, it must work towards the stabilization of Afghanistan rather than undermine it. The four decades of war in Afghanistan have taken a big toll, including in Pakistan. There are strategic experts in Pakistan re-imagining 1995 and the Taliban's quick victory and establishment of the Islamic Emirate of Afghanistan. This first example ended as a tragedy. A repeat might be farcical. Pakistan might suffer as a result of the strategic depth it seeks in Afghanistan.[7] If Afghanistan were to go down, or parts of its east and south were to come permanently under insurgent control, it could put a strain on Pakistan's polity, and in turn, pose an even greater security threat for India than it faces today. This consideration explains the restraint in India's policy towards Afghanistan.

The 2010 Afghanistan–Pakistan Transit Trade Agreement was not renewed in 2015 because of Pakistan's continued refusal to accept Afghanistan's request for two-way overland trade access to India. Pakistan wanted instead to maintain its connectivity with Central Asia through Afghanistan. An important consideration was that an Afghanistan disconnected from India would help in keeping Afghanistan weak and perennially dependent. To overcome this impediment to commercial exchanges, an India–Afghanistan air-freight corridor was instituted in June 2017. In the three years since then, this has entailed close to 1,000 flights, carrying goods valued at over $216 million. Another initiative the same year was the operationalisation of the Chabahar Port in Iran, which connects to the Zaranj–Delaram Road constructed by India. The port has begun handling cargo, proving its feasibility for transit trade with Afghanistan and reducing its dependence on Karachi.

Afghanistan faces a difficult situation: it is land-locked, surrounded by unstable neighbours and suffering from poverty, extra-legal power centres, weak governance and under-development. Underwriting Afghanistan's stability by them is difficult, as their own polities and social structures are fragile. It is the US and its allies and friends that attempted to guarantee Afghanistan's security since 2001. The US is now unsure or uninterested in a continued commitment to Afghan security.

Afghanistan's neighbour to the west, Iran, views the US's

role in Afghanistan as destructive, and wants US military forces out of there.[8] Iranian leaders have accused the US of pursuing its own priorities and sacrificing the interests of the Afghan people. The three northern neighbours of Afghanistan—Turkmenistan, Uzbekistan and Tajikistan—while working cautiously to increase commercial exchanges and connectivity with Afghanistan, and investing in energy projects that could feed Afghanistan's requirements and extend further east to Pakistan and India, want to insulate themselves against the terrorism and narcotics spreading from Afghanistan.

Afghanistan's other important neighbour, China, though against terrorism, separatism and extremism in principle, defers to Pakistan's policies in its dealings with Afghanistan. China hopes to step into the space created by the ongoing American disengagement in the Afghanistan–Pakistan region. China's emblematic Belt and Road Initiative (BRI) is a Sino-centric project meant to assist in China's transition from export-led manufacturing to services, high-technology and its hinterland's development. China says it's a win-win proposition, meant to build communities of common destiny. China co-opted other countries, including Afghanistan, to join in its super-fast train of progress. China's regional posturing has become markedly more assertive. India is not convinced that the BRI is only about geoeconomics, and that geostrategy has nothing to do with it. China has promised to extend the BRI to Afghanistan. So far, almost all of the BRI-related investments have been in the China–Pakistan Economic Corridor (CPEC) projects and not in Afghanistan.

A Steadfast Partner

India and Afghanistan are linked by their history and culture—through the civilizational contact between Bamyan, Kandahar and Kabul, and Pataliputra, Nalanda and Delhi. These have been buttressed by physical contact, through the movement of peoples and ideas, and through the building by Sher Shah Suri of what came to be known later as the Grand Trunk Road, from Kabul to Delhi, extending now to the Bay of Bengal. In recent years, India has sought to build connectivity and infrastructure to revive the links, despite the obstacle presented by Pakistan in blocking such activity.

There has been a remarkable consistency in India's development partnership with Afghanistan. This has sought to build Afghanistan's human and institutional capacities, besides focusing on humanitarian (India has been supplying high-protein biscuits for the World Food Programme's school feeding programme), social and infrastructure sector assistance. Two projects completed earlier by India include the construction of a transmission line over 3,000 metres high from Phul-e-Khumri to Kabul and the construction of Afghanistan's largest electricity supply sub-station at Chimtala to bring Uzbek electricity to Kabul, and the 212 km highway from Delaram to Zaranj, connecting the Kandahar–Herat highway to the Iranian port of Chabahar. India has also executed a number of quick-gestation, small development projects in Afghanistan: construction of schools, clinics, micro-hydel, solar electrification projects, sports stadiums and administrative infrastructure.

Since PM Modi took office, India completed two other emblematic projects, the construction of the Afghan parliament and the Harirud Dam, the first hydro project to be commissioned in Afghanistan since 2001, bringing electricity and irrigation to the Herat province. Much of India's $3 billion development assistance has gone into state-building, training of public servants and educating in India a new generation of Afghans, including in finance, agriculture and mining. The new commitments include construction of the Shahtoot Dam and drinking water project for Kabul, water supply for Charikar City, road connectivity to Band-e-Amir in Bamyan Province promoting tourism and low-cost housing for returning Afghan refugees in Nangarhar Province.

As a result, India has established an excellent entente with the Afghan people and successfully bridged the hiatus that had developed with them due to reduced Indian presence in Afghanistan, particularly from 1992–2001. While other countries have dramatically reduced their commitments to Afghanistan, India has maintained them. India is supportive of economic connectivity, infrastructure and energy projects, such as the Turkmenistan–Afghanistan–Pakistan–India (TAPI) and the eventual conversion of CASA-1000 into the Central Asia-South Asia Regional Electricity Market (CASAREM).

The policy of promoting projects for public welfare has paid India rich dividends. Successive surveys of public opinion across Afghanistan show that Afghans have a most favourable opinion of India and its activities, all of which have been undertaken in response to specific requests from the Afghan government. India has never sought Afghan support on Jammu and Kashmir, and neither has such support ever been voluntarily offered. Afghanistan, in turn, has not sought India's support on questioning the Durand Line, and neither has Indian support on this been ever on offer.

The Doha Agreement and Beyond

The February 2020 Doha Agreement was for the US to extricate its troops safely out of Afghanistan. For the Taliban, it was to rid Afghanistan of foreign forces and bring them a step closer to re-establishing an Islamic Emirate in the country. The Taliban intend to take control over the Afghan government, nothing less. Mawlawi Hibatullah Akhundzada, the Taliban's current chief, described the Doha Agreement as the 'Termination of Occupation Agreement,' while it is actually titled, 'Agreement for Bringing Peace to Afghanistan.' With the prospect of a full American withdrawal from Afghanistan, the Taliban sense a fresh wind in their sails. Over six months later, the Afghan Peace Negotiations teams of the Afghan government and the Taliban, led respectively by Abdullah Abdullah, chairperson of Afghanistan's High Council for National Reconciliation (HCNR), and Mullah Baradar, the deputy leader of the Taliban, met at the inaugural session in Doha on 12 September 2020. As of the beginning of December, negotiations were yet to begin.

The Afghan Peace Negotiations has the two sides pursuing fundamentally contradictory objectives concerning the end-state in Afghanistan: the continuation of pluralist democracy versus the re-establishment of an Islamic Emirate. The Taliban are keen to attain power without taking part in elections. The Loya Jirgah held in Kabul in April–May 2019 was convened to establish the framework for talks with the Taliban. It specified certain 'no-go' areas. There was a consensus that the Taliban could join the Afghan State and society. But it expected the Taliban to clarify its relationship with Pakistan. The limitations or red lines laid out by the Loya Jirgah about constitutional changes included: no change in the name of Afghanistan, democracy, right to freedom of speech and the rights of women to education and work.

The Doha Agreement gave the Taliban international legitimacy. The Taliban's profile went up, disproportionate to its gains on the ground. To win American acceptance, the Taliban sold the narrative of peace. Its interpretation of the US capitulation at Doha is that the US has been defeated and is ready to abandon Afghanistan. It follows from such logic that the regime and constitution put in place by the US in

Afghanistan should be dismantled. The Agreement, which blindsided the Afghan government, is seen by many as not a capitulation by the US to the Taliban, but as a capitulation by it to Pakistan. Pakistan's objective is to have a pliant, Taliban-led government in Kabul, which would limit India's presence in Afghanistan. Then, Afghanistan, not Pakistan, will become the home base for international terrorism, including jihadi groups targeting India.

Responsible US practitioners have stated that in the Doha Agreement, the US negotiated the terms of its surrender, and that Taliban commitments were made with prior knowledge that the US would not have the power to enforce them.[9] One of the commitments made by the Taliban was reduced violence. There is little sign of it so far. Another big commitment was to abjure relations with the AQ. Again, there is no evidence of it from the field and no unambiguous statement from the Quetta Shura avowing dissociation between the Taliban and the AQ. Most curious of all is the US expectation that the Taliban, the primary focus of US military counterterrorism and counter-insurgency efforts in Afghanistan since 2001, would henceforth assist in combatting the Da'esh. This has not happened.

The Taliban is being made to look respectable by holding the Da'esh responsible for the continuing violence in Afghanistan. The US logic is that since the Taliban is a lesser threat compared to the AQ or the Da'esh, a compact with the Taliban is preferable to dealing with a more truculent adversary. It has the additional, perhaps unintended, consequence of keeping Pakistan—the Taliban's primary mentor—off the hook. Afghan vulnerabilities will be tested in the coming months and years not so much by Da'esh, but by the Taliban, in search of buttressing its claim, already recognized through the Doha Agreement as enjoying political legitimacy in contrast to the AQ and Da'esh.

That the Taliban have not severed their connection with the

AQ and other like-minded terrorist organizations is testified by the 26th report of the Analytical Support and Sanctions Monitoring Team submitted on 23 July 2020, pursuant to the United Nations Security Council Resolution 2368 (2017) concerning ISIL, AQ, and associated individuals and entities. The report states that the AQ is active in 12 out of Afghanistan's 34 provinces. Its leadership, including Ayman al-Zawahiri, maintains 'close contact' with the Haqqani Network for their ongoing cooperation. Also, according to the report, the AQ in the Indian subcontinent operates under the Taliban umbrella in the provinces of Nimruz, Helmand and Kandahar. Most other terrorist organizations in Afghanistan operate with the active support of the Taliban. There are an estimated 6,000–6,500 Pakistani foreign terrorist fighters in Afghanistan.[10]

The AQ, the Taliban and other Islamist insurgent groups have an opportunistic and protean quality: adapting easily to new circumstances. Most of the Da'esh members are former members of the AQ and the Taliban. The elimination of Osama bin Laden in May 2011 by US Special Forces weakened the AQ and created space for the emergence of a new terrorist organization. The Wilayat Khorasan (Khurasan Province), encompassing Afghanistan and Pakistan, was constituted in early 2015. It could now have about 3,000 active fighters amongst its ranks. Afghanistan might be seen as a soft target, given the Taliban's ubiquitous presence in the majority of the country's provinces, the resultant absence of the Afghan State in different parts of Afghanistan and especially the countryside, the end of ISAF combat operations half a decade earlier, the progressively dwindling American military presence, the resurgence of terrorism and insurgency, and the systematic ceding of political space by the Afghan government.

The leadership of Da'esh in Afghanistan is populated by the Taliban. Its former deputy commander, Abdul Rauf Aliza, was a prominent Taliban leader and Guantanamo Bay detainee. The leader of the Wilayat Khorasan since July 2019, Aslam Farooqi, responsible for the April 2020 attack on the Kabul Gurdwara, is a Pakistan national and a former member of the Lashkar-e-Taiba. In that capacity, he had worked with the ISI. Farooqi, along with 47 other operatives in Kabul, was arrested by the NDS. Pakistan immediately wanted Farooqi to be returned to Pakistan. The Afghan government refused, citing the absence of an extradition agreement and the need to try him for crimes committed in Afghanistan. A spokesperson of the Afghan National Security Council tweeted after the arrests that in initial investigations, Farooqi 'confessed of strong relationship between the Islamic State-Khurasan and regional intelligence agencies'.[11]

The Price of Peace

For Afghanistan, this is a difficult moment. A major part of its territory is under Taliban control. The fall of Sangin has been critical, as it is the main crossover point between Kandahar, Helmand, Uruzgan and Nimroz, then connecting onward to Farah and Herat. Except Lashkar Gah, the rest of Helmand is under its control. The fall of Musa Qala in August 2015 perhaps signified the futility of the US and ISAF military effort in Afghanistan, since it was the object of much activity from 2006, when British forces surrendered the town, and later, when US Marines took it back after incurring casualties. Major towns, including Kabul and Ghazni, have been under attack. The situation in several provinces is grim.

Da'esh has gained adherents among the Orakzai and Afridi tribes, active in two Nangarhar districts in eastern Afghanistan. Thus far, it is a collection of criminals, disaffected Taliban and some Uzbek elements returning from Syria and Iraq. It is different from the Taliban, which represents a mixture of Islam and Pashtunwali. Da'esh is more sectarian and Wahabbist. Unfortunately, in order to strike a deal with the Taliban, the threat from Da'esh in Afghanistan has been exaggerated. Russia was the first to treat this threat as true, reorienting its policy towards the Taliban and Pakistan, partly to protect itself, and partly to reassert its presence in the region and as insurance against the possible misuse of Da'esh by others.

Afghans are tired of the incessant violence visited upon them over the past four decades. They see the peace process as an opportunity. They agree that the continuation of conflict serves the interest of no party. The question that arises is: what is the price of peace? Peace dictated by the Taliban and Pakistan may not be acceptable to the Afghan people and government. They will have to control the peace process themselves. Restoration of the status quo ante is ruled out. At the minimum, they will insist upon the preservation of pluralism and democracy, constitutionalism and the rule of law.

According to President Ghani, over 3,500 Afghan soldiers and policemen were killed and about double that number were severely injured in less than five months since the signing of the Doha Agreement. Instead of an immediate and permanent ceasefire to prepare for intra-Afghan peace, the Taliban carried out a full-scale onslaught against the ANDSF. Meanwhile, the Taliban has succeeded in their objective of securing the release of Taliban prisoners, including those accused of violent crime and drug-running, without any abatement in violence.

Afghanistan has three basic requirements: security, governance and economic development, with security trumping the other two. Maladministration and corruption have retarded Afghanistan's development, but are not primarily responsible for the lack of it. Much of the failures of Afghanistan's administration and economy result from the resurgence of terrorism and insurgency spearheaded by multiple factions of the Taliban, whose leadership and training centres have remained in Pakistan. In the quest for peace, Afghanistan has held on to a tenuous coalition, which is fraying around the edges. There is a flight of talent and capital, shrinkage of external assistance and investments and collapse of construction, logistics and transportation.

In crafting its future policy, India cannot forget that the Islamic Emirate of Afghanistan, defeated by American forces acting in concert with Ahmad Shah Massoud's forces, harboured terrorists from Pakistan training in camps to fight in Jammu and Kashmir. When, in September 1998, US cruise missiles rained down on a terrorist training camp in Jawher Khel near Khost, hoping to eliminate Osama bin Laden in reprisal for the East African bombings by the AQ, those killed or wounded were not Arabs or Afghans, but Lashkar-e-Taiba cadres and trainers from the Pakistani Army.[12] India shall have to guard against a similar arrangement by a future Islamic Emirate.

The problem with the Taliban leadership is that they want a share in the country's governance and to change the constitution, which will compromise the gains made by the Afghan people over the last few years. Its leadership is dominated by those bent on restoring the organization as a totalitarian force: undemocratic, inegalitarian and misogynistic. It wants the whole, not just a part of the government. It is argued by many that some Taliban members might have genuine grievances that could be redressed. How about its grievance that women are being educated and encouraged to join the workforce? Or that Afghanistan has embraced multi-ethnic, democratic ways? Or that it has adopted a secular jurisprudence, which is in tune with the culture and genius of the Afghan people, but does not base itself exclusively on the Sharia? Are Afghans willing to give up on their sovereignty and independence? History tells us that might not be the case.

India has advised leaders of different ethnicities to work in cohesion with others for the common purposes of peace and nation-building. It favours the reintegration of insurgents and groups that give up their links with terrorist groups and networks, resile from violence, are inclusive and embrace the Afghan Constitution. It opposes only the political accommodation of individuals, groups or organizations associated with known terrorist entities, since this will subvert the nascent Afghan democracy, undermine human rights—particularly women's rights—and destroy emerging Afghan institutions. India must, as it has been, remain supportive of the Afghan people and their government, and be far more proactive in doing so.

The erstwhile Indian policy was to eschew interaction with the Taliban. Modi changed that. India's external affairs minister participated in the inauguration of the Doha peace negotiations. The invitation to India was an acknowledgement that India has vital interests in Afghanistan. The external affairs minister's participation was not to suggest that India had suddenly warmed to the Taliban, but to underline that India has no reservations in interacting with the Taliban if the Afghan government has none. The policy of lining up behind the Afghan government has not been given up. India has underlined its willingness to engage with any party committed to peace and stability in Afghanistan.

In any eventual settlement arrived at in the Afghan Peace Negotiations, the Taliban must be disarmed, demobilized and reintegrated into society, in much the same way that the cadres of the Hizb-e-Islami (HeI) in Afghanistan, the Islamic Renaissance Party in Tajikistan and the Maoists combatants of the People's Liberation Army in Nepal were. The Taliban should become a political party and be given every chance to participate democratically in the Afghan polity. The Afghan State alone must, however, have a monopoly on force, as in Tajikistan and Nepal.

Henry Kissinger famously said that the US 'exit strategy' in Afghanistan was all about exit and not at all about strategy. For a viable exit strategy, he advocated a ceasefire, withdrawal of foreign forces, creation of an alternate government and an enforcement mechanism.[13] Without these, a US exit or disengagement will fail. American forces may not be required for Afghanistan's security, but continued support to strengthen the Afghan State will be required for several more years. Modi has confirmed that India has no exit strategy for Afghanistan. In association with the international community, India will continue to stand by Afghanistan and sustain its stabilization with long-term commitment. The regional solution, never given a fair trial so far, can only work if Iran is brought into it as an important stakeholder, together with Afghanistan's other major neighbours, such as China, India and Russia.

India shares Afghanistan's objective: to establish a stable, strong and sovereign Afghanistan, which is able to stand on its feet and take its own decisions. So long as that happens, India's short-term strategic interest in Afghanistan will be fully met. India believes that if Afghans have food, fuel and firepower, as well as the solidarity of its neighbours and the international community at large, it can hold its own and find appropriate political solutions with the reconcilable among the armed opposition, including the Taliban. The manner in which Gulbuddin Hekmatyar (who even contested the last presidential elections in Afghanistan) and the HeI cadres were accommodated within the country's political order was admirable. Contrary to what is conventionally imagined, India has no issues in having dealings with Islamist groups, so long as they resile from violence and embrace constitutionalism. Even in the late 2000s, a large number of Cabinet ministers and provincial governors had HeI antecedents, and the Indian embassy in Kabul maintained excellent relations with them.

In the long run, India would like to see Afghanistan as a trade, transportation, energy and minerals hub, linking Iran and Central Asia with China and South Asia. Throughout history, Afghanistan has been the crossroads or roundabout for the region. Even if such an objective might seem remote at this juncture, it is well worth striving for, as it could make Afghanistan's slow process of recovery sustainable.

2

PAKISTAN

Inimical Neighbour

APARNA PANDE

India and Pakistan, notwithstanding ties of history, culture, ethnicity and language, remain hostile neighbours, divided by the impact of the British–Indian Empire's partition in 1947. The split of a unified subcontinent along religious lines framed the fundamental relations between the two neighbouring states. To understand Indo–Pak relations, there is a need to comprehensively understand the underlying issues of their relationship.

The roots of the key areas of conflict between India and Pakistan lie in the legacy of Partition—whether it is the problems facing minorities, the dispute over Kashmir or issues such as Siachen or the Sir Creek and the water dispute. The two countries have fought four wars in the last six decades: three over Kashmir (1947 and 1965, and a limited war in 1999) and one that resulted in the creation of Bangladesh (1971).

Since Independence in 1947, Pakistan's identity and foreign

policy have been framed around India. A religion-based national identity was constructed for Pakistan based on the view of 'Hindu' India as the 'other' for an 'Islamic' Pakistan.[1] This feeling of mistrust towards India and the insecurity about India's larger size led Pakistan's leaders and strategists to argue that India never accepted the creation of Pakistan and seeks to undo the Partition.

Pakistan's foreign and security policy is driven by a fervent desire to check 'hegemonic' India from achieving its 'nefarious' aims in South Asia and beyond. Although there is no evidence that India seeks to reincorporate Pakistan, the fear of India undoing Partition has informed Pakistani decision-making for over seven decades. In fact, even in 1971, during the civil war in East Pakistan that created Bangladesh, India supported the Bengalis but withdrew its forces as soon as the war ended.

Every Indian prime minister, from Jawaharlal Nehru to Narendra Modi, has sought to improve relations with Pakistan based on the belief that it will lead to a peaceful neighbourhood. Only in recent years has a strong anti-Pakistan sentiment emerged in India, particularly in the aftermath of the 1999 Kargil War and the 2008 Mumbai terror attacks, both of which are seen as a reflection of Pakistan's use of peace initiatives as an opportunity to launch attacks.

In the last two decades, three successive Indian prime ministers—Atal Bihari Vajpayee (1996; 1998–2004), Manmohan Singh (2004–14) and Narendra Modi (2014–)—have attempted to rebuild relations with Pakistan. Although the Pakistani civilian leaders have reciprocated Indian initiatives, a hard core of Pakistan's national security apparatus remains wedded to the idea of India being a permanent enemy. In fact, civilian leaders who have initiated friendship towards India, such as Benazir Bhutto, Nawaz Sharif and Asif Zardari, have been targeted by their domestic opponents as 'security risks' or 'Indian agents'.

They have also lost influence and power soon after the initiation of a peace process with India.

Throughout the various ups and downs, India's argument has consistently been that the two countries must build people-to-people ties and economic relations before resolving outstanding issues such as Kashmir. In recent years, the rise in terrorism, including the 2008 Mumbai terror attacks, has made it difficult for Indian governments to consider a dialogue with Pakistan without any discussion of terrorism.

If the topic of terrorism is front and centre for India in any dialogue with Pakistan, for Pakistan, it is the topic of Kashmir.

Kashmir: 'The Unfinished Business of Partition'

The one issue that best epitomizes how the rest of the world looks at Indo-Pak ties is that of Kashmir. The divergence of views on Kashmir starts from how the two countries—India and Pakistan—refer to the issue: for Pakistan, Kashmir is the 'unfinished business of Partition', whereas for India, it is a settled issue that only needs dialogue and discussion.

India has always maintained that Kashmir is Indian territory and the Instrument of Accession signed by the Maharaja of Kashmir, Hari Singh, in October 1947, and successive elections within the province demonstrate that the people of Kashmir wish to remain with India. Pakistan's argument has always been that as a Muslim-majority area, Kashmir should have gone to Pakistan at the time of Partition.

The two countries have adopted differing policies when it comes to dealing with Kashmir. Pakistan has sought to internationalize the Kashmir dispute. Pakistan's leaders have consistently demanded that a plebiscite should be held in Kashmir in accordance with the United Nations (UN) resolutions to ascertain the will of the people about joining

India or Pakistan. However, the last of the UN resolutions was voted on in 1957, over six decades ago. India views Kashmir as a bilateral issue, not an international dispute.

For New Delhi, the Simla Agreement of 1972 remains the framework within which the two countries should discuss any problem areas, especially Kashmir.[2] The Agreement states that both countries are 'resolved to settle their differences by peaceful means through bilateral negotiations or by any other peaceful means mutually agreed upon between them'. The Lahore Declaration of 1999 reiterated the Simla Agreement 'in letter and spirit'.[3] However, Pakistan's military argues that the Simla Agreement was a treaty that was imposed after the devastating loss in the 1971 War, which resulted in the separation of East Pakistan and the creation of Bangladesh. They would prefer to ignore the agreement signed under duress and find a new basis for bilateral relations that deny India an upper hand.

However, Kashmir forms a subset of the broader issue of Indo-Pak relations and Pakistan's desire for parity with a much larger neighbour. Unable to maintain parity with India on the conventional military front, asymmetrical warfare in the form of terrorism was viewed by the Pakistani deep state as the cost-friendly yet potent alternative against a much larger neighbour. Pakistan has nurtured a hardline *'Kashmir bazor Shamsheer'* (Kashmir by the sword) lobby that portrays India as an existential threat to Pakistan—a view supported by Pakistan's politically dominant military.

Until a few years ago, India pursued a policy of sporadic engagement with Pakistan even amidst intermittent terrorist attacks. The hope was that these comprehensive dialogues— covering everything from Kashmir to Siachen and the economy to the visa regime—would help build a mechanism that would resolve both the larger and smaller issues between the two countries. But since 2015, New Delhi has made dialogue contingent on Pakistan, ending all support for Kashmiri terrorist groups and giving up the option of using force to gain control of Kashmir.

There has been no bilateral meeting between the Indian and Pakistani PMs since the December 2015 visit by PM Modi to Lahore to meet the then PM Nawaz Sharif.[4] Relations have only worsened since. The January 2016 Pathankot terrorist attack was followed by the Uri terror attack later that year, which resulted in India's surgical strike against Pakistan-based jihadi camps.[5] In February 2019, after one of the deadliest terror attacks against Indian security forces by a Kashmiri terrorist belonging to the Pakistan-based terror group Jaish-e-Mohammed (JeM) in Pulwama, India ended its traditional strategic restraint and struck at terror camps deep inside Pakistan in Balakot, Khyber Pakhtunkhwa.[6]

The two countries are at an impasse now. India does not believe it needs to restart a dialogue with Pakistan unless and until Pakistan takes actions against terrorist groups that target India. Pakistan believes it only needs to convince the global community to exert enough pressure that will bring India to the negotiating table.

On 5 August 2019, the Indian government amended India's constitution, removing article(s) 370 and 35A that conferred special status on Jammu and Kashmir (J&K), and divided the erstwhile state into two Union Territories (UTs).[7] The erstwhile state of Kashmir—the one Maharaja Hari Singh acceded to India in October 1947—now no longer exists. Part of its territory is with Pakistan, which has already ceded a portion to China, and the part that was with India is split into UTs, with autonomy less than that of a state under the Indian constitution.

The Indian government believes it has changed the reality of Kashmir on the ground, in the hope of resolving the long-standing dual issues of national integration and international legitimacy with respect to J&K. India's leaders think they have resolved the Kashmir issue and presented the world with a *fait accompli*. As of now, India has benefitted from its friends around the world, notably the US and most Western countries, being willing to give India time to restore normalcy in Kashmir.

Pakistan has received little support in its attempts to raise the matter of J&K at the United Nations Security Council (UNSC) or even at regional fora. Except for Turkey, Iran and Malaysia, Muslim countries have avoided castigating India on the Kashmir issue. There is an international consensus that terrorism is not acceptable as a means of focusing attention on any grievance. But if the internal situation in J&K, where suspension of civil liberties and severe militarization have accompanied the change in constitutional status, does not change for the better, the problem could come back to affect India's global standing. Like all defining decisions, this solution must stand the test of time before being described a triumph.

Blowing Hot and Cold

The two neighbours are at an impasse that cannot be broken unless one or both give up on the issue they define as the principal issue holding the relationship back. Moving forward requires that Pakistan backs away from demands relating to Kashmir in return for India no longer insisting on terrorism-related conditions being central to peace talks.

Turning to the broader Indo-Pak relationship over the last six years, we see a lot of continuity again. When Modi was the chief minister of Gujarat and the prime ministerial candidate of the Bharatiya Janata Party (BJP), he consistently attacked his predecessor PM Manmohan Singh in matters relating to national security. After the 2008 Mumbai terror attacks, Modi addressed a press conference and sharply criticized then PM Singh's address to the nation as 'disappointing' and went on to outright blame the Pakistani government for the terrorist attacks that killed over 160 civilians.[8]

However, one of Modi's first acts after winning the elections in 2014 was to invite all his counterparts in South Asia, including Pakistani PM Nawaz Sharif, to his swearing-in ceremony.[9] This was followed by a series of peace moves made by both governments. During the 2014 South Asian Association for Regional Cooperation (SAARC) summit at Kathmandu, PM Modi posed for a handshake with PM Sharif, and later both leaders went on to have an hour-long secret meeting.[10] In June 2015, PM Modi called PM Sharif to send his good wishes for the Islamic holy month of Ramzan.[11] In the following month, both leaders met once again on the sidelines of the Shanghai Cooperation Organization (SCO) summit in Ufa, Russia. In November, Modi and Sharif met once again, this time on the sidelines of the United Nations Climate Change Conference in Paris, where they decided to resume National Security Advisor (NSA)-level talks between the two countries.

In the last month of 2015, the NSAs of both countries met for a diplomatic summit in Bangkok and discussed a wide array of issues including terrorism and Kashmir.[12] A few days after the Bangkok meeting, India's external affairs minister Sushma Swaraj travelled to Islamabad in early December 2015 to attend the Heart of Asia conference, which led to the resumption of comprehensive talks to discuss all issues of disagreement between the two countries.[13]

In December 2015, PM Modi travelled to Lahore to attend the wedding of PM Sharif's granddaughter.[14] The trip marked the first time that India's PM travelled to Pakistan in over a decade, and the optics could not be better. Both leaders were photographed hugging and sharing very friendly moments.

Modi's surprise visit to Lahore revived the oft-desired hope that India and Pakistan would finally be able to live as friends, and not adversaries.

This was not the first time that an Indian PM had extended a hand of friendship towards Pakistan; what was different was the style: a sudden stopover in Lahore on the way back from Kabul. For many, this is reminiscent of former Indian PM Dr Singh's words in January 2007: 'I dream of a day, while retaining our respective national identities, one can have breakfast in Amritsar, lunch in Lahore and dinner in Kabul. That is how my forefathers lived. That is how I want our grandchildren to live.'

On the other side, two civilian governments in Pakistan had attempted to improve ties with India since 2008. However, they had been unable to do so because of the veto of Pakistan's military-intelligence complex. Sharif too came to power in June 2013 seeking to change Pakistan's policy with respect to India and Afghanistan. While in Opposition, he often spoke of the need for better relations between India and Pakistan. Unfortunately, as with previous civilian administrations, this time too the Pakistan military-intelligence establishment that runs Pakistan's foreign and security policies ensured that Sharif was unable to change policies.

From the Indian perspective, a democratic and civilian-led Pakistan has multiple benefits. In fact, Modi's overture to Pakistan was founded on the belief that Pakistan was facing tremendous international pressure from the US and that better ties with India would boost the civilian government by improving its global image. It would also help provide the civilians with leverage over the military-intelligence establishment at a time when the latter was facing pressure from radical groups—both domestic and foreign. Restarting talks also opened the prospects of boosting economic and commercial relations and people-to-people ties that would help change the narrative and eventually lead to peace in the region.

However, meetings alone do not change policies; paradigm shifts are required in how the Pakistani Army views India. That has yet to happen, and within a week of Modi's visit to Lahore in January 2016, an Indian Air Force base at Pathankot was attacked by militants.[15]

In a remarkable move, the Modi government allowed an investigative team from Pakistan—consisting of members of the Inter-Services Intelligence, Military Intelligence and police—to reach the airbase and investigate the causes of the attack.[16] While in the past, there have been occasions when the intelligence agencies of both countries have spoken with each other, or sent messages, there is a reason that mistrust exists. This mistrust also ensured that the idea of a joint intelligence mechanism mooted in 2006 went nowhere.

Predictably, after several days of investigation, the Pakistani investigators returned home and claimed that the Pathankot attack had been staged by the Indian government.[17] Prime Minister Sharif decided to suspend the ongoing peace talks with India, and then Pakistan's High Commissioner to India Abdul Basit stated that no meetings were going to be scheduled between the foreign secretaries of the two nations.[18]

Nine months after the January 2016 attack, in September 2016, tensions rose once again when 17 Indian soldiers were killed after Pakistani militants attacked an Indian army brigade headquarters in Uri, Kashmir.[19] In response, Indian troops crossed the Line of Control on 29 September in a move that was widely described as a 'surgical strike' by India's media establishment. While New Delhi did not release the official figures, reports in the Indian media claimed up to 50 casualties.[20] Pakistan sought to defuse the situation by asserting that nothing happened during this strike by India.[21]

So even though Modi, like his predecessors, started his premiership by seeking to resolve the 'Pakistan question', he faced the same issue that had plagued others before him.

In 2018, after elections in Pakistan, there was a revival of the view both regionally and globally that there would be a new beginning in relations with India. But Imran Khan's promise of a new Pakistan was easier for Pakistanis to believe than for the rest of the world. Nations tend to proceed cautiously when it comes to countries that have acted in an antagonistic manner or failed to keep promises in the past.

India and Pakistan know that good relations would benefit them both, but there are reasons why that knowledge has not translated into a workable strategy for positive engagement. Those reasons do not disappear just because one of the two countries has a new PM; one who has no experience of governance and a tendency to over-promise amidst incredible faith in himself.

In his first speech after being elected, Imran spoke about improving relations with India even though he had denigrated similar efforts by his rival, Sharif, whom he dubbed as *'Modi ka yaar'* (Modi's friend) in his election campaign. Elections in Pakistan might be won more easily by painting your opponent as too friendly to India, but the burden of office turns all hawks into doves.

Imran then wrote to Modi requesting that the two countries resume talks with a meeting of foreign ministers on the sidelines of the annual UN General Assembly (UNGA) meetings in September 2018. He indicated that Pakistan would be willing to discuss terrorism, but he asserted the need to make life easier for the people of J&K.

This was a major concession from the Pakistani side, even if it fell short of India's demand. For once, an ostensibly hawkish Pakistani leader was asking for improvement in the lives of Kashmiris without demanding resolution of the age-old Kashmir dispute.

The contents of Imran's letter, however, were not released first by the Pakistan government, making Indian officials wonder whether Pakistan's desire was just to create an illusion of a peace process to break out of international isolation. For India, it is important that negotiations with Pakistan's leaders be conducted transparently.

From the Modi government's perspective, it did not turn down an offer of talks. It initially accepted what it referred to as 'talk not dialogue' on the sidelines of the UNGA, seeing it as an opportunity to at least hear what Foreign Minister Shah Mehmood Qureshi might have to offer. India only backed off after the inhumane killing of an Indian Border Security Force jawan and the kidnapping and killing of J&K police by Hizbul Mujahideen terrorists.

Things worsened in February 2019, when over 40 Central Reserve Police Force jawans were killed in Pulwama, Kashmir, by a car bomber. The suicide attacker was a member of the Pakistan-based terrorist group JeM. Twelve days after the attack, on 26 February, the Indian Air Force crossed into Pakistan for what the government called a 'non-military pre-emptive strike' on a JeM terrorist camp.[22] Pakistan retaliated by launching airstrikes in Indian-administered Kashmir, which was followed by an air battle in which an Indian Air Force pilot, Wing Commander Abhinandan Varthaman, was captured by Pakistan.[23] After several days of uncertainty and hostility, tensions finally eased when Pakistan returned Varthaman to India.

The Pulwama attack led to a growing view within the Indian foreign policy establishment, and even the broader public, that it was futile to attempt to rebuild relations with Pakistan unless Pakistan's military intelligence establishment changed its strategic outlook and views on India. Therefore, for the last two years, the Indian policy has consisted primarily of using the issue of terrorism to isolate Pakistan in international fora, from the UN to the Financial Action Task Force, and at the regional level. In addition, against the background of heightened political and military tensions, the Indo-Pak relationship further collapsed with suspension of cross-border trade relations and official channels of communication.[24] On the other hand, the strongest political response that Pakistan managed in the aftermath of the Balakot air strikes was shutting down Pakistani airspace to India for over four months, even at the cost of financial losses to Pakistan.[25]

While India has often been an election issue in Pakistan, Pakistan was rarely an issue in India. This changed after 2014 and now Pakistan is an electoral issue even in state-level elections. The 2019 Pulwama–Balakot attacks played an influential role in helping the Modi government comfortably win a second term.[26] During the campaign, the PM and many Bharatiya Janata Party leaders asserted that India is not afraid of Pakistan's nuclear threats anymore and even suggested that India's nuclear weapons were not just for show.[27] The bilateral relationship between the two countries deteriorated even further in August 2019 with India's revocation of the special status of J&K. Pakistan's immediate reaction was the expulsion of the High Commissioner of India in protest.

While Modi has strong domestic and international support, his Pakistani counterpart does not have the same luck. After the initial shock of India's move in Kashmir, Islamabad's reaction was to either isolate India or to have the Indian action condemned by other Muslim countries or regional or the global community.

However, despite renewed tensions, the Indo-Pak relationship did not break down completely. In fact, after the

2019 election results were announced, Imran telephoned Modi and congratulated him while expressing the desire to improve the bilateral relationship.[28] Modi was receptive and reiterated his earlier suggestion of working together to fight poverty, develop further cooperation and enable an environment devoid of violence and terrorism.[29]

In November 2019, the two countries inaugurated the visa-free Kartarpur Corridor, allowing Sikh pilgrims from India's Punjab state to visit some of their religion's holiest shrines located across the border.[30] For India, the Kartarpur corridor is simply a corridor to ease access for Sikh pilgrims to their religious sites located across the border. It is an issue-specific concession, akin to offering visas for medical purposes that ties in with India's overall policy of improving people-to-people ties with Pakistan. It does not, however, reflect any change in Indian policy on substantive matters and, therefore, does not ease India's policy over the last several years of refusing direct high-level talks with Pakistan until the issue of terrorism is addressed.

The global community may have expressed a collective sigh of relief when India and Pakistan announced their latest ceasefire in end-February 2021.[31] However, this is not the first such ceasefire and will certainly not be the last. The ceasefire is, as of now, simply a limited ceasefire agreement, and like most agreements between India and Pakistan over the last several decades, they survive only till the next terror attack.

For those asking why this ceasefire happened right now, the answers lie more in domestic reasons than international. Pakistan is under considerable pressure on multiple fora. The civilian government is weak and not interested in foreign policy. As the institution that in effect has dictated Pakistan's foreign and domestic politics, the Army feels there is too much pressure on the country and that there is a need to alleviate that pressure.

However, there is no sign that the Pakistani Army has given up its strategic vision or view on India as an existential threat. It is simply seeking temporary reprieve from Indian pressure on Pakistan's border, and international pressure on the country's economy. If Pakistan is viewed as reaching out to India, that will lower the global pressure on Pakistan and buy the country some time and hopefully some economic assistance. The Indian side is speaking with the military because Delhi knows that at the end of the day, the Pakistani civilian leaders will not be able to guarantee any agreement unless the Army backs it. India currently has a live border situation with China and would like at least one of the two borders to be cold.

Since 1989, on every New Year's Day, India and Pakistan exchange lists of sensitive nuclear installations pursuant to a non-attack agreement between them. In 2020, too, the two sides successfully completed the 29th consecutive annual Agreement on the Prohibition of Attack against Nuclear Installations and Facilities that requires the countries to exchange such lists to prevent such installations from being attacked during any conflict.[32]

Starting from 2008, there has been growing Indian public opinion that has supported a tough hawkish policy towards Pakistan. This has only deepened since 2016 and even more after 2019. This has provided the Modi government with the necessary domestic support to continue with their policy and lay down strong conditions for the resumption of any diplomatic dialogue with Pakistan. At the international fora as well, India has been able to obtain support from the US, European countries, and even in the UNSC on calling Pakistan out on the issue of terrorism.

Stabilizing a Cold Peace

Indo-Pak crises are not new, nor are terrorist attacks by Pakistan-based groups or India's attempts to coerce Pakistan in their aftermath. What has changed over the last few years and was witnessed in 2019 was the regional and global reaction to both the 14 February 2019 terror attack at Pulwama and India's punitive action against Pakistan. Almost every major country, as well as the UNSC, have been unequivocal in condemning the terrorist attack and did not mince words in assigning the blame to Pakistan. Even China disregarded Pakistan's usual ploy of linking terrorism to the situation in J&K or demanding more evidence about those who orchestrated the attack in Pulwama.

This was in sharp contrast to the statements by countries that used to be allies of Pakistan—the United Kingdom (UK), the US and the European Union, as well as Gulf countries such as Saudi Arabia and the United Arab Emirates in the aftermath of the 26/11 Mumbai terror attacks that provided some leeway to Pakistan. Words such as 'non-state actors' were sometimes used alongside expressions of faith in Pakistan's promises of acting against the terrorists. That seems to have changed. No one is now willing to praise the Pakistan government's actions against domestic terrorists while asking for action against terrorists targeting India and Afghanistan. With both domestic and international support, the Modi government had the necessary support to back their slogan, 'terror and talks cannot go together'.[33]

The failure of attempts at resuming talks between India and Pakistan reflects the inability of both governments to make an extremely difficult political decision. Pakistan's leaders remain reluctant to admit that their desire for the intractable Kashmir dispute to be resolved will not be fulfilled any time soon. India finds it difficult to recognize that it might have to forego its demand for justice in past terror cases as the price for a future commitment to normal, good neighbourly relations.

Although both sides are currently raising the temperature for their respective domestic constituencies, it is important to remember the broader context of Indo-Pak peace-making and periodic phases of jingoism.

If Pakistan is really interested in improving bilateral relations, it will need to move beyond the 'Kashmir first' policy. Pakistan may have to bite the bullet and accept that normalization of relations with India would require that Kashmir is placed on the back burner not just for now but possibly forever.

There are some Pakistanis who understand that reality. Former ambassador Shahid Amin argued in an article that Pakistan needs to understand the 'Kashmir dispute cannot be solved by military means or through the use of non-state actors'.[34] Ambassador Husain Haqqani has argued in his books and articles for over two decades that improving relations with India is more important for Pakistan than resolving a specific dispute.

But currently, there are no such thinkers in Pakistan's government. On the Indian side, too, national pride and anger over terrorism preclude initiatives involving what some refer to as 'magnanimity towards Pakistan'.

Pakistan remains critical to India's view of its neighbourhood. It is the country that broke away from India, so to speak, and has maintained consistent hostility towards India. Every Indian PM has come to power hoping to leave as their legacy the resolution of the conflict with Pakistan. The fact that this has not happened points to the problem having deeper roots than is generally assumed.

For Pakistan, antagonism towards India has become an essential characteristic of its national identity. Until and unless the Pakistani military-intelligence establishment moves away from viewing India as an existential threat and stops using jihad as a lever of foreign policy, there is little hope for normal relations between the two countries.

India, therefore, must plan on the assumption that Pakistan will continue to be hostile to India and will act as an obstacle to India's rise. India would have to convince others, especially the US, that instead of mediating in some Indo-Pak dispute, their role should be to check Pakistan's implacable hostility and disregard for international norms when it comes to India.

3

CHINA

End of the Era of Expansionism

GAUTAM BAMBAWALE

The summer of 2020 saw Chinese military aggression against India on our undefined boundary (referred to as the Line of Actual Control) in Ladakh.[1] Although there were incidents between the Indian and Chinese militaries in that geography in 2013 at Depsang and in 2014 at Chumar, those incidents were different because in those instances, army patrols from the two countries had accidentally come face to face with each other while conducting normal patrolling activities. The summer of 2020 was completely different and was of another dimension altogether. That year, the Chinese People's Liberation Army (PLA) came to Ladakh in large numbers of several divisions with tens of thousands of soldiers. Also, it brought in arms and ammunition of an entirely different proportion, including tanks and artillery.[2] It also proceeded to engage the Indian Army at several different locations in Ladakh. From all these facts, we can safely assume that the current move by China is not merely premeditated but also well planned and aimed at achieving several political and military objectives. To this mix must be added the incident which took place at Galwan on 16 June 2020, where hand-to-hand combat took place between soldiers of the two armies. Twenty Indian soldiers, including an officer, lost their lives as did an unspecified number of Chinese troops. The People's Republic of China government has announced gallantry citations and awards for four dead soldiers as also for one more who was severely injured. While China may have announced these four casualties on their side at Galwan, intelligence sources continue to claim that many more Chinese soldiers died that night. Naturally, Indian public opinion is inflamed due to this violation by China of all the agreements that exist between the two nations aimed at ensuring peace along the borders.

However, it is imperative that we backtrack a bit and analyse what kind of relationship was inherited by Prime Minister (PM) Narendra Modi when he was elected to office by the people of India in mid-2014. Such a recapitulation would also provide some depth to the current assessment of India–China relations.

The 1988 Template: An Enduring Legacy

One has to hark back to December 1988 and the China visit of India's then PM Rajiv Gandhi, the first by an Indian PM in 34 years, to comprehend the template in which India–China relations have developed over the past three decades. During that visit, between 19 and 23 December, the two governments arrived at the understanding that while it was important to make efforts to resolve the Boundary Question, this process would take time and, hence, it was unlikely that a solution could be reached at in the near term. Hence, it was of utmost importance for the two sides to ensure that peace and tranquillity were maintained in the India–China border areas. This necessary condition would then permit the rest of the bilateral relationship to move forward. Towards this end, the governments agreed to the establishment of a Joint Working Group on the Boundary Question headed at the vice minister/secretary level and simultaneously also formed a ministerial-level Joint Group on Economy and Trade, Science and Technology.[3] If the two countries succeeded in ensuring peace and tranquillity in the border areas, the rest of the relationship could be normalized particularly in economic exchanges, trade, science and technology, tourism and people-to-people exchanges. This was the new template for India–China relations arrived at in December 1988 and it was this paradigm that has been followed since then until the summer of 2020. On the Indian side, the *modus vivendi* arrived at by PM Rajiv Gandhi has been pursued by all his successors including PMs V.P. Singh, Chandra Shekhar, Narasimha Rao, H.D. Deve Gowda, I.K. Gujral, Atal Bihari Vajpayee, Dr Manmohan Singh and Narendra Modi.

Having inherited this *modus vivendi* for the China relationship, the newly elected PM, Modi, accepted the proposed visit to India of China's new leader, Xi Jinping. One must keep in mind that as chief minister of Gujarat, Modi had visited China several times with the aim of learning from China's economic successes to understand if any of her experiences could be transferred to Indian conditions so as to bolster India's own development processes. He had clearly seen how foreign trade and foreign direct investment (FDI) were of great assistance in not merely boosting economic growth rates but also in modernizing certain sectors of the economy, which would then lead the way for the rest of the nation. In particular, Modi had understood the necessity of new thinking or out-of-the-box ideas, which could be translated to local conditions.

Chinese president Xi Jinping's visit to India took place between 17 and 19 September 2014, very soon after Modi became PM. Xi himself had taken over as general secretary of the Communist Party of China in November 2012 and as president of the nation in March 2013. Modi placed a fair amount of importance on building a rapport and relationship with the Chinese leader. Their interaction in Ahmedabad produced photographic moments for the cameras and more importantly for live television broadcasting to over two billion Indians and Chinese.

It was only after having tasted Gujarat's history, culture and cuisine that Xi moved to New Delhi for the formal part of his programme. This kind of diplomacy was not merely new to the Indian audience, but by all accounts, it made a huge impact on the Chinese people including when they saw Modi and Xi chatting with each other on a swing decorated in Gujarat's handmade finery.

On the substantive side, the two governments announced that their relations now comprised a 'Closer Developmental Partnership'[4] indicating a higher level of cooperation between the two. Sixteen agreements and memoranda of understanding were concluded and signed between the two sides including the opening of a new route for Indian pilgrims to visit Kailash Manasarovar via Nathu La in Sikkim, expansion of economic exchanges between the two countries as well as cooperation in space science and nuclear energy. China indicated it would set up two industrial parks in India and promised to bring in FDI amounting to $20 billion into them. A comprehensive joint statement issued at the end of the visit clearly gave the impression that relations were moving into a higher gear under the new leaders of the two nations.

For our purposes, one sentence in the joint statement is fundamental since it made the point of how peace on our borders was looked upon as a necessary condition for the relationship to continue its forward momentum. The joint statement clearly stated that 'peace and tranquillity on the India–China border areas was recognized as an important guarantor for the development and continued growth of bilateral relations'. The significance and importance of this principle will be revisited when we analyse the events of the summer of 2020.

Xi's visit to India was marred, however, by another dust up and close proximity situation between Indian and Chinese troops in Chumar in Ladakh. Just as the visit was taking off, a face-off occurred in this geography which made headlines in the Indian media, infuriating media handlers of the Chinese president. Modi took the opportunity to discuss the situation with Xi, who was still fairly uninformed of the developing situation. However, the face-off was resolved soon after the visit concluded. However, this also gave rise to speculation in some quarters in India that the PLA could have undertaken the face-off without clearance from the chairman of the Central Military Commission, namely, Xi himself.

Modi's return visit to China took place between 14 and 16 May 2015. Clearly, the bonhomie between him and President Xi seemed to have endured, with Xi greeting Modi in Xian to show him the culture and history of China as a reciprocal gesture to that made the earlier year by Modi in Ahmedabad. The Chinese president travelled out of Beijing to receive and greet a foreign leader—something of a rarity in China's communist epoch. The formal meetings in Beijing the next day produced 24 bilateral agreements as well as a joint statement on climate change. A broader joint statement was also issued, which indicated that the understanding amongst the leadership of the two countries visualized space for each of the emerging Asian giants as well as a partnership encompassing the political, developmental and social fields. The template set for the relationship as far back as 1988 seemed to be holding even 25 and more years later.

Again, a perusal of the India–China joint statement of 2015[5] reveals that, 'peace and tranquillity on the India–China border was recognized as an important guarantor for the development and continued growth of bilateral relations'. Even more pertinent from our point of view was the following sentence stating that, 'Pending a final resolution of the boundary question, the two sides commit to implementing the existing agreements and continue to make efforts to maintain peace and tranquillity in the border areas.'

Clearly, the first year after Modi's election as the PM of India seemed to indicate that bilateral India–China relations did not merely continue in the paradigm set in 1988 but had broadened further and deepened over the years. The equilibrium between the two nations continued to hold even as the economic, military and political asymmetry between the two enhanced and increased with each passing year.

Duality of Cooperation and Competition

However, alongside greater cooperation, the period commencing from 2014 also saw enhanced competition between India and China.

China launched its ambitious One Belt, One Road initiative in 2013 soon after the new leadership led by President Xi and Premier Li Keqiang took office in Beijing. The project aimed at utilizing the excess capacity available in China to help other nations build infrastructure that they required through loans and aid that the cash-rich Chinese government was willing to provide. The focus was on connectivity projects from mainland China to other parts of Asia and even Europe. Africa and Latin America were not ignored in what was rechristened the Belt and Road Initiative (BRI) in English, although in the Chinese language, it continued to be referred to as the One Belt, One Road project. The 'One Belt' refers to the Silk Road Economic Belt launched by Xi during a visit to Kazakhstan in September 2013, while the 'One Road' refers to the twenty-first-century Maritime Silk Road announced by Xi in October 2013 while visiting Indonesia. With China already having emerged as one of the world's largest trading nations, the BRI was not merely an initiative to keep China's factories humming and labour fully employed, but it also had the objective of ensuring that it was well connected to its markets around the globe through modern infrastructure, which in turn ensured its continued prosperity and growth. Looked at from this perspective, the BRI is not merely a geoeconomic strategy but a geopolitical one[6] as well. Its success can be seen in the manner in which the strategy enabled China to divide developed western Europe from lesser-developed central and eastern Europe.

The BRI took an ominous turn for India when Xi visited Pakistan in April 2015 and announced the launch of the China–Pakistan Economic Corridor (CPEC). Described as an important part of the One Belt, One Road initiative, China announced that it would invest $46 billion in power, roads, railways and the Gwadar port project, all of which would be constructed under the CPEC rubric. The fact that CPEC ran through territory claimed by India in Pakistan-occupied Kashmir (PoK) seemed to have been no obstacle to China's plans and Beijing did not even hesitate a little, leading India to observe that 'connectivity initiatives must be based on universally recognized international norms, good governance, rule of law, openness, transparency and equality. ... Connectivity projects must be pursued in a manner that respects sovereignty and territorial integrity'. India's statement went on to clearly enunciate, 'No country can accept a project that ignores its core concerns on sovereignty and territorial integrity.[7] With this insensitivity by China towards a matter of core concern for India, the battle lines on BRI were drawn between the two. There is no way India can resile from its articulated position on the BRI involving sovereignty over Pakistan-occupied Kashmir. How would China have responded if India had built a road through Chinese-claimed territory?

Meanwhile, China opposed India's entry into the Nuclear Supplier's Group and insisted that if India was admitted, then Pakistan must also be treated similarly. China continued to use all the tricks in the book at the UN 1267 Committee to ensure that Masood Azhar was not listed as a terrorist, enraging India. Increasingly, India worked closer together with the major Western powers such as the United States (US), France, United Kingdom and Germany on this and other issues such as Pakistan's grey listing by the Financial Action Task Force, the money laundering and terror-financing watchdog organization. The Quad or Quadrilateral Security Initiative was revived in 2017 pulling together India, the US, Japan and Australia in a possible future coalition against Chinese aggression in the Indo-Pacific. Since then, in little over three years, the Quad has gone from strength to strength with meetings of foreign ministers becoming commonplace. In November 2020, India included the Australian Navy in its Malabar Naval Exercise. The Americans and the Japanese have been part of these exercises for some time already. In this manner, the Quad countries have been able to exercise together with the objective of coordinating their navies and integrating them. The First Quad Leaders' Summit, which was held virtually in March 2021, is an indication of the seriousness with which the participant nations take this initiative, which aims to ensure that the Indo-Pacific remains a rules-based region and does not become authoritative in its orientation.

What China's foreign minister, Wang Yi, had once described as foam on a beach which fizzles out quickly, does seem here to stay as a possible future guarantor of good behaviour from China. That is why China has reacted negatively to the Quad and clearly recognizes that it could become a force to reckon with in the Indo-Pacific theatre.

In 2017, the one single incident that marred India–China relations significantly was the stand-off between their two armies at Doklam in Bhutan. On 16 June 2017, a PLA construction party came to the Doklam area of the Bhutan–China border to construct a road. A Royal Bhutan Army patrol attempted to dissuade the PLA from undertaking such unilateral activity in an area which was disputed between the two countries. Bhutan lodged a formal protest with China on 20 June 2017. The attempts of China to construct this road was in direct violation of agreements between the two nations on maintaining peace and tranquillity in their border and the eventual settlement of their border problem. Given the close political and military ties between India and Bhutan, Indian Army troops from Doka La in the Sikkim Sector approached the Chinese PLA and urged them to desist from changing the status quo.[8] The stand-off between the two armies continued for 72 days (16 June–28 August) till a mutually acceptable process of disengagement and de-escalation was agreed upon and took place in August 2017. In a democracy like India, this incident took a life of its own, with the Indian media covering it intensively throughout this period. The Chinese side also added grist to the mill by talking about it and giving their version through their foreign ministry and defense ministry spokespersons. Indeed, world media and political attention was focused on this stand-off. Atypically, Chinese official commentary was strong and shrill. Chinese diplomatic manoeuvres too were atypical during this episode, with insistence that India should withdraw first and only then would China withdraw. On its part, India took the high ground insisting that mutual withdrawals take place through discussion and negotiation. Coming on the heels of the face-offs of 2013 and 2014, the Doklam incident did inject a lot of strain and competition to bilateral ties.

Informal Summits: A New Normal?

So even as aspects of competition were buffeting the relationship, there was also the clear enhancement of China's comprehensive and economic power bringing in its wake a serious asymmetry between India and China. It was increasingly becoming obvious that the 1988 paradigm was not capable of guiding the relationship between the two nations and that perhaps a new normal or equilibrium was necessary. Thus, bilateral relations were suffused with hope for a balanced and forward-looking relationship between India and China after the two Informal Summit meetings between Modi and Xi at Wuhan in April 2018 and Chennai in October 2019. The optics from those meetings, including the news that the two leaders had advised their militaries to reduce tensions on the border, appeared to indicate that the two Asian giants were moving towards a new equilibrium in their relations.

These two Informal Summits between Modi and Xi were the manifestation of this search for a new *modus vivendi* for structuring relations so that they could continue forward without creating a major hiccup. Unfortunately, the process was incomplete even after two summit-level interactions and the new template or paradigm for the relationship was a work in progress.

In the meantime, the Chinese leadership also considered the military option on the Line of Actual Control and obviously went for that choice. However, by doing so, they have clearly indicated what kind of relationship they desire to establish with India. In their assessment, there is a huge asymmetry in power between China and India, implying China could gain on the ground through military coercion. However, in doing so, they have lost India strategically. They must ask themselves if the price has been commensurate to their tactical gains.

Deciphering China's Playbook

Many Indians ask the reasons for China's military aggression against India when the entire world is still embroiled in tackling the COVID-19 pandemic, which itself is known to have originated in Wuhan, China. A number of rationalizations have been advanced by Indian and foreign thinkers including:

- China was worried by India's road-building activity in the border areas
- India was beginning to get really close to the US and was actually colluding with it to contain China's rise
- India had changed the status quo in Jammu and Kashmir on 5 August 2019 by announcing the creation of two separate Union Territories and China wanted to clearly indicate what it considered its own borders
- Indian claims on Aksai Chin had spooked China
- To divert domestic public opinion in China from criticism of Beijing's handling of the COVID-19 pandemic
- Beijing's need to display and project strength particularly on sovereignty issues.[9]

Whether any of these reasons are correct is impossible to confirm as the Chinese decision-making system is opaque. However, the proximate cause of the Chinese military action in Ladakh could be a mix of these reasons and factors.

Whatever be the reason for China's military aggression

and attempted coercion on our borders in Ladakh, there are some very clear signals that China was sending India with its action. These include:

(a) Tactically, China was showing that there was a huge asymmetry between its own and India's comprehensive national power and that it could move its troops right up to what it considers its boundary with India. In other words, China was showing that it could unilaterally decide and define its border with India.
(b) Strategically, China was clearly implying that it is the regional hegemony in Asia and that India should understand its place in the power hierarchy on our continent. Moreover, the twenty-first century was not an Asian Century but solely a Chinese Century.

India's military moves on the ground to face up to and combat the Chinese military build-up with its own mirror strengthening of forces on the border[10] have clearly shown that we do not accept or agree with many of the above-mentioned propositions or contentions. The Indian Army has heroically and bravely blocked Chinese advances and even taken some proactive military measures of its own, which appear to have shocked the PLA. Clearly, India has indicated to the Chinese leadership that we shall not tolerate Chinese bullying and we shall reply to the aggression with our own show of force. India's displeasure towards China's attempts and measures has been conveyed through our military action on the ground in Ladakh.

Having sent these very clear signals to China through our own military responses in Ladakh, it is also very necessary to replicate or reinforce these messages through policy actions and measures. Why is this so? If we were not to do this, then the Chinese would jump to the incorrect conclusion that India does not take objection to the kind of military actions it has undertaken in the summer of 2020 in Ladakh. China would also believe that it is free to change things militarily on the ground but that the rest of the India–China relationship can and will continue merrily as it was before last summer. In particular, China is keen to ensure that economic relations between the two nations are not hampered as China makes approximately $50 billion each year through its trade surplus with India. Remember, China's trade policy is steeped in mercantilism. So, this is China's playbook—undertake military aggression on the ground but ensure that the rest of the relationship is maintained as it is.[11]

It Cannot Be Business as Usual

If India were to permit such a scenario, it would indeed be a win-win for China, where it would win on both counts—military and economic. Therefore, it is essential for India to show China that if there is no peace on our borders, our bilateral ties cannot continue as earlier. The template for India–China relations set during Rajiv Gandhi's visit to China in December 1988 and followed unswervingly by following administrations in India has been nulled and voided by China's actions in the summer of 2020. This is exactly what the Government of India has done by banning many Chinese apps on national security grounds from the India market. In fact, after India's decision, other countries have also replicated our measures. Hence, the Chinese app TikTok has now been banned in the US. Those who argue that India does not have sufficient economic leverage over China are wrong. We do have leverage and we must show our displeasure to the Chinese authorities. This is to be done by clearly showing them that in the aftermath of Ladakh, it cannot be business as usual.[12]

The Indian government has also taken other good first

steps by ensuring that we have the means to ensure that Chinese firms do not win competitive bidding procedures in public procurement. Similarly, an additional level of due diligence has been added to FDI procedures for Chinese entities by implementing just the government route for them. The automatic route is no longer open for Chinese investment. An important leverage that India has in its hands is the possibility of keeping Chinese firms such as Huawei out of our 5G trials and roll-out. Since Huawei has already been banned by the US, Australia, the UK and others, if it is kept out of the huge India market, it will be quite a setback for it. Indian telecom operators are already being advised by our authorities to be very careful in utilizing Chinese equipment in their existing and future telecom systems. A ban on Chinese firms is quite likely too. All these measures aim at raising the costs for China in undertaking the military action in Ladakh.

The telecom sector, particularly the manufacture of mobile phone handsets, is once again providing the lead in shifting global supply chains to countries like India so as to ensure reliability of supply. While economic factors are paramount in such decision-making, non-economic factors are also creeping into such corporate decisions. This can indeed be the right time for India to attract large amounts of FDI, although we must make it easier to do business in India not merely for foreign firms but for Indian entrepreneurs as well. Second-generation reforms are the need of the hour, particularly in the supply of land, labour, capital and management.

Auto ancillary manufacturers in India are also seeing the first indications of American and German companies significantly raising their procurements from India, perhaps as a result of this need for reliability in supply as well as due to advice to do so from their own governments. If this is indeed true and becomes a trend, the auto sector in India is likely to get a boost from international demand. We shall have to ensure that quality control measures are enhanced to meet such new demand. Also, India's own auto firms should see the writing on the wall and move to Indian suppliers as much as possible. The idea of 'Atmanirbhar Bharat' is not one of autarky, but it definitely aims at ensuring local manufacturing of key systems and products where India does have a competitive advantage. In the auto components segment, India can indeed compete with China. While we do not see a complete economic de-coupling between India and China, there is definitely a move to ensure greater symmetry in economic exchanges between the two countries and to provide a level playing field for Indian manufacturing firms in sectors where we do have a competitive advantage. Indian industry must take advantage of these conditions. How much India–China economic relations will be impacted will also depend on how long the Chinese aggression continues. The longer the Ladakh imbroglio continues, the more the rest of the relationship will be negatively impacted and the more it will deteriorate. However, even if the PLA were to restore the status quo ante, the course for the bilateral economic relationship is unlikely to deviate from the trajectory now set.

Similarly, in the pharmaceutical industry, India is far too reliant on the supply of active pharmaceutical ingredients (APIs) from China. Almost 70 per cent of the APIs used in our domestic pharma industry is sourced from China. India does have a competitive advantage in this product line. We used to domestically produce many APIs before predatory pricing and related policies forced the closure of such factories including the iconic Hindustan Antibiotics Limited and Indian Drugs and Pharmaceuticals Limited. With a more level playing field, India is set to manufacture more of these APIs at home and hopefully witness a revival of this sector. Such a development will also be in line with Atmanirbhar Bharat.

This brings us back to the argument we started with: that China has been able to commit military aggression against India in Ladakh due to the huge asymmetry between the two economies. It is only when India reduces this asymmetry by growing its own economy for an extended period of time that we shall be able to ensure that China will not commit military aggression against us. We have to find ways of increasing the share of manufacturing in our gross domestic product. This is what the 'Make in India' project is all about. No major power in the world has become number one unless it is able to make at least some of the arms and armaments it needs to protect itself, its territory and its integrity at home. We cannot become a major power by importing all the defence systems required by our Armed Forces. India has to pay more attention to its manufacturing sector so that it is able to achieve this goal. In turn, India can become a major power only if its economy grows at 7–8 per cent per annum.

Such relatively rapid economic and social progress will also reduce the asymmetry in economic size between India and China. In turn, this may also lead to changes in military asymmetry and the currently huge discrepancy in comprehensive national power between the two. Of course, we have to do all this for ourselves too. We need rapid growth to raise the living standards of our people, to eliminate poverty, to ensure that Indians live longer and have healthier lives and to make India an even more consequential power in international politics. The key is to rediscover our mojo for rapid 7–8 per cent annual economic growth.

Such reinforcing policy decisions, to indicate to China that it cannot be business as usual after its attempted military coercion in Ladakh, need to be taken not merely in the economic field but also in the political and strategic areas too. The meeting of the foreign ministers of the Quad countries—

namely India, the US, Japan and Australia—in Tokyo on 6 October 2020 was a clear signal that these nations would not tolerate any change in the rules-based systems which dominate issues pertaining to the global commons not merely in the Indo-Pacific region but all over the world. India's invitation to Australia to participate in the next edition of the Malabar Naval Exercise off the coast of India is a clear indication that the Quad nations will move forward purposefully to enhance interoperability of their militaries as a way to balance China, if and when found necessary. Intel sharing is also an area of cooperation among the four nation states, which will have a positive impact on their habits of working together. The entire Indo-Pacific region and its fundamental importance has also received a boost with the enunciation of a policy by Germany and the appointment of an ambassador for the Indo-Pacific by France. The Quad must be taken to its logical conclusion and amongst other actions India could also:

(a) appoint an ambassador for the Indo-Pacific region
(b) institute a Quad 2+2 dialogue of foreign and defence ministers
(c) institutionalize the four-nation Malabar Naval Exercise as an annual event held alternately off the coast of Japan and off the coast of India
(d) consider bringing in France as another member of the Quad
(e) join the Blue Dot Network[13]
(f) institute a Quad dialogue with ASEAN

The Indo-US relationship itself is strengthening immeasurably with the 2+2 dialogue between the foreign and defence ministers having taken place in end of October 2020. The signing of the last foundational agreement of the Basic Exchange and Cooperation is another move forward on this road. Economic aspects of the relationship also need reinforcing and strengthening and if we are able to conclude some kind of trade agreement that would be a signal to the rest of the world that the two nations are serious about working together. The trend of a closer India–US partnership is clear for all to see and has continued under the new Joe Biden administration. Closer defence cooperation is on the cards as is our coordination on issues at the United Nations, where India is a non-permanent member for 2021 and 2022. While human rights issues are likely to be taken up by the current US administration, these will not mar the relationship, as there are several proactive areas of cooperation which both sides are keen to pursue.

India must ensure that it cannot be business as usual with China in order to signal its displeasure against its military aggression as well as raise the costs of undertaking such misadventures. There are many in India who argue that such a policy that precludes business as usual with China will hurt India more than it will hurt China. That may be the case, but once a decision has been taken to stand up to China and stare it down on national security grounds, then all of us Indians should be willing to pay the higher price involved in sending a clear message to China and its leadership. How can we even expect that such strong decisions will not involve a cost to the people and our economy? The government and the people of India are resolved on this issue and have the perseverance and wisdom to see this through.

The plain and simple fact is that we as a society are willing to pay that price for the defence of the nation. A re-set and recalibration in India–China ties is happening even now and will have to be taken to its logical conclusion.

4

NEPAL

Old Friendship, New Freeze

MANJEEV SINGH PURI

The spectrum of India–Nepal relations has few parallels in the world with the strongest manifestation at the level of the people. Rooted in geography and history, these *Roti-Beti ke samband*[1] are unique ties of friendship and cooperation characterized by an open border of over 1,850 km with five Indian states: Sikkim, West Bengal, Bihar, Uttar Pradesh and Uttarakhand. It is, however, important not to conflate the close ties at the level of the people with state-to-state relations between India and Nepal. Furthermore, while the elite in Nepal have internalized and played up differentiation with India, particularly resenting 'big brother' attitudes,[2] the understanding in India, even among influential sections, is one of being an 'elder brother' and/or looking at Nepal from an employer's perspective.

State-to-state ties go back to before India's independence, with Nepal being among the first countries to set up a diplomatic post in New Delhi (in 1934) and the Embassy of

India functioning in Kathmandu from June 1947. The India–Nepal Treaty of Peace and Friendship of 1950 provides citizens of both countries 'national treatment', that is, citizens of both countries can avail opportunities of employment in the other country on par with citizens. Special relations between India and Nepal include an open border, recruitment of Nepalese in the Gorkha regiments of the Indian Army and close economic ties including the Nepalese rupee being effectively pegged to the Indian rupee. As regard to India's now huge development partnership programme, it bears noting that much of it began with Nepal in the late 1950s, with the establishment of the Indian Cooperation Mission, which supported construction of most of the basic infrastructure in Nepal, including the airports and highways.

Little wonder then that over and above the 'Neighbourhood First' policy, significantly improving India's ties with Nepal was a natural objective of the National Democratic Alliance government, given the Bharatiya Janata Party's strong belief in the societal ties that bind India and Nepal. Moreover, for many in the party, the shared link of Hinduism would work strongly to underpin a closer coming together of the two countries. In this view, Nepal's drift towards secularism and the abolition of the monarchy was encouraged by the United Progressive Alliance and evidenced by the fact that no Indian prime minister had paid a bilateral visit to Nepal in 17 years.[3]

Prime Minister Modi himself led the effort to boost relations with Nepal and visited Nepal for a record four times in his first term with the first visit taking place in 2014, just months after he assumed office. Development partnership and improving connectivity was made a high priority. The success of the first visit made 2014 a year of the highest expectation for India–Nepal relations. However, even by the end of 2014, expectations had diminished significantly. A similar situation arose four years later in 2018, but once again ominous dark clouds appeared to ensure that India–Nepal ties remained quagmire.

Nepal prides itself in never having been colonized and thinks of itself as a 'yam' between two big Asian giants—India and China. But given societal and religious similarities with India, Nepal has also been acutely conscious of its 'independent' identity from India. The Nepalese have internalized the angst of the small state and believe that if they do not actively differentiate themselves from India, they would be subsumed. Nepalese nationalism is a 'mask for [an] anti-India sentiment'[4] and is the key systemic reason for India–Nepal state-to-state ties not truly progressing.

Recent times have changed Nepal, and other important factors are now also affecting India–Nepal ties. These include globalization and the pervasive changes it has brought in Nepalese society, Left politics and the vastly increased influence of China in keeping both with its growing global clout and regional interest.

High-Level Interactions

Prime Minister Modi paid a bilateral visit to Nepal in August 2014 and received a tumultuous welcome in Kathmandu. His speech in the Constituent Assembly (Parliament) struck the perfect chord with the Nepalese people across the country and it was said that if he stood for elections in Nepal, no one could take him on. He also visited Nepal in November 2014 for the South Asian Association of Regional Cooperation (SAARC) Summit.

Modi invited the Nepalese prime ministers (PM) for his swearing-in both in 2014 and in 2019. Furthermore, the Nepalese PM was invited with other Bay of Bengal Initiative for Multi-

Sectoral Technical and Economic Cooperation (BIMSTEC) leaders for meeting with the BRICS Heads of Governments in Goa in September 2016. In keeping with the tradition of India being the first foreign country to be visited by a Nepalese PM after assuming office, PM K.P. Sharma Oli visited India in 2016 and 2018, while PM Sher Bahadur Deuba was here in 2017. Prime Minister Pushpa Kamal Dahal 'Prachanda' broke the tradition by first visiting China in 2017 after he assumed office in 2016, but was soon thereafter in India. In addition, after a gap of over a decade and a half, the president of India, Shri Pranab Mukherjee, paid a state visit to Nepal in November 2016. The return state visit was paid by the Nepalese president, Hon'ble Bidya Devi Bhandari, in April 2017.

Humanitarian Support

On 25 April 2015, Nepal was struck by a devastating earthquake. Reacting with all swiftness and support as could be expected from a friendly and caring neighbour, India was the first responder from outside, immediately sending specialized teams of the National Disaster Response Force along with significant air support and rescue and relief materials to Nepal. The total Indian relief assistance amounted to over $67 million apart from technical assistance, including in restoring three power sub-stations in Kathmandu valley. Medical teams from India were also made available in various parts of Nepal which played a critical role in the treatment of the injured at the Trauma Centre in the heart of Kathmandu, which was built by India and inaugurated a year earlier.

Underscoring India's support for Nepal at the time of the earthquake, Modi said in his monthly radio address: 'My dear brothers and sisters of Nepal, India is with you in this hour of grief... For 125 crore Indians, Nepal is their own. India will do its best to wipe the tears of every Nepali, hold their hands and stand with them.' India pledged the largest amount of post-earthquake reconstruction package of $1 billion ($250 million in grants and $750 million as a line of credit) during the International Conference on Nepal's Reconstruction held in Kathmandu on 25 June 2015. The grant covers four key sectors requiring reconstruction: housing, health, education and heritage.

Indian grant assistance worth $100 million has reconstructed 50,000 housing units in the districts of Gorkha and Nuwakot directly benefitting thousands of those worst affected by the earthquake. In the area of education, 70 schools and the Central Library at the Tribhuvan University, Nepal's main university in Kathmandu, are to be rebuilt with a grant assistance of $50 million. Work has already been completed at eight schools, and progress is ongoing in 56 other schools. India's premier institution, the Central Building Research Institute, Roorkee, is the consultant. The institute is also the consultant for reconstruction of 147 health facilities. Another premier body in India, INTACH, is the consultant for 28 culture heritage sites.

Development Partnership

Development partnership and building better connectivity with Nepal also proceeded at an accelerated pace since 2014. A special Oversight Mechanism, co-chaired by the Indian ambassador and the Nepalese foreign secretary was put in place to sort out project-related issues. It has representation at senior levels from across the Government of Nepal. Moreover, the India–Nepal Joint Commission co-chaired by the external affairs minister of India, Dr S. Jaishankar, and foreign minister of Nepal, H.E. Mr Pradeep Kumar Gyawali, met after a gap of many years in August 2019 in Kathmandu. India's budget for 2019–20 earmarked ₹1,200 crore as 'Aid to Nepal'. In addition, around $1.65 billion worth of Letters of Credit have been issued by India for financing development projects in Nepal during the past few years.

Hydroelectric power is seen as the economic panacea for Nepal. The reality, however, is that despite a potential of 40,000 megawatt (MW), the country barely produces 1,000 MW and in 2015–16, found itself faced with the severest of electricity shortages resulting in long hours of power cuts even in Kathmandu. The power situation in Nepal was then significantly ameliorated with agreements for the supply of electric power from India through three dedicated transmission corridors: Muzaffarpur–Dhalkebar, Kataiya–Kusaha and Raxaul–Parwanipur. Today, Nepal imports around 600 MW of power from India.

More significantly, after years of being in the works, things finally moved forward on big hydro projects between India and Nepal, with the Arun-III project. This is a project being developed by India's public enterprise, Satluj Jal Vidyut Nigam Limited, and would generate 900 MW once completed in the coming years. Not only would this project add considerably to the availability of electricity in Nepal, it would have huge and positive economic gains for the Nepalese economy. The laying of its foundation stone jointly by the PMs of India and Nepal in May 2018 was, therefore, a landmark moment. This is the largest engineering venture in Nepal and is moving ahead apace with its construction.

At around $8 billion, India accounts for over two-thirds of Nepal's external trade of about $12 billion and provides transit for most of Nepal's third-country trade. Improving connectivity is a key objective of both countries. This received a big boost in 2018 when the two PMs inaugurated the Integrated Check Post

(ICP) at Birgunj built with Indian assistance. Birgunj is the most important transit point for India–Nepal trade and for Nepal's third-country imports coming via Kolkata and Visakhapatnam ports. Trade connectivity was further boosted when another ICP was inaugurated at Biratnagar in January 2020. Another important aspect of better connectivity has been the enhanced direct bus services between different cities in India and Nepal.

Nepal imports much of its petroleum requirement through India and almost all is moved through tanker-trucks. This involved fairy long journeys of several days subject to the vagaries of road transport. For years, the idea of an oil pipeline connecting nodal points in India and Nepal was on the table but never executed. In 2018, this imbroglio was broken, and the PMs of India and Nepal jointly presided over the groundbreaking ceremony for the pipeline between Motihari in India and Amlekhgunj in Nepal. The pipeline was completed in November 2019 in a record 18 months, several months ahead of schedule. The benefits of this easy and hassle-free petroleum products delivery system were immediately visible at the people's level with PM Oli announcing a ₹2 per litre reduction in petrol prices in Nepal.

Progress has also been witnessed in other areas including railways and roads. Track upgradation to broad gauge has been completed on the Jayanagar–Janakpur stretch, the only passenger line in Nepal, and the line is being extended to Bijalpura and Bardibas. Work to complete a rail track to Biratnagar was held up for some time due to land acquisition issues on the Nepalese side but is expected to resume soon. The Nepalese are keen on a railway line to Kathmandu, and the Indian Railways has submitted proposals for linking Nepal's capital with Raxaul. Similarly, the two sides are looking at possibilities of cooperation for an east–west railway line along the foothills of Nepal.

Roads in the Terai region are a priority and India is financing the construction of 10 roads divided into 14 packages that would significantly boost connectivity in Nepal and with India. Seven of these packages are complete and the others should soon be completed too. Issues pertaining to land acquisition have been key impediments to progressing these road projects. Two new thrust areas of much relevance to both the countries—agriculture and use of inland waterways—were identified and are being progressed.

Ominous Dark Clouds

Yet, even as ties were sought to be developed, traditional fault lines ensured that the outcomes fell short of expectation and, indeed, newer fault lines appeared. Modi's visit to Nepal in 2014 is perhaps the best case in point. Despite all the public applause, it appears that for the disruptive elements in the political class of Nepal, popularity and public acclaim for an Indian leader was just not acceptable and growing India–Nepal ties needed to be stymied. The opportunity arose during Modi's visit in November 2014 for the SAARC Summit.

In contention was a request for him to drive from India to Janakpur, the home of Sita, which is close to the Indian border, address a public meeting and then proceed to Kathmandu. Citing security concerns, though the reasons clearly were intertwined with the ethnic politics of Nepal and the issues of the Madhesis, the Nepalese turned down this proposal much to the consternation of India. Only recently before this, Modi had addressed large gatherings in New York and London! There were no further prime ministerial visits to Nepal for the next four years.

A similar situation occurred during Modi's second bilateral visit to Nepal in May 2018. Contrary to the hullabaloo of his visiting Janakpur in 2014, he was received at the holy Janaki Mandir in Janakpur by PM Oli himself in 2018. Thereafter, Modi was accorded a huge civic reception by the city of Janakpur, which was attended by over 100,000 people from Nepal. This outdid the huge meetings of people of Indian origin addressed by Modi in other parts of the world. Modi's May 2018 visit to Nepal was followed by another visit in September 2018 for a BIMSTEC summit. A visible symbol of India–Nepal friendship, a huge dharamsala that would cater to pilgrims visiting the most revered Pashupatinath Temple was jointly inaugurated by the two PMs.

However, the second visit had barely concluded when Nepal was awash with political leaders crying hoarse to the fact that India wanted it to join a military alliance of BIMSTEC countries and that Nepal could never countenance this. The context of this was a counterterrorism exercise being carried out by militaries of BIMSTEC countries in India for which invitations had been extended months earlier to all the countries, including Nepal. Indeed, an advance contingent from Nepal was already in India when the political storm erupted, and they stayed back and observed the exercise even while the main Nepalese contingent was stopped from travelling to India. Later, Nepal fell short in calling out Pakistan for its fostering of terrorism in the aftermath of the Pulwama attack of February 2019.

A similar scenario took place in the wake of the 2015 earthquake when even as the relief operations were continuing, elements in Nepal seized on zealous and intrusive reporting from some media teams from India to swell an anti-India feeling. This forced repackaging of Indian relief material before distribution. Moreover, in keeping with the general tendency in Nepalese ruling circles to play down India, Indian assistance was not earmarked for any of the iconic heritage reconstruction works in central Kathmandu. Instead, projects were allocated to the Chinese, the Americans, the Japanese and the Koreans.

Pushing development partnership also came up against similar recalcitrance on the part of the Nepalese, though it must be admitted that India's delivery in some cases has been tardy. The delays in moving ahead on the construction of the National Police Academy, for which the foundation stone was unveiled in 2014, is often quoted in the context of poor delivery and juxtaposed with the academy built by the Chinese in just a few years for the Armed Police Force of Nepal.

The best example of Nepalese procrastination primarily because of its benefits to India as well is the 5,000 MW Pancheshwar Multipurpose Project on the Mahakali River. This project has remained on paper even more than two decades after the two countries signed the basic treaty on sharing the benefits of the river. Another long-standing example is that of a high dam on the Kosi, which would prevent flooding in both India and Nepal but for which no willingness has been expressed by the Nepalese for decades. It is, of course, pertinent to point out that river training works on the Indian side of the border have not proceeded apace even while the India-funded works on the same rivers have moved ahead in Nepal. Unwillingness to move even on grant projects has also been noticed. For example, in 2018, Modi announced a ₹100 crore grant for development projects in Janakpur. Till date, no proposals have been received from the Nepalese side.

Nepal is keen on developing an east–west rail line along its foothills. The economic viability of this track, if at all, squarely rests with it being linked with the Indian network as a shorter route for India to its north-east. Despite this, the Nepalese are insisting that the line be built using the standard gauge used by China and not the broad gauge used by the Indian Railways. Indian projects have also faced innumerable hurdles. In recent years, the most well-known is the case of the rescinding of the contract awarded to Infrastructure Leasing & Financial Services (IL&FS) for the fast-track road linking Kathmandu to Nijgadh, the site of the proposed new international airport for Nepal. On the other hand, the Chinese have been re-awarded the 1,000 MW Budhi Gandaki hydro project even after repeated disqualifications of their contractors.

But these irritants are par for the course. However, two happenings in the past six years have long-term problematic implications for bilateral ties. The first is what the Nepalese call 'blockade' of 2015 and the second is Nepal laying claim to the Indian territory in Uttarakhand (2020). Further, India–Nepal relations have also been seriously exacerbated by the growth of Chinese influence in Nepal.

'The Blockade'

In 2015, Nepal adopted a new constitution declaring it to be a federal democratic republic. The concept of federalism was new in Nepal, which had been a unitary state under the monarchy. Seven provinces were created including one (Province No. 2) that fell almost wholly in the region known as Madesh. This was a half-hearted compromise to address the issue of ethnic divisions in Nepal, in particular with the Madhesi community in the Terai, who were identified by the Paharis with India and have been traditionally discriminated against in Nepal along with the tribal communities.

Particularly contentious were clauses denying easy citizenship rights to foreigners marrying Nepalese. This greatly affected Madhesis, who have age-old customs of marrying across the border. This has now been codified in legislation with a mandated waiting period of seven years. For many, this is part of the effort to loosen the *'roti-beti'* ties and goes to the heart of India–Nepal relations at the level of people.

The other contentious decision was to declare Nepal a secular state, doing away from its status as a Hindu country (in 1962, Nepal had proclaimed itself a Hindu kingdom). For many in Nepal, secularism undermined the societal character of Nepal, which has more Hindus as a per cent of its population than any other country in the world, including India. For India, it undermined the societal links between the two countries. Most accounts indicate that in parleys with senior leaders in India, Nepalese politicians assured that the country's status would be maintained as a Hindu Rashtra. But this did not happen and Indian suggestions to reconsider and hold back the adoption of the new constitution were brushed aside. Though having encouraged establishment of democracy in Nepal for years, India only 'noted' the adoption of the new Constitution.

Although the constitution was adopted in the Constituent Assembly with a huge margin, with Members of Parliament (MPs) even from pro-Hindu parties voting in favour, the Madhes was disaffected and a great deal of unrest and *andolan* (movement) was witnessed. The fact that the Madhes traverses the key transit routes from India to Nepal obviously meant huge disruptions over a long period in supply of goods, including petroleum products, which are almost all imported by Nepal through India. For Nepalis, especially in the Kathmandu valley, the resulting shortages were regarded simply as a 'blockade' by India. As the disruption in supplies caused serious difficulties over a reasonably long period, it has left an indelible and strongly negative feeling in Nepalese minds about India's action. This sentiment was hugely leveraged by the Communists led by PM Oli in Nepal during the elections in 2017.

An Eminent Persons Group (EPG) was set up by the two governments in the aftermath of the 'blockade' to discuss issues between India and Nepal and suggest ways forward. Its report is ready but has yet to be received by the two governments. Though not public, reports suggest that among its recommendations could be measures to regulate movement of people across the border apart from revising the 1950 Treaty of Peace and Friendship.

Red Lines Breached

In May 2020, Nepal issued a new map and laid claim to around 350 sq. km (140 sq. miles) of Indian territory, breaching, perhaps, the darkest of red lines between two neighbouring and friendly countries. The territories cartographically included now in Nepal are those of Kalapani, Lipulekh and Limpiyadhura, which have traditionally been used for the Kailash Manasarovar yatra by pilgrims from India. The areas are in Uttarakhand near the Chinese border and were not even included in the map of Nepal till the recent claim.

The incorporation of these areas by Nepal is being justified by declaring a stream flowing from the east in Limpiyadhura as the source of the river Kali, which demarcates the western extremity of Nepal in the 1816 Treaty of Sugauli. Traditionally, the Kalapani stream from the north is the accepted main tributary. This new interpretation flies in the face of maps and other documentation, both Indian and Nepali, in particular from 1879, when the first official survey of the region was carried out.

Nepal's present coat of arms or national emblem includes its map in outline. This coat of arms was introduced in the 2015 Constitution—earlier there was no map in the coat of arms. The coat of arms clearly did not feature the territory to Limpiyadhura, which juts out as an elongated finger into India. A constitutional amendment adopted by an overwhelming majority in Parliament, including the ruling and opposition parties, 'updated' the coat of arms that now includes Indian territory. This is clearly untenable and furthermore raises practical issues with India because the 'updated' national emblem, showing a part of Indian territory, will be on the letterheads of the Government of Nepal.

Nepal's Changing Face

The past 15 years have seen the end of monarchy and the Hindu kingdom in Nepal after 250 years. This is the most obvious change and brought the Maoists, who had waged an insurgency for over a decade, into the mainstream of multiparty democracy. This was also an era of globalization and the rise of China, both of which have had major impacts on Nepalese society and polity.

Left Politics

Nepal has an old history of Left politics and a well-established Communist Party, the Unified Marxist Leninist (UML). The addition of the Maoists brought about a substantial accretion to Left polity in Nepal and heightened the challenge for the Nepali Congress that prided itself in leading the fight for democracy in Nepal. With the end of the Koirala era, the Nepali Congress also started witnessing ineffectual leadership. The weight of the Left was reflected in results of various elections held in Nepal since 2005, with one or the other Left party invariably being in the government and many a time, the post of PM being held by a communist leader.

Following the adoption of the new constitution in 2015, elections were held in 2017 in Nepal for all three tiers of the government: federal, provincial (for the first time in the history of Nepal) and local. The Left weight was significantly reinforced towards the end of the year when the Maoists joined the UML and the two fought the federal and provincial elections together.

The result saw a sweep by them across Nepal. Surprisingly, the world did not notice that, perhaps, for the first time in the world, a communist (not socialist) party had won federal elections in a multiparty democratic election. The only hold-out was Province 2, the Madhesh province, where two Madhesi parties joined hands and formed the provincial government—the result reflecting the sentiment in the Madhes.

A key manifestation of the Left's nationalism in Nepal has been to try and undo the special relations of Nepal with India. To this end, the expression 'special relations' was not mentioned in the joint statement issued during PM Oli's visit to India in 2018. In an earlier visit to India in 2016, even a joint statement was not issued. Prime Minister Prachanda had earlier broken the tradition of a Nepali PM making his first foreign visit to India by instead first travelling to China.

Tilt towards the Chinese

Nepal shares a 1,400 km land border with China (Tibet) and the conventional view was that the high Himalayas acted as a natural barrier, which was difficult to transcend. Chinese goodwill is important for Nepal given that vast tracts of Nepalese territory in the north share links across the border in Tibet. To this end, in the past decade, they have acquiesced to Chinese pressures for tight vigilance at the border. The Chinese, on their part, have taken further advantage by building infrastructure that provides easier sustenance for these areas given the almost absence of roads on the Nepalese side.

Recent years have, however, seen hugely stepped up Chinese efforts to reach into Nepal not only on the economic side but also on the political and societal sides. China is now Nepal's second-largest trading partner and is also billed as the largest foreign investor in the past few years in terms of pledges of investment. The Chinese were awarded two major airport expansion projects in Pokhara and Bhairahawa and under the pretext of having Buddhist links, are undertaking several developmental works in and around Lumbini. The number of flights into Kathmandu from China rival India's and the number of tourist arrivals is just short of the figure from India (these figures only account for air travellers, thereby vastly undercounting visitors from India).

The Chinese are also active in Nepal in the hydro sector, and the Nepalese would like Indian purchasing power from such projects even though the beneficial owners are really the Chinese. Technology and finances have now enabled the Chinese to reach a point where they may be able to develop cross Himalayan infrastructure into Nepal. A rail line is being considered, linking China with Kathmandu and beyond. While the viability of such an expensive project would appear to hinge on further connectivity with India, if built, it can effectively alter geography by providing connectivity of an order not seen before and impact trade and societal links of Nepal and India. It can also have security implications for India.

The China card has always been important for Nepalese politicians in their dealings with India under the pretext of maintaining a balance in their relations with their two big neighbours. This has now been amended to say that Nepal would like to play the role of a bridge between India and China. Obviously, growth and development in China and its increasing salience in global politics are also factors that influence Nepalese thinking. Nepal also signed a memorandum of understanding with China on the Belt and Road Initiative (BRI) in 2017. While indicating a certain reluctance to go along with BRI, nonetheless, Nepal remains a participant though only with a limited number of projects.

Visits by Nepalese PMs to China have become part of the political discourse in Nepal. The 'blockade' of 2015, coinciding with a time of greater assertiveness and expansionism by China, saw the Nepalese trying to reach out to China as a substitute for India. In this context, PM Oli made a major trip to China in 2016 and signed various trade and transit deals, including for the Chinese supply of petroleum products to Nepal. Not much came of this. Later, PM Prachanda made his maiden prime ministerial trip to China in 2017. Interestingly, one of the purchases the Nepalese were 'persuaded' to make was of several Chinese-made small aircrafts. Not only were these unviable white elephants, their possession appears to have been a millstone for Nepal remaining on the no-fly list of the European Union.

The Chinese have also made inroads into the Nepal Army by providing several courses and training opportunities but more importantly becoming a supplier for equipment, though not major lethal equipment. This has been done through the expedient of making available grants for purchases in China. This is naturally worrying for India, given the Indian Army's traditional links with the Nepal Army including as the main source for their equipment. Surprising as it may seem, government-to-government supply does not sit well with the Nepalese, who would prefer grants to make purchases that would also presumably line pockets.

In recent years, the Chinese have been not only active in the internal politics of Nepal but also increasingly visible. This has certainly been aided by a liberal use of the chequebook across the board with all the political parties, including visits to China by politicians (and bureaucrats, media personnel, etc.). The Left parties, though, have been special targets and the Chinese have leveraged 'fraternal' communist ties. Obviously, they would like to see that the communists in Nepal remain united and in power. The high point of Nepal–China ties in recent years was a state visit by President Xi Jinping to Nepal in October 2019, a high-level visit to Nepal by a Chinese leader after more than two decades. This being a visit the Nepalese had been longing for, Xi was naturally accorded a grand welcome. Though the visit itself did see a showering of 'bounties' for Nepal, it has opened the way for the Nepalese showing a clear 'tilt' towards the Chinese.

Globalization and Western Influence

In 1990, when democracy was restored in Nepal, the issuance of passports was liberalized, and Nepalis started availing work opportunities, especially in the Gulf and South East Asia, making these regions major destinations for labour in the years to come. Migration, including students and skilled personnel, also started to Europe, the US, Australia, Thailand and even to Japan and South Korea. This was fuelled by security uncertainties at home with the Maoist insurgency from the mid-1990s. Today, nearly a quarter of Nepal's population, from all parts of the country, is reportedly overseas. The international carrier with the maximum number of flights to Nepal is Qatar Airways.

In so far as India is concerned, economic development in Nepal and the opening up of destinations across the globe for Nepalese has meant that today many of the leaders of Nepal, especially younger ones, are not schooled in India. This lack of common collegiate roots has removed a natural bond of previous generations that had provided for constant communication and better understanding and even empathy between the two countries. Moreover, while most Nepalis understand Hindi, courtesy the popularity of Bollywood, articulation in Hindi has become quite another matter.

The spread of information technology throughout the country, smartphones and Facebook not only helped Nepalese keep contacts with their kin abroad but also exposed the world to Nepal bringing with it a certain Western cosmopolitanism. These ideas have also been pushed by Leftist ideology at the grassroots and by the large presence of international non-governmental organizations ostensibly in Nepal to resolve conflict and help alleviate poverty.

Underreported but exceptionally large is the presence of Christian missionaries, who gained entry into Nepal during and in the aftermath of the Maoist insurgency. 'Faith Houses', as churches are euphemistically called in Nepal, can be found in villages and towns across the country, including the Terai regions, and represent not only European and American organizations but Korean ones too! Similarly, posters advertising education opportunities in Australia, US/Canada and South East Asia are all over Nepal.

At $8 billion, nearly 30 per cent of Nepal's gross domestic product is accounted for by remittances making it one of the most remittance-dependent countries in the world. With a nominal per capita income of just above $1,000, Nepal only ranks 159 out of 186 countries in the International Monetary Fund's 2019 ranking. It is now in the process of graduating from its LDC (least developed countries) status. The huge remittance economy, however, has helped Nepal build a semblance of middle-class prosperity and raised Nepalese ambitions significantly, raising the bar for India to satisfy these growing aspirations in Nepal. This is, in fact, one of the biggest issues for India given the limitations of its economy. This also makes it imperative for India to encourage its best-performing corporates to work in Nepal (this used to be the case in years gone by, but the growth story of these corporates and India makes Nepal relatively unattractive to them). A metropolitan Nepal is, of course, a far cry and not the priority for its political class, which remains rent-seekers rather than wealth-creators.

In so far as the government, long-standing efforts to spread

Nepal's options beyond India are witnessed across the board. Multilateral development banks are by far the major lenders and players in the country's development efforts with the European Union being Nepal's biggest donor. Interestingly, the Millennium Challenge Corporation of the US has offered the single-largest bilateral assistance package to Nepal and this 'deal' has become a bone of contention in domestic Nepalese politics—the pulls and pressures of China and the US!

India and China are not the only players for big projects—western and South East Asian players are in the game too. A long-delayed project to bring water to Kathmandu through a pipeline was with an Italian company and the upgradation work at Kathmandu Airport was with a Spanish company. A big investor in the telecom sector is Malaysian. And there is clear visibility of Koreans and Japanese products in Nepal even if several are made in factories located in India. Interestingly, westernization has helped see an increased presence of China in Nepal through affordable Chinese-made imitations of Western brands that are flooding Nepal's market.

Lockdown and Nepali Politics

The year 2020 will be known for the coronavirus pandemic and the global lockdown necessitated by it. But even this most trying of economic and health situations did not keep Nepali politics in lockdown.

The victory of the Nepal Communist Party (NCP) in the elections held at the end of 2017 is generally attributed to its capitalizing on the strong anti-India sentiment among the Pahari community after the 'blockade' of 2015. However, equally critical was the merger of the two Left parties, the UML, led by Oli, and the Communist Party of Nepal-Maoist Centre (CPN-MC) of Prachanda. The election was, thus, fought with a power-sharing deal but after two years of leading the government, PM Oli was not willing to relinquish either the prime ministership or the leadership of the NCP solely to Prachanda.

The simmering factionalism boiled over in 2020 with PM Oli under severe pressure to accommodate the rival faction, which also included his arch-rival from the UML and another former PM of Nepal, Madhav Kumar Nepal. This scenario saw the Chinese lean into Nepal become very public when their ambassador was most visibly seen perambulating through Kathmandu to keep the NCP together and PM Oli in power. It appeared that the Chinese were now not just influencers but major brokers of the political scene in Nepal. Given the armed clashes between India and China in June 2020 in Eastern Ladakh, there was a feeling in some quarters that the cartographic adventurism with India in the Limpiyadhura region indulged by PM Oli may have had some tacit encouragement of the Chinese.

However, the Chinese soon had to reckon with the avarice of Nepali politics when, within a few months, they were not only forced to accept a possible fall of the government of PM Oli, but also a collapse of the NCP's unity, for which they had strived so hard. Perhaps, the last straw was when PM Oli preempted matters and, in December 2020, suddenly dissolved the Nepali parliament even though more than two years of its term was remaining. Earlier, he had reversed tack from the anti-India rhetoric that he had spewed through much of the first half of 2020 and reached out to India. This process saw three senior-level visits from India to Nepal including the Research and Analysis Wing Chief, the Indian Army Chief and the Foreign Secretary. Thereafter, the Nepali foreign minister came to Delhi and a meeting of the India–Nepal Joint Commission was held. It, of course, bears noting that even throughout the turbulent days of 2020, India kept up a steady supply of COVID-related medicines to Nepal, including vaccines, as their roll-out began in India in early 2021.

On the political front in Nepal, matters were complicated when the Nepali Supreme Court ruled in February 2021 that the dissolution of Parliament was not legal and ordered its reinstatement. Further, in a separate judgement, the Court decreed that the 2018 merger of the UML and MC was not legal. Now the NCP, which controlled nearly two-thirds of the House of Representatives, would be two separate parties—UML and MC—with neither having a majority by itself in the House of Representatives. For many, such political anarchy is a recipe for disaster, but it is par for the course in Nepali politics, where make-and-break, align-and-realign are the general norm. By early March 2021, it is unclear as to which combination will prevail with every possibility of PM Oli retaining his position or Nepali Congress leader Sher Bahadur Deuba taking over. And the leaders of the revolt in the NCP, whose actions brought about this topsy-turvy travail, could be left out in the cold or holding a junior position in government.

Blaming India for the ails of its politics is the default position in Nepal. Incredibly, the happenings of late 2020 and early 2021 have seen no finger pointing towards India. Instead, the nature of Nepali politics has been brought to the fore for the world to see with the Chinese possibly having to swallow a lesson.

The Eternal Way Forward: *Ekla Chalo Re*

Nepal is India's closest neighbour and so it hurts in India when things go wrong in our ties with Nepal. Stepping back or withdrawing, as is suggested by some in the wake of Nepal repeatedly spurning Indian efforts to strengthen ties, is not an option. No root-and-branch examination should give in to efforts of certain groupings in Nepal, which would like to do away with the special relations between India and Nepal. This would include placing curbs on the open borders, revising the terms of recruitment of Nepalese Gorkhas in the Indian Army and/or upending the currency peg between the two countries.

India–Nepal ties must be pursued bilaterally without giving even friendly external players an outsize role—*Ekla Chalo Re* (Walk alone). India has pre-eminent equities with societal and economic ties that are unmatched in Nepal. This is also important given India's regional position and global aspirations. Nepal needs attention from Delhi and India must constantly engage with all sections of the political class in Nepal, especially those with the highest salience in Nepali politics. High-level and official interactions must be strongly supplemented by engagement by political players and playing down domestic imperatives. Indian efforts must add to the well-being of the people at large in Nepal with stepped-up interface with the youth and nurturing of long-standing cultural ties. Cross-border flows of people, goods, services and investment, more air connectivity and development of India's border areas must be actively encouraged, keeping in mind a changing and aspirational Nepal. No matter the machinations of Nepalese politicians and regional geopolitics, the oldest partnership cannot go into a freeze.

5

BHUTAN

Druk Bond

V.P. HARAN

'India and Bhutan enjoy a unique and special relationship, which has been forged by ties of geography, history and culture. Therefore, Bhutan as the destination for my first visit abroad as Prime Minister is a natural choice.'

—Prime Minister Narendra Modi, in a statement on 15 June 2014, prior to his departure for Bhutan

India and Bhutan signed the Treaty of Perpetual Peace and Friendship in 1949 but did not have diplomatic relations till 1968. Given their experience at the hands of Tibet and British India, Bhutan's suspicion of other countries was understandable. Pandit Jawaharlal Nehru's visit to Bhutan in 1958 and his statement that India wished Bhutan to 'remain an independent country' thawed the ice.[1] Bhutan started opening up to India, facilitated largely by successive governments in

India abiding strictly by what Nehru had said on Bhutan's independence. However, our cooperation with Bhutan in the military and development spheres preceded the establishment of diplomatic relations.

India's special relations with Bhutan is rooted not only in history and geography but also in religion and culture. Trust, mutual understanding and respect for each other's concerns and interests characterize these relations. Bilateral relations are an outstanding example of how two countries so dissimilar in size and population could coexist and cooperate peacefully for mutual advantage. The bond between the two countries has been carefully nurtured by both countries.

In 2014, when Narendra Modi became the prime minister (PM), there were no major outstanding issues between India and Bhutan. There were delays in execution of hydropower projects and consequently, the target of 10,000 megawatt (MW) export of power by 2020 from Bhutan had become impossible to achieve.[2] India's dealings with the elected government in Bhutan and the new political set-up under the Constitution enacted in 2008 had transitioned smoothly into the new groove. The important change[3] in the revised Indo-Bhutan Friendship Treaty of 2007, on Bhutan's external relations with India, did not come in the way of close cooperation on issues of interest and security to either country, as there is full realization that these issues of both countries are interlinked. This was evident during the Doklam crisis, when both India and Bhutan were on the same page.

Bhutan has witnessed sweeping changes in less than two decades. The Fourth King abdicated voluntarily in favour of his son, Jigme Khesar Namgyel Wangchuck, in December 2006. Before that, he set in motion the process to transform Bhutan into a democratic constitutional monarchy, with an elected Parliament, which had powers defined in the Constitution.

The education system underwent significant changes too. The younger generation of Bhutan is well-educated, exposed to the outside world through social media and has its own expectations and aspirations. This is bound to impact Bhutan's foreign policy.

In this background, Bhutan and India decided to work towards strengthening economic relations through creating interdependencies. In turn, bilateral relations were placed on firmer footing in the long-term context.

High-Level Contacts

The swearing-in ceremony of Modi on 26 May 2014 saw leaders of all South Asian Association for Regional Cooperation (SAARC) nations being invited to the event. This was the beginning of the evolution of PM Modi's 'Neighbourhood First' policy. The PM of Bhutan Tshering Tobgay also attended the event. In the bilateral meeting, the two leaders committed themselves to further strengthening relations. This was the first of the frequent contacts at the highest level between the two countries, since the National Democratic Alliance was voted back to power in India in 2014.

Modi's first foreign visit after taking over as PM was to Bhutan on 15–16 June 2014, less than three weeks after assuming office. This underlined the importance that the new government attached to relations with Bhutan. During the highly successful visit, Modi addressed the joint sitting of the two Houses of Parliament, laid the foundation stone of the Kholongchhu hydro project and announced that India will provide assistance in establishing a digital library (e-library) in Bhutan's National Library and in all the 20 districts of Bhutan. Discussions with leaders of Bhutan reassured them of continuity in India's policies towards Bhutan.

President Shri Pranab Mukherjee had dealt with Bhutan for many years, in his more than four decades of public life. As External Affairs Minister, he had taken active interest in the negotiations on updating the bilateral Friendship Treaty, which was signed by him from the Indian side in 2007. He paid a state visit to Bhutan on 7–8 November 2014, when all issues of mutual interest were discussed. On conclusion of the successful and 'most memorable' visit, the president said, 'India is proud to be a privileged partner in Bhutan's advancement and growth. I am happy that our assistance is being effectively utilized in important sectors.'[4]

The King of Bhutan, His Majesty Jigme Khesar Namgyel Wangchuck, visited India from 31 October to 3 November 2017, two months after the Doklam stand-off between the troops of India and China was resolved. This timely visit helped to focus on security-related issues and discuss ways to handle the growing concerns on China's activities along the northern border. Under the Constitution of Bhutan, security issues are dealt with directly by the King. The King of Bhutan later visited India in August 2018 for the funeral of former Indian PM Atal Bihari Vajpayee, which indicates the closeness between Indian and Bhutanese leadership.

Among the first few countries to be visited by PM Modi, in his second term, was Bhutan, on 17 and 18 August 2019. Reflecting the expanding areas of bilateral engagement, 10 memorandum of understanding (MOUs) were signed in diverse areas such as space research, information technology, power, education and aviation. India increased the currency swap limit, which is used effectively by Bhutan when needed, by $100 million. The two PMs jointly inaugurated the Indian Space Research Organization's Ground Earth Station and SATCOM network, which enabled Bhutan to utilize the South Asia satellite to enhance coverage of public broadcasting and communications. To augment the digital library project Modi had announced during his first visit to Bhutan, India's National Knowledge Network and Bhutan's Druk Research and Education Network were interconnected. India and Bhutan will remain a unique model of relations between two countries, PM Modi said. Bhutanese leadership felt confident that India will continue to accord high priority to relations with Bhutan.

The former PM of Bhutan, Tshering Tobgay, participated in the Advantage Assam Global Investor's Summit in Guwahati in February 2018. Bhutan has a long border with Assam but exchanges are limited to border areas. Bhutan's PM and Assam's chief minister Sarbananda Sonowal jointly inaugurated the newly established Consulate General of Bhutan in Guwahati. Sonowal said that the establishment of the Consulate General marks a new beginning for trade, cultural and other relations between Bhutan and Assam. The PMs of India and Bhutan held bilateral talks in Guwahati, covering a range of issues.

Tshering Tobgay paid an official visit to India on 5–7 July 2018, when the two countries resolved to enhance India–Bhutan ties in all areas of mutual interest and agreed to take the exemplary bilateral partnership to 'new heights'.[5]

The newly elected PM of Bhutan, Dr Lotay Tshering paid a visit to India on 27–29 December 2018. His request that increased focus be given to the health sector in the plan assistance provided by India, was welcomed. India announced an assistance of ₹4,500 crore for Bhutan's 12th Plan, as requested by Bhutan. The Plan assistance is at the same level as for the 11th Plan. The two sides announced that they are looking at expanding trade ties beyond hydropower, but nothing concrete has emerged on this so far. Prime Minister Dr Lotay Tshering visited India again in May 2019 to participate in the swearing-in ceremony of Modi as PM for a second term.

There have been several visits at ministers' and senior

officials' levels between the two countries to continue the tradition of frequent consultations. This has contributed greatly to strengthening bilateral relations through increased understanding and cooperation on various issues.

Security Cooperation

Since 1962, when the Indian Military Training Team was sent to Bhutan following bilateral discussions, the Indian Army has been training and equipping the Royal Bhutan Army personnel. This followed Chinese manoeuvres across Bhutan's northern boundaries in the early 1960s. Security interests of Bhutan and India are strongly linked. Landlocked Bhutan's only practical land access to the outside world is through India. Much of its trade passes through the narrow Siliguri corridor, which is less than 100 km from China's Chumbi valley. This corridor is also the lifeline for India's North-East. Over the years, security cooperation has expanded and strengthened. India's Border Roads Organisation's project Dantak has been building roads in Bhutan since 1961. Many of the arterial roads in Bhutan were built by Dantak, whose services are widely appreciated in Bhutan.

Article 2 of the 2007 India–Bhutan Friendship Treaty of March provides that Bhutan and India 'shall cooperate closely with each other on issues relating to their national interests. Neither Government shall allow the use of its territory for activities harmful to the national security and interest of the other'. This mutually beneficial provision provided the basis for security cooperation in recent years in the context not only of Chinese action across the border but also of the activities of anti-national forces along the India–Bhutan border. The two countries have been exchanging information, including actionable intelligence on the activities of anti-national forces along the 699-km border. Cooperation in this area has been progressing smoothly during the National Democratic Alliance years also.

Security cooperation has acquired added salience in view of the activities of China along the border with Bhutan as well as the India, Bhutan and China tri-junction areas. China has been nibbling away at Bhutanese territory, despite the agreements of 1988 and 1998 between Bhutan and China, providing for the maintenance of peace and tranquillity in border areas pending a final settlement on the boundary question and the maintenance of status quo along the boundary. In recent years, China has made some major moves such as the Doklam incident in June 2017 and the subsequent strengthening of their presence in the region, China's objection to the Global Environment Facility (GEF) funding for a project in the Sakteng wildlife sanctuary on the grounds that it is a disputed area and the construction of a new settlement by China in Pangda village, which as per published maps, is within the claim line of Bhutan.

Of the four areas under dispute between Bhutan and China, Doklam is the most important for strategic reasons. The 89 sq. km Doklam plateau to the south of Chumbi valley has been an important subject of discussion in the Bhutan–China boundary talks since 1984. China was not physically present in Doklam on a continuous basis till 2017. It had completed a road from Chumbi valley through Sinche La (Pass) to the northern part of Doklam in 2004. From 2013, the People's Liberation Army (PLA) has been coming from the end of that road to the southern side by foot, all the way up to the security post of Bhutan. The plateau is bisected by Torsa Nala, which is a deep gorge and can't be crossed. Men belonging to the PLA have to come to the western end of the plateau, where the Nala begins, to go to the southern side, passing close to the Indian border post at Doka La.

On 16 June 2017, China started work on extending the road to the southern side when India intervened and stopped them physically from going ahead with the work. This resulted in a stand-off, which was resolved on 28 August 2017, after 13 rounds of talks between India and China. The two countries agreed to withdraw their soldiers from the stand-off point and China had agreed to withdraw its equipment also. Indian forces withdrew to their post in Doka La. The PLA withdrew its men and equipment from the stand-off point, but not from the plateau; they moved to the eastern side of the plateau. The PLA has significantly altered the status quo by strengthening its forces and building new structures, helipads and a road on the eastern side, towards Torsa Nala. They are now permanently present on the northern and eastern parts of the plateau, whereas before 2017, Doklam was never inhabited during the harsh winter months.

The PLA is keen to come over to the southern side of the plateau and reach the Jampheri ridge, the highest ridge to the south that separates Chumbi valley from Doklam. From Jampheri ridge, one can get a clear view of movement along the Siliguri corridor, which would be of enormous strategic advantage in the event of a conflict. China's presence in the Jampheri ridge will also push the boundary tri-junction about 6 km to the south, from Batang La to Gyemochen, which China claims to be the India–Bhutan–China tri-junction.

China's recent activities on the northern side of the Doklam plateau indicate that it will continue its efforts to reach the Jampheri ridge and we need to prepare ourselves to handle the situation, should it arise. Doklam is part of Bhutan and the tri-junction is located on the ridge to the west of Doklam. India has a direct interest in the location of the tri-junction. This was also recognized by China; the 2012 Agreement between the Special Representatives of India and China provided that the tri-junction would be decided in consultation with the third country concerned, namely Bhutan. No trilateral consultations have taken place so far on the issue. Chinese attempts to occupy the Doklam plateau are in violation of its bilateral agreements with both India and Bhutan to maintain status quo and is clearly a unilateral attempt to dictate the location of the tri-junction, which has serious security implications for India and Bhutan.

India and Bhutan should hold immediate consultations under Article 2 of the Friendship Treaty of 2007, referred to earlier, on steps to handle an aggressive China. Available options could be examined. Such options include trilateral discussions on the issue, strengthening the presence of Bhutanese forces on the southern side of Doklam plateau and the establishment of Bhutanese security posts on the Jampheri ridge, among others. Such consultations would help in deciding the course of action to be followed in the face of the creeping occupation of Doklam by China and facilitate taking immediate preparatory action if necessary. Steps to counter any adventurous move by China should also be agreed upon.

As mentioned earlier, in the GEF Council meeting held in June 2020, China objected to GEF funding for a project in the Sakteng wildlife sanctuary on the grounds that it is a disputed area. This was an astonishing assertion by China, since Sakteng had never figured as a disputed territory in the border talks between the two countries that have been ongoing since 1984. Sakteng is in the far east of Bhutan, in the Trashigang district. This sanctuary is located below the Tawang district of India. It is well away from the tri-junction as also any section of the Bhutan–China boundary. China's claim also raises questions on the eastern tri-junction of India, Bhutan and China.

The GEF Council approved the project, but China insisted on recording that it is opposed to the funding for the project and did not join in the Council decision stating that Sakteng is located in Bhutan–China disputed areas 'which is on the agenda of China-Bhutan boundary talk'.[6] Bhutan rejected China's claim and said that Sakteng 'is an integral and sovereign territory of Bhutan' and that Sakteng had never figured in the border talks as a disputed area.[7] The motivation of China in raising such outrageous claims is political and is to bully a small neighbour to agree to boundary demarcation as dictated by China. In any case, India needs to be watchful and hold regular consultations on the issue with Bhutan since it will have implications for India too.

Development Cooperation

Since Bhutan launched its five-year development plans in 1961, India has been its most important development partner. Our development cooperation programme is highly successful. Focus areas for assistance all through the plans were roads, public health, education and public infrastructure.

India's assistance for Bhutan's 11th Plan (2013–18) was ₹4,500 crore. This constituted 21 per cent of the Plan outlay. An additional ₹500 crore was provided for the Economic Stimulus Plan of Bhutan. Most of the projects agreed upon were implemented after the NDA came to power in India in 2014. As in the past, Bhutan implemented the plan successfully. Average gross domestic product (GDP) growth rate during the Plan period was 5.59 per cent. During the 10th and 11th plans, the GDP of Bhutan trebled, and the per capita income increased from $1,815 to $3,438. The per capita income was $2,700 in 2014.

When the PM of Bhutan, Dr Lotay Tshering, visited India, in 2018, India's contribution for Bhutan's 12th Plan (2018–23) was decided at ₹4,500 crore, which will be 14.5 per cent of the total plan outlay. An additional ₹400 crore was offered for transitional Trade Support Facility, to help Bhutanese exporters, whose competitiveness in the Indian market was affected by the implementation of goods and services tax (GST) in India.

Among all our overseas development cooperation programmes, the one India has with Bhutan is the most successful. The government and people of Bhutan are highly appreciative of India's contribution to Bhutan's development. It is gratifying to note that Bhutan will be graduating from the UN's list of Least Developed Countries in 2023.

Trade and Transit

Article 5 of the 1949 Treaty of Friendship provided for free trade between India and Bhutan and for transit rights for Bhutanese products. This was formalized through the Agreement on Trade and Commerce of 1972. This Agreement has been renewed periodically, the last time on 12 November 2016, for the next 10 years. To facilitate Bhutan's industrial development, the Agreement provides that it can impose non-tariff restrictions on Indian goods.

India's exports to Bhutan, which was $356 million in 2013–14, increased to $657 million in 2018–19, a growth of 85 per cent. Major items of exports were petroleum, oil and lubricants (POL) products, motor vehicles and food items. India's share in Bhutan's imports averaged 88 per cent during the period 2014–19. It must be added that India's exports to Bhutan is somewhat inflated, since it includes Chinese-origin goods which are exported by Indian traders as 'Indian products'.

India's imports from Bhutan jumped from $152 million in 2013–14 to $356 million in 2018–19, an increase of 134 per cent. Bhutan used to export mainly primary products before inexpensive power became available; now the export basket has expanded and undergone significant changes. The main items of imports from Bhutan were electricity and Ferro silicon, accounting for 36.8 per cent and 34.9 per cent, respectively. India's share in Bhutan's exports to the world was 92 per cent during the period 2014–18.

A study by the Indian Council for Research on International Economic Relations (ICRIER) on potential for additional bilateral trade indicated that India can increase its exports to Bhutan by $51 million and its imports by $55 million.[8] This would be approximately 10 per cent of the current levels of bilateral trade and is not surprising given that India is the main trade partner of Bhutan accounting for nearly 90 per cent of its total trade. There is potential for increasing import of electricity, dolomite, cement and mineral products from Bhutan.

Such overwhelming dependence of Bhutan on India for its foreign trade is due primarily to its geographical location. It is a landlocked country, with only India and China as its neighbours. For political reasons, trade with China was officially banned in 1960. Even otherwise, trade with China would not be easy as the major markets are far away from the border and the mighty Himalayas stands between the two countries.

The bilateral Agreement on Trade and Commerce also provides for transit rights for Bhutan's trade with other countries and the for movement of goods from one part of Bhutan to another. The latter is important for Bhutan as it does not have an East–West Highway near the border with India. Visa-free travel between the countries facilitates the movement of people and goods. The two countries have designated more than 20 entry–exit points for the movement of goods. India has been responsive to Bhutan's requests for additional entry–exit points.

A few trade- and transit-related issues need to be addressed expeditiously. There have been complaints from Bhutanese traders on the problems they face at the border and in bordering areas, much of it is security related. This needs to be addressed expeditiously.

A major issue that remains to be addressed is the request of Bhutan, agreed to by India, for shifting the land customs station in the border town of Jaigaon on the Indian side to near the Bhutanese town of Pasaka about 5 km away. Nearly 90 per cent of Bhutan's external trade passes through the congested border towns of Jaigaon and Phuentsholing in Bhutan, causing traffic problems on both sides. Further, many trucks passing through this customs station carry items meant for use in the industrial units in Pasaka and can reach Pasaka directly if the land customs station is shifted to near Pasaka. India has not been able to persuade the Government of West Bengal to allot a suitable plot for the land customs station. A few months ago, an arrangement was worked out on an alternate route for movement of trucks due to issues caused by COVID-19. This gives hope that a permanent solution to the problem may be on the horizon.

Another issue is the inadequate and inefficient infrastructure at the Jaigaon land customs station. With increased paperwork necessitated by implementation of GST by India, facilities at the Jaigaon customs station need urgent upgradation.

Connectivity

India and Bhutan have been working constantly on improving connectivity to promote trade and facilitate the movement of people. SAARC decided to improve connectivity and facilitate smooth and seamless movement of motor vehicles. The SAARC Motor Vehicle Agreement, which was expected to be signed at the Kathmandu SAARC Summit in November 2014, ran into last-minute objections from Pakistan and the Agreement was not signed. Following this, Bangladesh, Bhutan, India and

Nepal (the BBIN group of countries) signed a Motor Vehicles Agreement (MVA) in June 2015 at Thimphu, under the Bay of Bengal Initiative for Multi-Sectoral Technical and Economic Cooperation (BIMSTEC) framework, which provides for subregional cooperation. The Agreement was, however, not ratified by Bhutan due to pressure from the transporters lobby. Bhutan conveyed that pending its ratification, the other countries can implement the MVA. It was the expectation of the other signatories that India will persuade Bhutan to ratify, but India, aware of Bhutanese sensitivities on such issues, rightly decided not to take it up with Bhutan. The MVA remains on paper, though some trial runs have taken place. Cooperation with Bhutan at the bilateral level on this important issue is, however, continuing.

Economic Relations

The two countries took a conscious decision to place long-term relations on solid foundations by strengthening economic cooperation. Hydropower offers immense potential for this. As PM Modi observed during his 2014 visit, hydropower cooperation 'is a classic example of win-win cooperation and a model for the entire region.'[9]

Cooperation in the hydropower sector started in the 1960s. By 2014, three major India-assisted hydro-electric projects (HEP), namely, Chukha, Kurichhu and Tala, with a combined capacity of 1,416 MW, were operational contributing enormously to the development of Bhutan. In 2017, the hydropower sector contributed 13 per cent of the GDP, 10 per cent of national revenue and nearly a quarter of its exports revenue.[10] Cooperation in the hydropower sector has transformed relations to one of economic partnership between the two nations.

India financed these projects through grants and loans and contracted to buy all their surplus power at a price that will ensure a guaranteed return on investment. This has worked well: India got green power at competitive rates and Bhutan earned revenue and precious foreign exchange. The success of these projects gave Bhutan the confidence to strengthen cooperation in this area.

An agreement on hydropower cooperation was signed in July 2006, providing for increasing Bhutan's hydropower exports to India to 5,000 MW by 2020. This target was raised to 10,000 MW in May 2008, during PM Manmohan Singh's visit, at the request of the first elected government of Bhutan. The achievement of this target would have transformed Bhutan into a middle-income country, but unfortunately, the target has been missed by years.

The only project that has been completed in the last six years is the 720 MW Mangdechhu project, which started generating power in 2018 and was inaugurated by PM Modi during his 2019 visit to Bhutan. In fact, this is the first project to be commissioned after Tala, in 2006–07. Two major projects, Punatsangchhu I and II, with a total capacity of 2,220 MW ran into geological problems and are delayed by several years. The 600 MW Kholongchhu project, for which foundation stone was laid by PM Modi in June 2014, is also delayed with construction yet to begin. There is lack of movement on the other projects identified as part of the 10,000 MW plan.

Projects hitherto were intergovernmental. In respect of four projects, a joint venture (JV) model between an Indian public-sector undertaking (PSU) and Bhutan's Druk Green Power Corporation was agreed upon. Kholongchhu was the first of the JV model projects, and so far, the only one to be taken up for implementation. Following lack of progress in JV projects, Bhutan is not keen on JVs and would prefer the tried-and-tested intergovernmental model. Bhutan would now like to proceed with the mega 2,560 MW Sunkosh storage dam project. This is now under discussion between the two governments. Sunkosh will be downstream from Punatsangchhu I and II, which have experienced serious geological issues. It would be necessary to reassess the geological data before a final decision is taken on the project.

It would be desirable for India to have in-depth discussions with Bhutan on the 10,000 MW target in view of the delays and changes in market conditions since 2008, and rework the schedule and the model. This could also provide for the sale of electricity to third countries in the region.

Part of the reason for the delay in the Kholongchhu project is the ill-conceived guidelines issued in 2016 by the Ministry of Power, India, for cross-border trade in electricity. It provided for trade in electricity, after one-time approval, only by projects owned 100 per cent either by the Government of India or Bhutan or by a PSU owned entirely by the Bhutan government or by entities in which Indian ownership is at least 51 per cent. Requests from other entities would be considered on a case-by-case basis. This raised doubts in Bhutan on the export of the Kholongchhu power since ownership in it was 50 per cent each by India's SJVN Limited and Bhutan's Druk Green Power Corporation. The guidelines made no mention of trilateral cooperation in the energy sector. The tariff, if it had been agreed upon by the two governments, would continue to be determined in the same manner. This closed the door for Bhutan to explore the more lucrative commercial power market in India.

These issues were addressed in the revised notification issued by the Central Electricity Regulatory Commission in March 2019. It opened the door for export to third countries through India. The tariff was to be determined through competitive bidding. Conditions on ownership of entities that can export power to India were rescinded. The revised guidelines reassured Bhutan and would facilitate implementation of the Kholongchhu project.

Concerns have been expressed frequently in Bhutan on mounting hydropower debt, delays in projects and cost escalation. Increasing cost should worry India more, since the price of power is fixed on a cost-plus basis. Debt should not be a cause for concern since repayment commences only when the project starts generating revenue. A joint analysis on debt serviceability by the World Bank and the International Monetary Fund noted that India covers the construction and financial risks and offers assured market for the surplus power. Further, price for power is worked out on the basis of cost plus a net 15 per cent return. The analysis concluded that Bhutan is at a moderate risk of debt distress.

During his visit to Bhutan in 2008, PM Manmohan Singh announced that a railway line will be built from Hasimara in West Bengal to Toribari in Bhutan, near the border town of Phuentsholing. The rail link, to be called the 'Golden Jubilee Railway Line', was to mark the golden jubilee of Pandit Nehru's visit to Bhutan in 1958. This would have been the first railway connection to Bhutan, giving it access to the Indian Railway network. The project could not be implemented since the Government of West Bengal was unable to provide land for the proposed alignment. It would be worthwhile to consider alternate alignments for providing rail connectivity to Bhutan.

Investments

Bhutan came out with a foreign direct investment (FDI) policy in 2002 and this has been reviewed and fine-tuned over the last

18 years. Bhutan has opened many sectors to foreign investors. The services sector has attracted maximum investment so far.

Investments by the Indian private sector in Bhutan during the period of July 2007 to March 2019 were $50.12 million. Forty-two per cent of this was in electricity, gas and water sectors and 26 per cent in wholesale trade, retail trade, hotels and restaurants. Manufacturing attracted only about 14 per cent of the total Indian investments so far. India accounted for 32.6 per cent of the total FDI in Bhutan. Over the last five years, there has not been a single major investment in Bhutan from India.

Low levels of Indian investments in Bhutan is surprising given the advantages that an investor from India will have, such as free trade arrangement, double taxation avoidance agreement, electricity at a lower rate than in India, a big market next door, etc. Bhutan's FDI policy and operating environment are friendly. Part of the reason for the low level of investments is that Bhutan has not been aggressively marketing itself as an FDI destination and the Indian industry is perhaps not fully aware of the advantages that investment in Bhutan offers. This information gap can and should be bridged by Industry associations and Apex chambers in India.

Human Resources Development

Education has been accorded high priority in Bhutan since the 1950s. India has contributed enormously to the development of this sector by deputing teachers, developing infrastructure and offering scholarships for studying in India. Most of the elder generation in Bhutan was educated in India or was taught by Indian teachers. They had warm sentiments towards India. The situation has changed now. Educational facilities have improved in Bhutan. Further, those who can afford to, look beyond

India for higher education. For medical education, Sri Lanka and Bangladesh are the preferred destinations since a special arrangement has been worked out with them. Part of the reason for these developments is that Bhutanese students are finding it difficult to get admission in reputed Indian institutions because of the high cut-off marks, way above that of Bhutan's toppers. Also, unlike in the past, Bhutanese students are now required to pay fees payable by foreign students studying in India.

The number of Bhutanese students coming to India for higher education is still high, but most of the toppers do not come here. The ministries of human resource development and external affairs should jointly work out a scheme to attract the toppers, who will go on to occupy important positions in the government and industry in due course. Like earlier, seats should be reserved for them in reputed institutions and the entire cost of education should be met by India or at least be provided scholarships. We should also respond positively and promptly to Bhutanese requests for deputing professors to their universities. This would help Bhutan in updating its curriculum and teaching methods. Investment in the education sector would pay rich dividends in due course and we will have an important section of the population favourably disposed towards India.

India has been assisting Bhutan in skills development by organizing special training programmes, and by meeting the entire demand of Bhutan for Indian Technical and Economic Cooperation slots. The ₹205 crore Chiphen Rigpel or Total Solutions project aimed at providing information and communication technology skills to a fourth of Bhutan's population was launched by the PMs of the two countries in April 2010. This five-year project has helped Bhutanese all over the country to acquire information technology skills and contributed immensely to preparing them for the digital age.

India too could consider setting up a skills training institution in Bhutan.

Culture

'My country is the country of Dharma. I am of no caste and no creed. I am sustained by perplexity; and I am here to destroy lust, anger and sloth' was the message that the Indian Buddhist master Padmasambhava carried to Bhutan in the eighth century. He is venerated in Bhutan even today as Guru Rinpoche. Since then, religious and cultural ties between the people of India and Bhutan have gone from strength to strength. After Bhutan opened up to the outside world during the time of the Third King, the two countries have paid particular attention to strengthening religious and cultural interaction.

The Nehru-Wangchuck Cultural Centre was established in Thimphu in 2010 by the Indian Council for Cultural Relations to strengthen people-to-people contacts and to disseminate information on Indian culture. It organizes music and yoga classes, exhibitions and cultural programmes and runs a library and reading room. In its outreach efforts, it maintains constant contacts with schools and universities. The centre should expand geographical coverage of its activities beyond Thimphu.

Established in 2003, the India-Bhutan Foundation has promoted research, educational exchanges, seminars, exhibitions, cultural events and the exchange of visits by artists and artistes. The important role played by the foundation is visible in the number of proposals received by it. Constraint of funds due to declining returns on the endowment has hampered its ability to support some important initiatives. Given the important objectives that the foundation is fulfilling, its resources require to be augmented further.

Keeping Hearts and Minds Open

In 2018, India and Bhutan celebrated 50 years of establishment of diplomatic relations by organizing a series of events. The close bilateral relations built on trust and mutual understanding and respect for each other's interests and concerns over the past decades have been nurtured carefully and the momentum has been sustained. The challenge lies in maintaining this level of trust and understanding in a fast-changing and increasingly shrinking world, which influences the thinking and outlook of the younger generation. For them, the close bilateral relations are a historical fact but may merit constant reassessment. There are, undoubtedly, some natural factors that dictate the need for India and Bhutan to work together. The key to strengthening relations in the longer term would lie in strengthening mutually beneficial economic interlinkages.

The two areas to focus on for achieving this are hydropower and education. Both countries have derived benefits from cooperation in the hydropower sector. But, the power market in India is changing: generation is less than 60 per cent of the installed capacity. Renewable energy, to which the Government of India has accorded priority, has become highly competitive with thermal and newer sources of hydropower, and the price of power in the private power exchange has become highly volatile. As a result, it can no longer guarantee competitive price. In view of these factors, there is the need for urgent consultations with Bhutan regarding the priority to be accorded to the projects agreed upon, the mode of execution and marketing of power from Bhutan, including export of power by Bhutan to third countries.

In the field of education, Bhutan has seen the benefits that accrued in the past. India lost the initiative a couple of decades back, when Bhutanese students lost access to reputed higher educational institutions. India, in consultation with Bhutan, should work out a special scheme for high achievers from Bhutan, reserve seats for them in premier institutions and offer them full scholarship. They will in due course become ambassadors for close bilateral relations.

Another issue that requires urgent attention, in view of China's aggressive actions at the border, is the Bhutan–China boundary issue, which is of interest to India also since it would involve the two tri-junctions. India should work with Bhutan in addressing this issue on a priority basis.

Prime Minister Modi had said during his first visit to Bhutan that India and Bhutan are close not because of the open borders but because we have opened our hearts to each other. With careful nurturing of relations, it can be ensured that the hearts on both sides will remain open to each other in the future also.

6

BANGLADESH

A Golden Chapter in Bilateral Ties

PINAK RANJAN CHAKRAVARTY

'India desires a peaceful and stable environment for its development. A nation's destiny is linked to its neighbourhood. That is why my Government has placed the highest priority on advancing friendship and cooperation with her neighbours.'[1]

Prime Minister (PM) Narendra Modi's words while addressing the United Nations General Assembly in September 2014 underscored the importance of a peaceful, politically stable and economically secure neighbourhood to foster peaceful cooperation regionally and globally.

India's South Asian neighbours constitute the first circle of civilizational linkages, security and socio-economic ties and, therefore, have always had a special niche in India's foreign policy. And it is this shared heritage of the Indic civilization, history, language, culture and a common border (the longest that India shares with any other neighbouring country) that define ties between the People's Republic of Bangladesh and the Republic of India.

The shared struggle of the 1971 War of Liberation remains a special bond. Echoing Abraham Lincoln's famous words, Sheikh Mujibur Rehman, the leader of Bangladesh's freedom struggle and the country's first president, firmly emphasized the principles of peaceful coexistence and of friendship towards all and malice towards none.[2] He played a seminal role in laying the foundation of bilateral ties. The 1972 Indo-Bangladesh Treaty of Friendship and Cooperation (lapsed in 1997) was a significant guarantee of strong bilateral engagement.

Bangladesh has emerged as a pivot in subregional groupings such as the the Bay of Bengal Initiative for Multi-Sectoral Technical and Economic Cooperation (BIMSTEC); Bangladesh, Bhutan, India, Nepal (BBIN) initiative and India's 'Act East' Policy. Bipartisan political consensus in India for upgrading relations is a key driver. Bangladesh too has reciprocated substantially, despite opposition parties promoting a narrative that PM Sheikh Hasina has become subservient to India and giving too many concessions and not receiving enough in return.

It would be fair to say that when Bangladesh has had the Awami League (AL) in power, bilateral ties have progressed much faster. Military dictators and political parties cobbled together by them, namely the Bangladesh Nationalist Party (BNP) and the Jatiyo Party, maintained distance from India, nurturing a covert and sometimes overt hostility. The Jatiyo Party later changed its stance and moved away from its unfriendly position. Military dictators also promoted Islamization and emphasized Bangladesh's Islamic identity, as opposed to secular Bengali nationalism that had guided Bangladesh's War of Liberation.

A Country in Transition

Secularism was one of the four fundamental principles of Bangladesh in the first Constitution adopted in 1972. After a period of political instability, and following the assassination of Sheikh Mujibur Rahman on 15 August 1975 along with members of his family by Army personnel, General Ziaur Rahman, the Army Chief, usurped power in 1977. To consolidate his power, Zia promoted Islam as the primary identity of Bangladeshis, 90 per cent of whom are Muslims. He pardoned and rehabilitated all the Jamaat-e-Islami (JeI) leaders and other pro-Pakistani organizations and militias who had collaborated with Pakistan to thwart the freedom struggle. He passed an indemnity law prohibiting the prosecution of those who took part in the assassination. This law was repealed by PM Hasina after 2009.

Zia also rammed through an amendment to expunge secularism from the constitution (5th amendment) and replaced it with the phrase 'absolute trust and faith in Almighty Allah'. As an officer trained and nurtured in the Pakistani Army, Zia's ethos and mindset had a Pakistani orientation. He believed that Bangladesh's nationalism should be anchored in Islam. This was amply reflected in his political decisions and attitude towards India.

Zia was assassinated by his military colleagues in 1982 and succeeded by his deputy, Gen. Hussain Muhammad Ershad. He too was a Pakistani-trained officer and his mindset was similar to that of Zia. Ershad rammed through another Constitutional amendment (8th), declaring Islam as the state religion.

Political developments in Bangladesh have invariably had their impact on bilateral ties. After restoration of democracy in 1991, ideological orientations of the AL and the BNP-JeI, and the bitter personal equation between Sheikh Hasina and

Khaleda Zia led to fractious domestic politics, with India as an issue for debate. Divisive domestic politics continues to dominate the political landscape, though with less intensity, since the opposition political parties were decimated in the last election.

In 2009, when Sheikh Hasina returned to power, her government moved the Supreme Court, which restored the principle of secularism in the constitution. However, she left the amendment relating to Islam untouched to prevent her political opponents to hurl charges of being anti-Islam against her. The contradiction between secularism and a state religion in the Bangladesh Constitution[3] is, perhaps, a unique feature.

There is little doubt that the Islamization of Bangladesh has gained pace over the years and led to home-grown radical organizations that have carried out bloody terrorist acts. Sheikh Hasina and senior leaders of the AL were subjected to a public assassination attempt in 2004, organized by the BNP–JeI government, utilizing terrorist organizations such as the Harakat-ul Jihad Islami and Jamaat-ul-Mujahideen. The role of countries in the Gulf and the Bangladeshi diaspora[4] in promoting and funding an extremist and intolerant version of Islam is a cause for concern for both countries. These trends have influenced the younger generation towards greater religiosity. In Bangladesh today, the hijab and burkha are more ubiquitous among the young. Many Bangladeshis, however, have resisted this overt Arabization and Islamization through their passionate embrace of secular Bengali cultural mores such as 'Poila Boishak' (first day of Bengali calendar), music, dance and secular festivals.

Bangladesh has always had anti-Indian lobbies and people motivated by political ideology and religions sentiments. In fact, the JeI has always been seen as pro-Pakistan and their cadres, along with Qaumi Madrassa students, with their worldview coloured by religion, are easy to mobilize against 'Hindu' India. Social media and cyberspace today are vehicles to vent their feelings unfiltered and remain a useful tool for fanning anti-Indian sentiments.

One can identify such trends as strands in the legacy of Partition and the War of Liberation. It would not be incorrect to say that a section of the population in Bangladesh did not want Pakistan to break up and blame India for making it happen. They view ties with India via the prism of religion and through issues such as occasional killings along the border, water sharing, India's so-called 'big brother attitude' and even difficulty in obtaining Indian visas.

Unique Model of Cooperation

Over the years, a series of high-level interactions between the PMs of both nations contributed immensely in strengthening the bond between the two countries. During Sheikh Hasina's first tenure as the PM, the Ganges Water Sharing Treaty was signed in 1996. This 30-year treaty has stood the test of time and will come up for renewal in 2026. The first direct road connectivity link—the Dhaka–Kolkata bus service named Shouhardya—was jointly inaugurated by PMs Sheikh Hasina and Atal Bihari Vajpayee in Dhaka, in July 1999.

During the Army-backed Caretaker Government (2007–08) which arose out of domestic political crisis, the first passenger train from Dhaka to Kolkata, Maitree Express, was inaugurated in April 2008 on Poila Boishak. Cooperation in the security domain also started during this period. Then Indian external affairs minister and later president of India Pranab Mukherjee took personal care in guiding India's policy approach to Bangladesh during this period that witnessed incarceration and prosecution of top political leaders and businesspersons.

India played a supportive role in the return of democracy to Bangladesh.[5]

Bilateral ties started improving over a decade ago, after PM Sheikh Hasina returned to power in 2009. This positive trend has continued after she won the 2013 and 2018 elections, thereby creating history by becoming the PM for three consecutive terms. This is unprecedented in Bangladesh's history, hitherto witness to alternation between the two national parties—the AL and the Begum Khaleda Zia-led BNP—with their respective coalition partners.

Earlier governments headed by military dictators and the BNP have provided refuge and arms to Indian insurgent groups from the North-eastern states, in the hope of leveraging policy to develop pressure on India. This policy was a legacy of East Pakistan. The BNP carried on with this policy. Pakistan was an eager partner of such Bangladeshi governments, pursuing its goal of eternal hostility towards India. Military intelligence of the two countries, Inter-Services Intelligence and Directorate General of Forces Intelligence, collaborated in providing refuge and arms to Indian insurgents.

Prime Minister Hasina firmly clamped down on this policy in 2009, sending a clear signal that she will not permit the use of Bangladeshi soil for anti-Indian activities. This was the change that provided a catalyst to bilateral ties. The crackdown on leaders, members and camps of Indian insurgent groups led to increased confidence and trust in security and intelligence matters. Both governments made the strategic choice of cooperation on these issues, boosting mutual confidence.

Prime Minister Hasina's government has also cracked down effectively on terrorist groups. She fulfilled her electoral promise of bringing the leaders of the JeI to book and many of them have been convicted and executed for war crimes committed in 1971. On the other hand, she has coddled some of the other

Islamic organizations, such as the Hefajat-e-Islami and similar conservative outfits which control the Qaumi Madrassas, in a political move to balance the harshness of her government's crackdown on terrorist groups.

Bilateral ties received a boost with PM Manmohan Singh's visit to Bangladesh in September 2011, after a 12-year gap. However, the visit was marred by two issues: the failure to sign the Teesta River water-sharing deal and an agreement for transit connectivity, facilitating transportation of goods through Bangladesh to the North-eastern states of India. Bangladesh had linked the Teesta deal to the transit connectivity agreement. The Teesta deal fell through because the chief minister of West Bengal, Mamata Banerjee, refused to agree to the water-sharing formula. Notwithstanding these setbacks, the visit produced some important agreements.[6] The Framework Agreement on Cooperation for Development of 2011 is important for laying out a fundamental paradigm for cooperation.[7]

The Maritime Boundary dispute, which arose from differing and overlapping claims in the Bay of Bengal followed by years of discussion and negotiations, led to a deadlock. This had begun soon after independence from Pakistan. Bangladesh inherited this dispute after its independence. The Maritime Boundary demarcation was important when seen through the prism of Exclusive Economic Zone in the United Nations Convention on the Law of the Sea Agreement. Resolution of the boundary was seen as a lingering dispute and was referred to the Permanent Court of Arbitration (PCA) by the Hasina government in October 2009. Prime Minister Hasina may have also concluded that any bilateral agreement to settle this outstanding dispute based on give and take, would have inevitably led to charges of 'sell out' by the political opposition led by the BNP, along with their supporters and anti-Indian groups in Bangladesh.

India did not object to Bangladesh's move and participated in the PCA process, as a result of a well-considered policy option. In July 2014, the PCA announced its award which reduced India's claimed maritime territory and awarded Bangladesh some of the maritime domain from India's claimed area.[8] India accepted the PCA award, putting behind a lingering dispute that had been an irritant in bilateral ties since 1972.[9]

The 100th Constitutional Amendment in May 2015 gave affect to the Land Boundary Agreement (LBA), which was required to change the international border between the two countries.[10] The LBA of 1974 was pending implementation for a variety of reasons. This issue was revisited in 2009 and India took the decision to propose a formula for resolution to Bangladesh.

Ties Enter a Golden Phase

With the Maritime Boundary dispute resolved and the LBA signed, PM Modi undertook his first visit to Bangladesh in June 2015, beginning a defining phase in strengthening bilateral ties between the two countries.[11] The visit led to the opening up of new vistas in bilateral cooperation, outlined in the Joint Declaration termed, 'Notun Projonmo-Nayi Disha' (New Generation, New Direction).[12]

Prime Minister Hasina's visit to Delhi in 2017 was focused on the process of consolidation in bilateral ties. Thirty-four new agreements were signed, many by private Indian companies, indicating a shift towards public–private partnership.[13] Her visit in 2019 reinforced bilateral ties calling it 'a bond transcending strategic relationship'. Prime Minister Modi referred to bilateral ties reaching a 'Sonali Adhyay' or 'golden phase'. The emphasis during this visit was on border management and security, defence cooperation, combatting terrorism, expanding business partnerships, boosting connectivity, development cooperation, cross-border energy cooperation, education and cultural exchanges and the issue of displaced persons from Rakhine State of Myanmar. India has extended bilateral humanitarian assistance to Bangladesh to bear the burden of Rohingya refugees who fled Myanmar and sought safe haven in Bangladesh. The return with security and resettlement of these refugees has been sought by Bangladesh, and India has supported the repatriation of these refugees, extending help to build homes in Rakhine State for refugees who return to resettle.

This visit also led to a memorandum of understanding (MOU) for setting up a Coastal Surveillance System Agreement on standard operating procedures for the movement of Indian goods, withdrawal of a fixed quantity of water from Feni River for Sabroom town in Tripura, Lines of Credit Implementation Agreement, MOU of cooperation between Hyderabad and Dhaka universities and the renewal of the Cultural Exchange Programme.[14]

Earlier in March 2019, both PMs jointly inaugurated four bilateral developmental projects via video-conferencing for the supply of 500 trucks, 300 double-decker buses and 200 AC buses under the second line of credit; extension of National Knowledge Network to Bangladesh; establishment of 36 community clinics in five districts of Bangladesh and establishment of 11 water-treatment plants in Bangladesh. Three more projects were launched in October 2019, which included the inauguration of the Vivekananda Bhaban at Rama Krishna Mission in Dhaka; import of bulk liquefied petroleum gas from Bangladesh and inauguration of the Professional Skill Development Institute at the Institution of Diploma Engineers, Bangladesh, Khulna.

Trade and Economic Relations

Bangladesh is India's largest trading partner in South Asia with an annual turnover of around $9.5 billion, plus an estimated cross-border informal trade (smuggling) of around $8–9 billion, across the 4,097 km-long porous border. The adverse balance of trade has been a bilateral trade issue, though its salience is now relatively muted. To address this trade imbalance and permit the flow of more Bangladeshi exports into India, duty/quota-free entry was granted in 2011 under the South Asian Free Trade Area. This has helped increase exports from Bangladesh to over $41 billion.[15]

In Bangladesh, three special Exclusive Economic Zones for Indian manufacturing companies have been mooted and notified. When operational, this will encourage Indian companies to manufacture there and export to India, thereby reducing the trade imbalance further. Private-sector Indian investment in Bangladesh has reached $3 billion. In 2017, 13 agreements worth around $10 billion have been signed in the power and energy sectors.[16]

A major driver of bilateral ties has been the impressive performance of Bangladesh's economy. In the pre-COVID era, Bangladesh's per capita income was growing faster than that of other South Asian countries. This is remarkable for a country, once the poorest in the region, that emerged from egregious exploitation by the ruling elite in West Pakistan when it was East Pakistan. Soon after independence, Bangladesh was battered by natural disasters, famine and poverty.

Bangladesh's economy rebounded in the early years of this century and by 2006, the gross domestic product growth rates had started climbing, overtaking that of India and many Asian countries. Bangladesh's population started stabilizing with growth of 1.1 per cent and per capita income touching

$1,750.[17] People below the poverty line (earning under $1.25 per day) have dipped to 9 per cent of the population. The UN Committee on least developed countries (LDC) designation has approved Bangladesh's removal from the LDC list and the country is set to be designated as a developing country by 2026. A buffer of a few years has been provided because of the adverse economic impact of the COVID-19 pandemic.

New Sectors of Cooperation

Cyberspace has emerged as a new domain for cooperation. Bangladesh has provided cyber connectivity between the international gateway at Cox's Bazaar to Agartala for faster Internet services in India's North-eastern states. Cost will be borne by India. Bilateral cooperation in Bangladesh's nuclear power programme has started with the beginning of construction at the Rooppur nuclear power plant.

Energy cooperation has reached a new high. India is poised to export around 1,600 megawatt (MW) of power to meet the energy deficit in Bangladesh. Over 3,600 MW of power projects are under implementation by Indian companies. Foreign direct investment from India into Bangladesh has reached $3.2 billion, with a potential to increase to $9 billion, as per the statement of the Bangladesh Minister of Industries.[18] Bangladesh–India Development Cooperation is valued at around $10 billion, consisting of grants and lines of credit.[19]

The number of 'Border Haats' (border markets) has been increased. These markets started in 2011 to help local people exchange limited goods for daily use across the border without going through complicated customs procedures. Though very small in value, they are people-oriented and help provide additional livelihood in certain areas that are relatively remote.[20]

India has granted Bangladesh generous lines of credit and

grants with commitments reaching $10 billion. While the lines of credit mainly cover infrastructure and connectivity projects, grants flow into social sector development. Capacity-building under the Indian Technical and Economic Cooperation programme and people-to-people interaction are important pillars in bilateral ties.[21]

Bangladeshis form the largest group of tourists coming into India. The visa regime has been liberalized. To strengthen people-to-people contact, six new Indian visa application centres were opened in Comilla, Noakhali, Brahmanbaria, Satkhira, Thakurgaon and Bogra in Bangladesh in 2019, raising the total number of such visa application centres to 15. In 2019, the number of visas issued to Bangladeshi citizens crossed the mark of 16 lakh. The opening of two new Assistant High Commissions in Khulna and Sylhet in 2019 has also helped in facilitating an efficient and quick visa processing for Bangladeshi nationals.

Bi-annual Director General (DG)-level talks between the Border Security Force and the Border Guard Bangladesh, meetings between Naval and Air Force Chiefs, the Annual Defence Dialogue, Tri-services staff talks and DG-level talks between the Coast Guards have expanded the interface of defence interaction. The Army Chiefs of the two countries have been exchanging visits for quite some time. There is growing cooperation in UN Peacekeeping operations. Bangladesh has emerged as the largest contributor to the UN Peacekeeping Force. The two armies have developed good working relations.

Though Bangladesh's Army and its intelligence wing and the Directorate General of Forces Intelligence have had a history of intervention in domestic politics, they have gradually changed and have become less involved. Their interests today are also aligned with national objectives that believe that good relations with India are in Bangladesh's long-term interest. The defence forces have also moved away from their earlier doctrine of planning the defence of Bangladesh with India as the 'enemy' country.

Joint coordinated patrols by the border-guarding forces at designated vulnerable border areas have expanded security interaction. Bilateral joint anti-terror military exercise Sampriti and the International Multilateral Maritime Search and Rescue Exercise are held under the umbrella of the Indian Ocean Naval Symposium. Exchange of intelligence and cooperation in investigating terrorist strikes are growing features of bilateral collaboration.

Defence and security issues will require greater cooperation with the rise of religious radicalism and terrorism. Bangladesh has taken strong and effective steps against those who have been inspired by the ISIS (Islamic State of Iraq and the Levant) and indulged in terrorist incidents within the country. Islamist organizations have been breeding grounds for religious radicals and extremist views. These forces will pose a considerable challenge for governance in Bangladesh in the future.

Connectivity

Connectivity has emerged as one of the crucial pillars in bilateral ties. Recognizing the importance of connectivity for better trade, commerce and movement of people, the two countries have moved ahead rapidly, discarding the shibboleths of the past. Connectivity will also help speed up development in the eastern region of the subcontinent, including in the BBIN.

India is participating in the Padma Multipurpose Bridge Project and the Akhaura–Agartala rail link, which will dramatically change connectivity within Bangladesh and with India. With the completion of the Padma Bridge, a potential economic corridor can be crafted for mutual benefit. The bridge over the border river, Feni, has been opened. This will connect Sabroom in south Tripura to Ramgarh in Bangladesh. Earlier, goods were being shipped from Haldia to Chittagong port and then transported by road to Tripura. This important transshipment arrangement has opened a new and cheaper route and will help Tripura connect to Chittagong port. Waterway connectivity has been expanded with more ports of call being included in the Inland Water Transit and Trade Treaty, facilitating reduction in transport costs.

Bilateral grid connectivity has enabled power purchase agreements for the transmission of 1,600 MW from India to Bangladesh, ensuring energy security for Bangladesh. New power projects, Coastal Shipping agreement, revival of pre-Partition nodes in cross-border railway movement, new routes (Agartala–Akhaura), new passenger trains, new bus routes, movement of goods from West Bengal to Tripura via Chittagong by multi-modal sea-road routes and other connectivity projects have brought the two countries closer, providing mutual benefits. Containerized goods traffic by railways is bringing down transportation costs and benefiting business ties.

Addressing Bilateral Challenges

The main issues that dominate the bilateral agenda are: sharing of river waters, border management, smuggling and human trafficking and delays in obtaining Indian visas. Bangladesh remains unhappy on the issue of Rohingya refugees in Bangladesh, on which it expected more robust support to pressurize Myanmar. The military coup in Myanmar, public protests and crackdown by the military government have complicated matters further.

There are 54 rivers that flow from India into Bangladesh. Politics over river-water sharing is a hardy perennial in bilateral ties. It began with the construction of the Farakka Barrage in West Bengal, with the consent of Bangladesh, to divert water into the Hooghly. The Farakka Barrage was built to keep the Hooghly river navigable and prevent salt water ingress from the sea. On the issue of sharing of Ganga waters, an interim bilateral agreement was reached in 1977, under PM Morarji Desai's government. The 1996 Ganga Waters Treaty, valid for 30 years, solved the issue of sharing Ganga waters at Farakka, during the lean season (January to May).

On the unfinished bilateral agenda is the Teesta Water Sharing Agreement. In 1984, the Joint Rivers Commission[22] had attempted to allocate 42.5 per cent of the water during the lean season to India and 37.5 per cent to Bangladesh. Bangladesh's complaint is about less water flow from upstream during the lean season, thus affecting paddy and fisheries, which in turn impact livelihood. West Bengal asserts that water flow has decreased and can meet only one-sixteenth of the demand in both countries.[23]

There is diversion of water from the Gajoldoba Barrage (Jalpaiguri District) into the Teesta–Mahananda canal to meet the water requirement of agriculture and urban areas around Jalpaiguri and Siliguri. Receding Himalayan glaciers as a result of climate change, several run-of-the-river power generation plants on the upper reaches of the river in Sikkim and proliferation of paddy cultivation in West Bengal and northern Bangladesh have been responsible for the reduced flow of water. Governments are reluctant to educate and motivate farmers to diversify into less water-intensive crops.

The ball is in India's court. But the implementation of the draft agreement has been blocked by domestic Indian politics.[24] There is a deadlock and the COVID pandemic and forthcoming elections in West Bengal have complicated matters further.[25] Bangladesh has every right to be frustrated.

Migration of people from East Bengal, East Pakistan and Bangladesh into different parts of India is a historical fact. Poverty, unemployment, population displacement by communal riots, floods and natural disasters have been actors in migration. Partition caused a huge spike in migration, both ways, following communal riots. The most impacted were Hindus fleeing from East Pakistan in 1947. Migration again spiked during the wars of 1965 and 1971. The number of Hindus in Bangladesh has dropped from around 28 per cent in 1940 to around 9 per cent in 2018.

It has been argued by Prof. Abul Barkat, an eminent economist at Dhaka University, in his book *Political Economy of Reforming Agriculture-Land-Water Bodies in Bangladesh* that there will be no Hindus left in Bangladesh after 30 years. He says: 'The rate of exodus over the past 49 years points to that direction.' He further adds that 'from 1964 to 2013, around 11.3 million Hindus left Bangladesh due to religious persecution and discrimination'. According to him, 'on an average, 632 Hindus left the country each day and 230,612 annually', mainly during military governments after Independence. Prof. Barkat's study indicates that before the 1971 war, the daily rate of migration was 705, while it was 512 during 1971–81, 438 during 1981–91, increasing thereafter to 767 persons each day during 1991–2001, while around 774 persons left the country per day during 2001–12.[26]

The Enemy Property Act (EPA), enacted by the Pakistan government after the 1965 war, gave powers to appropriate enemy property, mainly Hindu owned. Bangladesh renamed the EPA the Vested Property Act (VPA, 1974), whereby properties previously seized under EPA came under the ownership of the government. This discriminatory law continued to be used against Hindu-owned properties. The AL government attempted to restore vested Hindu properties to their rightful owners in 2001 but with little success. People who had grabbed Hindu properties were politically powerful and prevented implementation.

It is estimated that 1.2 million Hindu families, or 44 per cent of Hindu households, have been affected by the EPA/VPA. Over 2 million acres of land has been confiscated and even after the VPA came into force, land encroachment continued, mostly under BNP governments. Hindus have been victims of ethnic cleansing and illegal usurpation of their properties. Their temples continue to be desecrated and their women targeted by property grabbers, forcing them to flee and seek refuge in India.[27]

In recent times, cross-border migration from Bangladesh has declined, but it has not stopped. 'According to the ILO, each year more than 400,000 workers leave Bangladesh for overseas employment. One estimate indicates that as of November 2016, a total of 21,657,632 Bangladeshi migrant workers went abroad for work.'[28] Migration into India, bulk of it illegal, takes place via smuggling networks across the porous borders. Many travel to India illegally and do not return, and there have been instances of Bangladeshi nationals acquiring Indian passports fraudulently. Considerable effort has been put in by Bangladesh on building a narrative which argues that Bangladesh's economic progress has diluted any push factor on economic migration. A counternarrative has been built up also about Indians working illegally in Bangladesh. This seeks to balance the debate on illegal migration.

On this sensitive issue, there have been comments made by a few Indian political leaders, during the heat of domestic electoral campaigns and in Parliament during the debate on the Citizenship Amendment Act (CAA). Such comments have caused concern in Bangladesh, leading to the cancellation of ministerial visits to India. It has also raised anxiety levels about India's National Register of Citizens (NRC) and the subsequent CAA.

Bangladesh denies any systemic persecution of non-Muslims and resents its clubbing with other Islamic countries such as Afghanistan and Pakistan, where persecution of non-Muslims is State-driven. Bangladesh has taken offence for being named in the CAA as a country that persecutes non-Muslims.[29] Bangladesh remains concerned about reverse migration, though the official position of Bangladesh is that there are no illegal migrants from Bangladesh in India. Bangladesh's sensitivity is heightened because of the influx and burden of Rohingya refugees.

The NRC's purpose is to document all the legal citizens of India, so that the illegal immigrants can be identified and deported. The NRC process was started by the Congress-led United Progressive Alliance government but brakes were put on it for electoral reasons. So far it has been implemented for the state of Assam, as directed by the Supreme Court. The recent NRC attempted to identify Indian citizens and undocumented migrants (non-citizens) who could not prove that they entered India before the midnight of 24 March 1971, just before Bangladesh's War of Liberation broke out. This date was mutually agreed upon by Bangladesh and India.

Another area of frequent debate and concern in Bangladesh is 'border killings'. The media in Bangladesh sometimes highlights this as 'killing of innocent Bangladeshis' by India's Border Security Force (BSF). The border along West Bengal is the most important theatre for criminal activities by the smuggling mafia on both sides, the most lucrative being the smuggling of cattle from India into Bangladesh. For various reasons, mostly religious sentiments of Hindus, live cattle has been banned for exports for decades and the government has banned export of all live animals from India in 2018.[30]

This has led to India having the largest cattle population in the world, which leads to huge oversupply and motivates smugglers to meet the growing demand in Bangladesh, where cattle meat is the cheapest source of protein. To meet this demand, smugglers in India round up cattle and take them to border villages in West Bengal and hand them over to their Bangladeshi counterparts, who send couriers to collect them, thereby illegally transgressing India's border.

This cattle trade is a well-oiled machine with political patronage in both countries. In Bangladesh, a cattle tax per head of cattle entering Bangladesh is collected. Current estimates of annual numbers of cattle smuggled are under 100,000.[31] India's BSF, which guards the border and is tasked with tackling smugglers, often gets involved in violent skirmishes with smugglers. Sometimes, these skirmishes result in shooting and deaths of smugglers, both from Bangladesh and India. Unfortunately, a few innocent people who try to walk across the border for various reasons, including social interaction or shopping, are sometimes accidentally shot by the BSF.

Most of the border has a barbed wire fence 150 yards inside Indian territory, which is frequently cut by smugglers for ferrying cattle and other purposes such as drugs and human trafficking and smuggling of fake Indian currency notes. The actual border or the zero line is marked by concrete border pillars, which run through open fields and villages. Where a river is the border, the median principle aligns the border in the middle of the river. These riverine sections are also used for smuggling since there is no fence there. People inhabiting villages along the border mostly seek their livelihood in smuggling.

The media outcry in Bangladesh is generated by the political powerful smuggling mafia, in tandem with other stakeholders in the cattle smuggling trade. Bangladesh's media is usually silent on the issue of Indian smugglers who are killed by the BSF, since the narrative of a 'trigger-happy' BSF is unnecessary for India–Bangladesh ties. A widely held public perception in Bangladesh is that the BSF shoots the smugglers when they are not paid off.

In India, the perception is that politicians in border districts and the BGB are hand in glove with the smuggling mafia and their illegal income depends on cattle smuggling. The media outcry generates pressure on the Bangladeshi government to protest and make it a bilateral issue. The smuggling mafia knows that if the BSF intercepts Bangladeshi cattle smugglers, causing casualties, then their agents and couriers may be deterred from entering India, impeding channels of smuggling and causing huge financial loss.

Bangladesh does not deny that smugglers transgress the border but demands that they should not be killed and should be arrested and legal action taken against them. Bangladesh considers killing of smugglers a violation of human rights and denial of justice. The BSF contends that they sometimes have to open fire in self-defence when attacked by smugglers.

Such killings are unfortunate on a border between friendly countries. India has taken steps to instruct the BSF to be very careful and use non-lethal means to apprehend smugglers. Yet, a few incidents occur regularly, though the numbers have come down through joint patrolling and better border-management methods. Bangladesh has taken important steps to encourage farmers, via subsidies, to breed more cattle for meat. This is helping to meet demand internally and reducing demand for smuggled cattle from India. But it is unlikely that cattle smuggling will stop completely.

The influx of Rohingyas into Bangladesh for refuge was a

humanitarian crisis, which burdened Bangladesh with over a million refugees. Bangladesh expected India to intervene with Myanmar to take back the refugees, but was disappointed when India was seen to be diffident in applying pressure on Myanmar. While India has tried to be helpful, it was not feasible to pressurize Myanmar beyond the threshold of persuasion. Myanmar is also an important neighbouring country for India, a member of BIMSTEC and ASEAN, a stakeholder in cooperating on security issues and an important partner in connectivity projects such as the Kaladan Corridor and the India–Myanmar–Thailand Trilateral Highway. Perhaps, Bangladesh expected more from India but such expectations are unrealistic.

The China Factor

China's security and economic footprint has grown in South Asia and managing this will remain a challenge for both countries. The option to use an external power, in this case China, by India's neighbours as a balancer has become more pronounced in recent years. Both China and India are engaged in development partnerships with Bangladesh and the latter's policy is now geared towards extracting maximum benefits from the two big powers. By itself, this is unexceptionable. India has never objected to Chinese projects such as bridges, trade centres, auditoriums and other similar infrastructure. China's financial muscle now gives it greater ability to fund infrastructure projects in Bangladesh.

Bangladesh's overwhelming dependence on military hardware from China is a source of Chinese influence in the military. The decision to acquire two submarines from China in 2016 has introduced a higher level of capability in the Bangladesh Navy. Bilateral professional cooperation between the security and armed forces of Bangladesh and India has increased. India has provided a $500 million line of credit to Bangladesh for the procurement of defence-related goods from India.[32] This momentum must be maintained and intensified.

China has promised billions of dollars worth of loans for infrastructural development, encouraged Pakistan to mend ties with Bangladesh and offered duty-free entry to 97 per cent of tariff lines for Bangladeshi goods. China's Belt and Road Initiative (BRI) is a geoeconomic and geostrategic project, funnelling huge Chinese investment for infrastructure development, thereby attracting many countries into China's sphere of influence. India has opposed the BRI because one section of it—the China–Pakistan Economic Corridor—goes through Indian territory under Pakistan's control. All of India's neighbours, except Bhutan, have joined the BRI.

India will have to take note of Bangladesh–China cooperation in the maritime sector too. Bangladesh facilitating China's entry into the Bay of Bengal will have consequences for India's maritime security environment. China is stepping up assistance in the digital sector to Bangladesh and Huawei 5G technology will be introduced there.[33] Security implications could be considerable for India. An industrial zone near Chattogram (Chittagong) hosting Chinese manufacturing companies will provide another avenue for cheap Chinese exports into India, since Bangladesh enjoys duty-free access to the Indian market. India will have to implement strict rules of origin criterion for imports from Bangladesh to check entry of Chinese goods.

Prime Minister Hasina appears conscious of and sensitive to India's concerns and has put on record at the World Economic Forum gathering in China that Bangladesh will not step into any 'debt trap'. She has also said that Bangladesh's ties with India are 'organic' and go beyond a few billion dollars. She is being cautious and has openly said that Bangladesh has no military ambition and seeks out China as a development partner only.[34] Bangladesh's development cooperation with China is not the issue and is unexceptionable as long as it does not impact India's national security concerns.

With China and India locked in a military confrontation in Ladakh, there is rising concern in India about China's proposal to fund, build and manage the Teesta basin project. If the project takes off, Chinese companies linked to the People's Liberation Army (PLA) and Chinese Communist Party will bring in thousands of workers, including PLA personnel, into areas along India's border and south of the sensitive Siliguri Corridor. Security experts in India have little doubt that the Chinese will use the opportunity for terrain mapping, gathering intelligence and planting devices for eavesdropping and jamming India's communications. China has also been awarded the project for the upgradation of Sylhet Airport, which is 54 km from Dawki on the Indian border in Meghalaya.

Can Bangladesh guarantee a firewall against such anti-India activities by the Chinese from Bangladeshi territory? This will require bilateral consultation and measures on the ground to monitor Chinese activities, at a time when China has adopted a threatening posture on the Himalayan border and when Indian sensitivity about China is at its highest. China's sudden benevolence towards Bangladesh cannot be altruistic. It has geostrategic dimensions with India in mind. If Bangladesh is playing the China card regarding the Teesta, then it has to be cautious about overplaying it, lest it impacts adversely on Indian security interests. Lessons from the past during the BNP–JeI government must be absorbed for protecting mutual interests.

Contours of the Future Road Map

Bangladesh and India are destined to cooperate despite hiccups in bilateral ties. Asymmetry creates special dynamics and challenges in bilateral ties which impinge on policy choices, as does the legacy of Partition and religious identity. Yet, Indian political leaders, from Indira Gandhi to Narendra Modi, have contributed to the development of ties with Bangladesh in a politically bipartisan manner. In Bangladesh, the maximum strides in bilateral ties have taken place under the leadership of Sheikh Mujibur Rahman and his daughter, Sheikh Hasina.

The future of Bangladesh–India ties lies in creating a web of connectivity that integrates roads, railways, waterways and coastal shipping for the faster and easier transportation of goods. Connectivity remains the bedrock of a more efficient transportation infrastructure for India's Act East Policy and bringing the North-eastern states into the mainstream of the Indian economy. Hence, Bangladesh and Myanmar are bridges to connect to India's North-east with ASEAN countries. Both countries must bring BIMSTEC into play, with its headquarters in Dhaka, for intensifying cooperation and allocating more resources for its functioning and expanded activities. Connectivity to the East, via Myanmar and Thailand, by members of both BIMSTEC and ASEAN needs vigorous implementation. India will have to step up implementation of bilateral projects to dispel the prevailing perception of tardiness in delivery schedules.

The post-COVID-19 pandemic situation will be an era of 'Relief, Rehabilitation and Regeneration'. It will open up opportunities for bilateral cooperation, particularly in the following sectors:

1. Upgrading the health sector, joint medical research, disease surveillance, telemedicine-COVID-19 Vaccine

2. Climate-smart agricultural technologies for sustainable and increased productivity to ensure food security
3. Climate change issues, preserving the biodiversity of the Sundarbans via joint projects
4. Attracting manufacturing as international companies diversify and disperse value chains out of China
5. Facilitating smoother travel both ways to boost tourism
6. Blue Economy projects
7. Water management and disaster management
8. Indian investment in special economic zones in Bangladesh, Bilateral CEOs Forum
9. Cyberspace security, information technology start-ups, online workshops, consultancy
10. Greater investment in innovation, technology infrastructure and digitization[35]

The post-COVID-19 era is expected to throw up several challenges in bilateral cooperation, particularly joint monitoring of projects and schemes, which are essential to maintain delivery schedules. In spite of temporary hurdles, the foundation of the relationship is firmly anchored in the convergence of mutual interests and is much stronger today than ever before. There is no escape from closer bilateral engagement, if future prosperity of the peoples of the two countries has to be secured.

7

MYANMAR

Time to Act East Harder

GAUTAM MUKHOPADHAYA

Narendra Modi began his first term of office as Prime Minister (PM) of India in May 2014 with a series of high-profile foreign policy initiatives bearing a personal stamp. Notwithstanding some pragmatic and defining moves that India has made since the end of the Cold War, they signalled a more self-confident Indian foreign policy and promised to overcome the remaining challenges posed by the dissolution of the erstwhile Soviet Union in 1991 and the nuclear tests of 1998.

With Myanmar, India has been able to develop relations on multiple fronts including security and defence cooperation with the Myanmar military. However, the military coup of 1 February 2021 overthrowing the newly elected Parliament that was to form a new National League for Democracy (NLD) government, and the ensuing widespread crackdown and violence against unarmed civilians by the Tatmadaw—Myanmar's military—has raised questions about both Myanmar's future and India's relations with an immediate neighbour that may take time to resolve. Although the Indian government has expressed 'deep concern' over the military takeover, called for the release of those detained including the president and Daw Aung San Suu Kyi and a restoration of the democratic process and transition and condemned the violence, its reluctance to criticize the military openly and its formal response to refugees on its borders in the north-east of India has attracted negative attention.

First Steps

Prime Minister Modi's very first act on winning the 2014 general elections was to invite the leaders of SAARC countries including PM Nawaz Sharif of Pakistan[1] for his swearing-in ceremony, thus displaying his ability to think big and think out of the box. Myanmar was not present, but its exclusion from the ceremony was more because of it not being part of the core group of SAARC invitees rather than any inattention or deliberate act of omission. However, it did underline the psychological amnesia that five decades of insular military rule in Myanmar and autarky in India had induced in both for the two countries to practically forget that they are close neighbours sharing 2,000 years of history, more than a century of colonial rule and long shared borders through the north-east of India, the Bay of Bengal and the Andaman Sea.

Modi followed up this early outreach to the neighbourhood with highly successful visits to Bhutan and Nepal in 2014, Bangladesh in June 2015 and Afghanistan, followed by a surprise visit to Pakistan to attend PM Sharif's grand-daughter's wedding in December 2015 to showcase his 'Neighbourhood First' policy. This proclaimed the priority that the National Democratic Alliance (NDA) government attached to its immediate and closest neighbours based on traditional ties, mutually beneficial relations and growth for all.

That this velvet glove concealed an iron hand was manifest in the prompt retaliation against Indian insurgent camps along the India–Myanmar border after a fierce ambush on an Indian Army convoy in Manipur in June 2015 killing 18 troops, reportedly by the National Socialist Council of Nagaland-Khaplang (NSCN-K). The operation carried a stern message to Indian insurgent groups sheltering outside India, but its larger message was clearly directed at another neighbour on the other side of India with whom PM Modi's early friendly overtures did not lead anywhere—that the latter would not hesitate to retaliate in case of terrorist attacks by non-State actors from across the border.[2]

The stinging episode was followed by a joint visit by National Security Advisor Ajit Doval and then foreign secretary Dr S. Jaishankar to secure Myanmar's understanding and support for a more robust policy against the now outlawed NSCN-K and other Indian insurgents using Myanmar as a safe haven and a training and staging ground for attacks inside India. If Myanmar was upset by what the media and a few ministers boasted was a 'cross-border' attack, they kept their sentiments in check at least in public. Indeed, the incident did not prevent Myanmar from inviting India to join as an official observer of the Nationwide Ceasefire Agreement with several of its own Ethnic Armed Organizations (EAOs) later that year in October 2015 along with the United Nations, China and Thailand. Although the Nationwide Ceasefire Agreement was an extremely important initiative of the U Thein Sein government and the NSCN-K was one of Myanmar's EAOs that the government was trying to draw into it, they did not finally press them into signing the Agreement out of deference to India's concerns.

Act East

While Myanmar was not an immediate beneficiary of Modi's Neighbourhood First policy, the Indian PM chose to visit Myanmar in November 2014 to attend the ASEAN Summit. An important purpose of the visit was to unveil his second flagship foreign policy initiative that has a bearing on India's relations with Myanmar—that is the re-branding of India's long-standing 'Look East' Policy launched by PM Narasimha Rao in 1991 into a new 'Act East' Policy. The new avatar enveloped earlier initiatives too, such as BIMSTEC[3] (1997), the Mekong-Ganga Cooperation Initiative (2000) and India's Duty Free Trade Preference (DFTP, announced in 2008) covering Cambodia, Laos, Myanmar and Vietnam as part of India's commitment to Least Developed Countries. Under the DFTP initiative, India extends zero duty or preferential access to more than 98 per cent of tariff lines to 28 Least Developed Countries since 2015.[4] More recently, India has also become a 'Development Partner' of the ACMECS,[5] a grouping of countries covered by the major rivers of the Greater Mekong Subregion (GMS).

'Act East' too was articulated in terms of an intensification of ties with South East Asia, with the ASEAN as its heart. The policy marked a continuity with its precursor and reiterated the importance of Myanmar as its gateway to the east. Several features distinguish the Act East Policy from its precursor though: first, an expansion on the concept to include not only Japan, Korea and Australia, but also the Pacific islands; second, a stronger emphasis on the cultural dimension of the relationship particularly the bonds of Buddhism; third, a greater role for the Indian diaspora where present, in which Hindu organizations have played a prominent role; but fourth and more importantly, the growing salience of the China factor in the relationship as a result of China's increasingly assertive strategic ambitions in the region. Officially, China has never figured in India's Look or Act East policies, but its very exclusion from an expansive Act East Policy is an indication of its presence in absentia. With time, as China has become more aggressive in its territorial claims in its neighbourhood resulting in clashes and a stand-off at the Line of Actual Control since May 2020, its presence has become inescapable.

Fifth, recent official statements make it apparent that at its Pacific end, India's Act East Policy now dovetails with its Indo-Pacific strategy.[6]

Multifaceted Ties

Myanmar is important to India for several reasons. First, it lies along four sensitive, sometimes insurgency-affected North-eastern border states of India with which it shares 1,643 km of land borders, which are still prone to ethnic tensions. These borders have been demarcated under a 1967 India-Myanmar Boundary Agreement but for a section at the tri-junction of India, Myanmar and China.

Second, it is India's terrestrial 'gateway' to the rich South East Asian landmass marked by great rivers[7] and north–south hill ranges and plateaus, with which the North-eastern states of India share various ethnic and cultural affinities.

Third, it is an incredibly resource-rich country endowed with an abundance of sun, water, land, forests, minerals, precious stones and metals, oil and gas, on and off shore, and a long coastline that should make it an attractive investment destination for India.

Fourth, it is strategically sandwiched between two of the world's most populous countries and largest economies that are in an uneasy relationship. Lastly, it is a strategic bridgehead for India's Act East and potentially Indo-Pacific policies.

The Modi government inherited a largely positive relationship with Myanmar, built up over two decades of patient diplomacy to overcome frosty relations going back to General Ne Win's coup in 1962 and its impact on Indians especially businesses and properties. These were aggravated by the military's suppression of democracy and ethnic rights over decades but especially in 1988. Over the last decade, however, India has built on and consolidated this relationship, successfully negotiating unexpected twists and turns emanating from Myanmar's domestic politics and their international repercussions. These are once again being put to the test with the recent coup.

Political and Strategic Context

Prior to the coup, the setting for India–Myanmar relations had changed quite dramatically. First, the elected civilian Union Solidarity and Development Party (USDP) government consisting of retired military officers with the tacit backing of the Tatmadaw embarked on political and economic reforms charted by former military strongman Senior General Than Shwe as part of his 'seven-stage road map to democracy'. This diplomatic opening to the world offered exciting prospects of Myanmar as a new market and 'emerging' economy in South East Asia.

Second, Modi, in addition to energizing and rebranding India's 1991 'Look East' Policy into 'Act East' Policy towards the ASEAN and East Asia, also subsequently embraced the 'Indo-Pacific' construct. Myanmar falls within these initiatives and India's 'Neighbourhood First' policy in varying degrees, and it also has a major role to play as a springboard for India into the GMS.

Third, landmark elections in Myanmar in November 2015—the first open, multiparty and reasonably free and fair elections in Myanmar since 1960 that were honoured[8]—brought in the democratic opposition led by Daw Aung San Suu Kyi and the NLD to power in an uneasy power-sharing arrangement with the Tatmadaw. That arrangement has now been shattered.

Although it took more than two years for the Modi government to demonstrate its Neighbourhood First policy towards Myanmar, it tried to make up for lost time after the elections. It sent Doval as Special Envoy of PM Modi to congratulate Daw Aung Sang Suu Kyi on winning the elections in June 2016. This was followed up with a high-level bilateral state visit by the new president of Myanmar U Htin Kyaw in August 2016 and by State Counsellor Daw Aung San Suu Kyi, for the BRICS-BIMSTEC Outreach Summit. But it was not until September 2017 that Modi himself could undertake a bilateral official visit to Myanmar.

These were followed up by President Ram Nath Kovind's Myanmar visit in December 2018 and President U Win Myint's India visit in February 2020. State Counselor Daw Aung San Suu Kyi visited India again for the ASEAN–India 25th Anniversary Commemorative Summit in January 2018. They were supplemented by visits at the level of foreign and commerce ministers, national security advisors and meetings of some 25 institutionalized bilateral working-level mechanisms ranging from boundary, border and security issues to new ones on power, oil and gas and science and technology, amongst others. They also served as occasions for India to express support for Myanmar's critical political and economic priorities notably Myanmar's peace process with its EAOs through the 'Twenty-First Panglong Peace Conference', amongst others. This momentum has now suffered a shock.

Fourth, internal developments in Myanmar relating to its restive and autonomy-seeking EAOs, and in particular the Rohingya issue, catapulted Myanmar once again into unwelcome international attention. The Rohingya issue all but negated the diplomatic breakthroughs with the West until 2016, alienated the Islamic world, dragged Myanmar to the International Court of Justice, where the Organisation of Islamic Cooperation filed a suit against Myanmar for 'genocide' against the Rohingyas and threw Myanmar once again into the grip of China. Even as Myanmar was fighting for room to manoeuvre from international censure over the Rohingya issue, it now finds itself in a new *cul-de-sac* over its nationwide crackdown on its entire population.

On the other hand, China's long-standing ties with some of the unreconciled EAOs in the north, and more recently with the militant and armed Rakhine nationalist Arakan Army, introduced a new irritant in Myanmar's relationship with China, serious enough for Sr. Gen. Min Aung Hlaing to comment on, on a visit to Russia in July 2020. The coup will not erase that but might make it worse.

The NDA government did not let the Rohingya crisis and its regional and international implications, particularly its fallout on Bangladesh (which hoped that India could bring pressure on Myanmar to reverse its Rohingya policy and take back the refugees), negatively impact India–Myanmar relations, though it did temper it by making it more even-handed. At this point, however, although the military has made overtures to Bangladesh over it, the Rohingya issue has been forced to take a back seat.

India's first reaction to the Arakan Rohingya Salvation Army (ARSA) attacks against Myanmar border guards and armed forces in August 2017 on the eve of the PM's official visit to Myanmar in September 2017 was highly sympathetic to the Tatmadaw at the expense of the Rohingya. Since then, however, India has tried to counsel the return of the Rohingyas to Myanmar under conditions of security, extended humanitarian assistance to both Bangladesh and Myanmar and assisted in reconstruction and development efforts in Rakhine with the aim of facilitating the process. India, however, did not take a strong position against the scorched-earth response of the Myanmar Army to the attacks that have resulted in charges of ethnic cleansing and genocide by sections of the international community, sanctions by the United States on individuals complicit in the reprisals, blacklisting of social media accounts of military authorities and some criticism of India for not standing up for the human rights of the Rohingya against egregious violations by the Myanmar Army. On the contrary, India's strong denunciation of ARSA terrorism in 2016–17 helped maintain a friendly and cooperative relationship with Myanmar and eased the way to build on past diplomatic, developmental, defence, security, cultural and people-to-people initiatives to position India more favourably in Myanmar.

Development Partnership

A similar pattern can be seen in India's development partnership with Myanmar although there has been some legitimate criticism about delays in completion of major connectivity projects. All the major projects in Myanmar such as the Tamu–Kalay–Kaleywa road, the Kaladan project, the Trilateral Highway, the Myanmar Institute of Information Technology, the Advanced Centre for Agricultural Research and Education (ACARE) and Rice Bio Park, to name a few, were initiated, and many completed, pre-2014. Though this is not well realized,[9] successive Indian governments have committed close to $2 billion in official development assistance out of the Ministry of External Affairs's budget and lines of credit.[10]

Some of these projects are still ongoing, some have matured under Modi's stewardship and some are new. One new initiative is the five-year, $25 million Rakhine State Development Programme modelled on the Border Area Development Programme, under which India has taken up some farm mechanization, housing, medical and reconstruction programmes in Rakhine state. These have entered its third phase. Others are extensions of previous initiatives that have worked such as the opening of a new Centre of Excellence in Information Technology and Software in Myitkyina; Industrial Training Centres at Monywa and Thaton (in addition to earlier ones at Pakokku and Mingyan); new basic defence and women police training centres and other initiatives relating to cooperation in the maritime domain, disaster management and the application of information technology to governance.

However, there were a few new inter-governmental initiatives in the power, petroleum, financial and education sectors that were potentially game changing. These relate to proposals for grid connectivity between the Indian and Myanmar power grids;[11] refining, development and retailing of petroleum and petroleum products; launch of RuPay card, creation of a digital payment gateway and settlement in local currencies to facilitate cross-border trade and financial transactions; and the extension of the National Knowledge Network to Myanmar universities. These were supplemented by cultural initiatives to build on earlier assistance to refurbish the Ananda Temple at Bagan to include the conservation of 92 pagodas in the Bagan UNESCO World Heritage site damaged by an earthquake in 2016. Other measures have also been taken to facilitate easier cross-border road travel between the two countries such as the 2018 Land Border Crossing Agreement enabling cross-border travel through Tamu–Moreh and Rhi–Zawkathar. Cumulatively, they had the potential of connecting India and Myanmar much more closely and lifting bilateral relations to a new level. It is unclear how these can be pursued after the military takeover that is being determinedly opposed by the people.

However, in spite of several noteworthy initiatives, there is hardly any comparison between people-to-people connectivity between Myanmar and India and Myanmar and its other major neighbours in terms of flights, tourism, business, leisure or road travel, educational ties, bus services, medical visits, etc. It was hoped that the Imphal–Mandalay Bus Service would make a big difference to this. There is also a need for a big push by the civil aviation authorities to pool in existing travel to Myanmar via Thailand into direct air services to and from destinations in India and Myanmar with the large Persons of Indian Origin (PIO) community in Myanmar as a ready base for that. This is only possible if Myanmar returns to normalcy.

Defence

One area where the relationship had genuinely gained in trust and cooperation was the defence and security relationship. While the thaw had started in the late 1990s and early 2000s, it had built up over successive visits by Sr. Gen. Min Aung Hlaing and Indian service chiefs in the last few years and diversified. At the time of the coup, it covered increased training of Myanmar Army and Naval officers in Indian defence-training institutions, cooperation on maritime security and coordinated Naval patrols, a growing defence equipment supply relationship especially to the Myanmar Navy culminating in the supply of a refitted Indian kilo-class submarine to the Myanmar Navy late last year (2020) and Army-to-Army cooperation and coordinated operations against Indian insurgent groups and cadres in Myanmar, notably the Myanmar Army operations in May 2020 which resulted in 22 IIG cadres being handed over by Myanmar to India.

The unusual October 2020 joint visit of the Indian foreign

secretary and Army chief was a sign of increased synergy between the defence diplomatic arms of our relationship with Myanmar, and the comfort of the civilian government in Myanmar in India's relationship with Tatmadaw that was based on Myanmar's defence and India's security needs as well as India's support for democracy internally.

It is unclear how these will develop with the February 2021 coup. One of its prime outcomes is that all countries will have to choose which side they are on. India's statements have been firmly pro-democracy, but in line with other Asian countries, it has stopped short of condemnation of the coup until now and kept channels of communication with the Tatmadaw open to assess the situation and take a position. India understands that Myanmar needs a strong army for its national defence, but India's preferred option would be to try to preserve a defence and security relationship with a professional army under civilian rule.

Trade and Investment

One area where India's performance post 2014 has been disappointing is commercial relationship. At the time of the transition from military to USDP rule in Myanmar in 2011, India was Myanmar's fourth-largest trade partner with a trade volume of around $1.3 billion, which composed overwhelmingly of imports of beans, pulses and timber from Myanmar. Taking into account India's fast-growing economy at the time, its huge market, geographical proximity, historic ties, its Look and Act East policies, India's development assistance, the DFTP scheme and ASEAN–Free Trade Agreement (FTA) on the one hand, and the trade- and investment-friendly economic reforms introduced by the USDP and NLD governments on the other, it was expected that economic ties would increase and expand in volume and depth. Initially, bilateral trade rose to approximately $2.2 billion in 2016–17[12] but declined to around $1.5 billion by the end of the decade, far below the $3 billion trade target set in 2011 for 2014. India's ranking on bilateral trade with Myanmar fell from the fourth to the fifth place, and investments from the ninth to 11th or 12th. Private-sector investment that could have made up for a number of handicaps vis-à-vis Myanmar's other neighbours such as China, Thailand and other trade partners, has been particularly disappointing.

While the government has officially invested close to $2 billion in connectivity and development projects, and Indian public-sector undertakings have invested over $1 billion in the oil and gas sector,[13] the only major non-extractive Indian private-sector investment has been a $200 million investment by Adani Terminals on a container port terminal in Yangon. This has come under pressure post coup. Indian industry has also been unable to take advantage of ASEAN and FTA markets and the DFTP with India to expand their presence in Myanmar.

There are various reasons for this poor performance in trade and investment such as lack of sufficient volume of trade through the year to sustain regular shipping services, poor direct banking services, higher transaction costs of trading largely through Singapore and lack of commercial lines of credit or risk cover for outward investment and transition issues in Myanmar. However, policy decisions have also played a part.

One reason for the stagnation in bilateral trade was a decline in India's imports from Myanmar. Myanmar's two primary export commodities to India—timber and beans and pulses—which had an overwhelming share in the bilateral trade, suffered on account of market factors and decisions by both Myanmar and India. The timber trade suffered because of a ban on export of raw timber on environmental and economic grounds by Myanmar in 2014. The beans and pulses trade, which could be worth $1 billion on a good year, suffered when

India abruptly set limits to imports of beans and pulses with shipments mid-sea in 2017 on account of higher domestic production and supply agreements entered into with other countries to stabilize domestic prices in the past.

As a result, a trade relationship in which Myanmar farmers grew beans and pulses for the Indian market that had survived all the vicissitudes of bilateral relations and international sanctions since the 1980s and virtually held up the India–Myanmar relationship through a hard period, suffered. Efforts were under way prior to the coup to stabilize the trade for which India had committed in advance to procure 1.5 lakh tonnes of *urad dal* from Myanmar until March 2021.[14]

However, more needs to be done. Indian exports to Myanmar, which were negligible until the middle of this decade because of a hiatus in trade relations as a result of political disruptions in Myanmar and the deterrent effect of US sanctions, had picked up over the last five years of Myanmar's opening. However, these exports were dominated by just two products, pharmaceuticals and steel, and lately sugar that was re-exported to China. It did contribute to a better balance in trade but was not enough to preserve India's trade position in Myanmar. Indian consumer goods that used to have a strong presence in the early decades of Burma's independence have hardly any presence in Myanmar now. Trade relations are likely to suffer even more as a result of the coup, though shortages of daily items may also lead to more imports from neighbouring countries.

Prior to the coup, Indian industry had identified bottlenecks inhibiting Indian exports to Myanmar and also identified products and sectors to promote two-way trade.[15] These will have to await a return to normalcy. But while these efforts may increase trade from present levels, they are unlikely to overcome India's structural disadvantages vis-à-vis Myanmar's other major trade partners such as China, Thailand, Singapore, Vietnam, Japan and Korea. These countries are either better connected to key commercial and industrial centres, are part of the ASEAN Economic Community or have deeper FTAs. They are also better placed commercially than Indian companies manufacturing and exporting out of India that face higher transaction costs and duties. This will get worse once the Regional Comprehensive Economic Partnership (RCEP) that India has opted out of enters into force.

The massive disruption and dislocation caused by the coup to the economy as a whole, including trade, banking, logistics, port operations and targeted sanctions, is bound to impact Myanmar's trade relations with all its partners heavily. But if things return to normal, instead of relying on an export-oriented strategy, India could consider investing in the high-resource, low-cost economies of Myanmar (and the rest of the CLMV [Cambodia, Laos, Myanmar and Vietnam]) and the ASEAN Economic Community in general) for an investment-led regional trade strategy to target the huge 2.5 billion RCEP market and the 1.4 billion Indian DFTP market, amongst others. Besides large conventional investments in oil and gas, mining, power, infrastructure, etc., the government could encourage and support smaller Indian investments in Myanmar's agricultural and allied resources, which constitute the mainstay of its economy. Other areas could be light industries, including the textiles and garments, where Myanmar has GSTP (Global System of Trade Preferences) quotas in OECD markets, autos and auto parts and the services sector including education, training, information technology and tourism, which together have the maximum potential of deepening the relationship through value adding, employment and partnership.

The Modi government had made a small beginning in this direction in 2015–16 with a Project Development Fund for the CLMV countries. The fund was administered by the Eximbank of India to incubate small Indian investments. But the approximately $70 million outlay is too small to make a difference and is directed mostly towards the health sector. The lack of a sizable Indian commercial presence in Myanmar that can act as a base for the GMS as a whole, has also handicapped its Act East Policy as a whole.

The North-East as a Gateway to South East Asia

The development of North-east India has been one of the foremost rationales for India's Look East Policy and its Act East avatar. One of its central pillars has been improvements in internal connectivity in the North-east and cross-border connectivity with Myanmar and beyond into South East Asia.[16]

Although often projected as more talk than substance, much of what constitutes Modi's Act East Policy can be traced to the Look East Policy before 2014. This is also true of the North-east and Myanmar components of 'Act East'. It provided a basis for the overture to Myanmar in the early 1990s at a time when the then military government of Myanmar was still cool to India over its support for the pro-democracy movement in Myanmar. India has since followed up with cross-border confidence-building, connectivity and development initiatives. The Border Trade Agreement of 1994–95, the Tamu–Kalewa–Kalemyo 'Friendship' road and the Land Customs Stations at Moreh and Zawkathar, all commenced operations during this period.

The big-ticket, flagship connectivity projects symbolizing 'Looking' and 'Acting' East on the ground, such as the Trilateral Highway and the Kaladan Multi-Modal Transit Transport Project (KMMTTP), too owe their origin to this period, as do the five-year $25 million, Border Area Development

Programme, the Integrated Check Post (ICP) at Moreh and the realignment and reconstruction of the Rhi-Tiddim road linking Zawkathar in Mizoram with the Trilateral Highway at Kalay.

Progress on ongoing projects has been mixed. While the 160 km Tamu–Kalewa–Kalemyo Road has served trade and development on the Myanmar side well, the Land Customs Stations in Moreh and Zawkathar have been functioning highly sub-optimally. The Modi government has been able to start the Trilateral Highway projects that were held up on various grounds. He also officially inaugurated the delayed ICP in 2018–19 and made its immigration post functional. But its trade terminal is still to be fully operationalized. Plans are afoot to construct Phase 1 of a modern ICP in Tamu on the Myanmar side of the border as well.[17]

The much delayed KMMTTP, which was expected to be operationalized by 2016,[18] was affected by the sudden emergence of the Arakan Army in Rakhine and Paletwa from 2016. The port component of the project with an Indian port operator was ready to start operations by the first quarter of 2021. Progress on internal connectivity by road, railways and waterways within the North-east and through Bangladesh is visibly greater.

In the area of trade infrastructure and soft connectivity, a Land Border Crossing Agreement facilitating travel with passport and visas was signed in 2018 and formalized with the partial operationalization of the ICP at Moreh in 2018–19. The potentially game-changing Imphal–Mandalay Bus Service that was expected to commence operations in 2020 and the India–Myanmar–Thailand Motor Vehicles Agreement facilitating vehicular movement from India to Thailand via Myanmar will have to await better times.

While the overall balance sheet on the implementation of cross-border projects and connectivity has been positive, there have been problems on trade through the North-east and these have been aggravated over the years.

On border trade, the Modi government inherited a very limited border trade arrangement with Myanmar through the North-east through four officially approved border trade points at Moreh (Manipur), Zawkathar (Mizoram), Nampong (Arunachal Pradesh) and Avankhu (Nagaland) under the Border Trade Agreement of 1994–95. Of these, only two, Moreh and Zawkathar, were truly functional. In addition, some nine points had been identified and agreed on for border haats from Arunachal to Mizoram. None of these haats were however operational in 2014. They remain so even now although there was a push in 2020 to start at least one in Mizoram as a pilot project, for which the government had allocated funds. 'Border trade', so defined, took the form of 'head-load' trade through barter, which was subject to modest monetary limits in a fixed number of commodities overseen by banks and local customs authorities. Moreh, the best connected and closest to commercial centres on both sides (through the Tamu–Kyigone–Kalewa Road), became the most important land trading point between India and Myanmar. The Namphalong market across the border flourished as a source for local and third-country goods mainly from China and Thailand through a parallel gate that facilitated trade outside customs parameters.

Over time, availing the lower duties applicable for border trade, Moreh became an important conduit for betel nut trade, not only from elsewhere in Myanmar, but also South East Asia. Third-country trade quickly became the most important component of border trade evading customs because of lack of regulatory clarity and systems and facilities for formal trade. As volumes rose, the border trade arrangement began to be seen as unnecessarily restrictive and a demand grew to permit most-favoured-nation (MFN) trade as permissible through other ports.

In 2016, the Indian government announced an abrupt change in the border trade regime to normal MFN trade in foreign exchange. Its immediate impact was to raise customs for items that were imported with duty concessions under the border trade regime without putting in place systems to levy duties on MFN trade, including third-country trade, and few checks, if any, on informal trade. That was left to be taken care of by the ICP. Formal betel trade plummeted to be replaced by an explosion in informal trade in third-country goods. This was evident in long queues of vehicles at Assam Rifles check points along the Moreh–Imphal route that are allegedly 'taxed' by various outfits. The government has not had the political will to formalize trade.

Despite what is often called India's 'gateway' to South East Asia, there are hardly any Indian goods exported through this 'gate'. The website of the Inland Port Authority of India that constructed and operates the ICP has recorded only one official trade and export transaction since its operationalization, a consignment of methyl bromide for export and no imports.[19] More importantly, neither past governments nor the NDA have given sufficient thought to how connectivity, development and trade projects (on which they have spent around $1 billion) can be integrated to serve India's trade, commercial, economic and strategic objectives. It has tended to see connectivity as an end in itself, leaving the market to do the rest.

In reality, India's connectivity projects have so far only contributed to imports of consumer goods from third countries. These are monopolized by a handful of traders on both sides who are in league with local power brokers, bypassing normal customs duties levied at other ports of entry. Also, there is no corresponding growth in exports. While Chinese, Thai and other third-country products can be found in the markets of Imphal and beyond, few Indian goods can be found even across the border in Namphalong market, Tamu or Kalay, let alone further ahead. Ironically, at a time when the government was trying to plug loopholes that permitted unfair advantage to Chinese goods and investments into the country post the Ladakh crisis of 2020, Chinese goods continued to enter the country through the North-east duty-free, albeit not in large quantities because of the very infrastructure constraints that the government is trying to address. The COVID pandemic and the coup too have constrained this booming informal trade somewhat.

The reasons for this are complex, but are linked to the lack of an appropriate development and export strategy for the North-east—a mismatch between security, development and foreign policy imperatives mirrored in different departments reflecting contradictory missions, and a lack of a coordinating mechanism.[20] Together, they have given rise to a well-founded perception that the North-east has been too heavily viewed through the prism of security and the Centre, and that it cannot play a serious part in our Look East or Act East policies except as a zone of transport and transit.

Balancing China

While China is not central to India's Myanmar strategy, neither India can ignore the China factor in Myanmar, nor can Myanmar. China has pursued its strategic interests in Myanmar by various means—political, economic and covert. At different stages, it has used the ethnic and expatriate Chinese community in Myanmar, the Burmese Communist Party, EAOs, the Tatmadaw, party-to-party relations, Myanmar's international isolation and sanctions against it post 1990 and, since 2015, the peace process and the Rohingya issue, to extract political, economic and strategic concessions from Myanmar, including for its Belt and Road Initiative (BRI).

China's objectives in pursuing the BRI are three-fold: to overcome its Malacca dilemma; to open a line of communication to the Bay of Bengal and Indian Ocean and to establish itself as a two-nation economic power. However, China's investments in Myanmar predate the BRI with major projects such as the controversial 6,000 megawatt (MW) Myitsone hydropower dam that was suspended by the U Thein Sein USDP government in September 2011; the Letpadaung copper mine that the government decided to continue; oil and gas pipelines from Kyaukpyu port in the Bay of Bengal to Yunnan province of China and the Kyaukpyu Special Economic Zone (SEZ) that was rushed through the USDP-dominated Parliament during the transition from USDP to NLD rule in 2015–16.

The years post the transition coincided with a determined effort by China to push the BRI and its flagship project, the China–Myanmar Economic Corridor (CMEC), in Myanmar. It invited Daw Aung San Suu Kyi for the First and Second Belt and Road Forums in Beijing, and offered dozens of small and large projects under the BRI to Myanmar. China also tried to make full use of the top priority she accorded to end Myanmar's ethnic armed insurgencies and discomfiture on the Rohingya issue in the UN Security Council to extract the maximum concessions it could. But while China has had some success in its efforts, it has also faced resistance. This is likely to be exacerbated by the military coup, which the Myanmar public behind the Civil Disobedience Movement widely believes is tacitly supported by China. It has also found expression in visible anti-China sentiment in the country.

The exact scope of the BRI in Myanmar and the CMEC is not clear. There is no single comprehensive listing of the projects covered by either, and what is apparent is an amorphous label that includes past investments, official projects and grey zone investments and businesses[21] in real estate, mining and plantations that add up to a grand design covering the GMS as a whole.

Its backbone is the CMEC that includes the oil and gas pipelines from Kyaukpyu to Yunnan, the Kyaukpyu SEZ and Deep-Sea Port that it obtained with the SEZ, and a whole series of projects from Kyaukpyu to the Myanmar–China border that are part of a larger blueprint. These include the revived Muse-Mandalay railway, a new Kyaukpyu–Nay Pyi Taw highway, and three Border Economic Cooperation Zones on the China-Myanmar border.[22] In addition, China is also undertaking the development of the New Yangon City at Yangon as part of its official BRI projects in Myanmar.

Chinese and Myanmar partners are also involved in a number of real estate development projects and industrial zones in different parts of Myanmar that fall into a grey zone. Interesting examples of these are a $400 million investment in Myitkyina Namjim Border Economic and Industrial Zone in Kachin state being developed by a Yunnan company with a local militia; the Mandalay Yida Economic and Trade Cooperation Zone;[23] and a grandiose $15 billion real estate development project being built by a Chinese company in Myawaddy on the Myanmar–Thai border that has drawn the attention of the US Congress and been described in detail in a report by the International Crisis Group.[24]

However, despite strenuous efforts up to President Xi Jinping, the Chinese have made only modest headway on their BRI projects in Myanmar. Learning from the experience of BRI projects elsewhere, the Myanmar government has been wary. The only significant new success is the proposed investment in the Kyaukpyu Deep Sea Port, where Myanmar has been able to renegotiate its exposure from $7 billion to $1.3 billion. These, together with the oil and gas terminals and pipelines, are however enough for China to seek to securitize the CMEC in future. These are, however, also coming under increasing public scrutiny and risk, post the coup. A restoration of democracy or continued instability will have a negative impact on Chinese projects and plans.

Weaving the Missing Links

Myanmar offers a strategic springboard for India's Act East and Indo-Pacific policies. But although not as advanced as the CPEC, China's BRI projects in Myanmar (and the GMS of South East Asia) also pose a strategic challenge for India by their sheer scale and ambition. In view of Myanmar's historical tradition of independence, strategic autonomy and neutrality between major powers, the odds of China succeeding in getting all that they want from Myanmar as part of its strategic outreach (of which the BRI is a part) is low and will be aggravated by public and political opinion post coup. The Chinese will, of course, continue to exert pressure through vested business and political interests including ethnic parties tied to it. Myanmar's ability to resist such pressure will depend on its ability to leverage its other international relationships especially the US, Japan and India but its strained relations with the West—to a large extent of its own creation—has not helped. This could change if democracy triumphs or China drops its tacit support for the Tatmadaw.

Part of the burden of balancing China in Myanmar will thus fall on countries such as India and Japan, which have maintained constructive relations with Nay Pyi Taw despite its multiple mis-steps. By and large, India has taken the right steps to develop this relationship in the political, diplomatic, defence, security, development and cultural spheres. Yet, the trade and investment and people-to-people relationships remain hugely under-developed. In addition, beyond the Trilateral Highway and Kaladan projects that have yet to take effect and whose benefits can be double-edged, there is a lack of big ideas to animate this relationship to a strategic plane. Post coup, the defence relationship could also come under strain.

The centrepiece of India's Myanmar policy should therefore be its closer economic integration to the Indian economy across both its land and maritime borders. This can be achieved by a multipronged post-coup strategy that is built on a relationship with the people rather than an unpopular army—one that uses Indian investment in the Myanmar economy in the areas of its agricultural and natural resources, which constitute the base of its economy and livelihoods, along with India's Northeast, through the land route. Emphasis should also be laid on working on an industrial route linked to global value chains building on connectivity and investment through the Bay of Bengal and a digital route using applications tried and tested in India that can be expanded to include South East Asia.

India's inability to join the RCEP would pose a problem for this goal. One way around it would be to strive for a Comprehensive Economic Cooperation Agreement with Myanmar, which could be extended to the CLMV countries and the GMS as a whole drawing in India's Act East, BIMSTEC, Mekong Ganga Cooperation and ACMEC initiatives under one larger umbrella and also extending its 'Atmanirbhar' policy to the region as a whole. With the situation to the west and north of India looking bleaker than ever, India has no option but to Act East harder.

Yet, much will depend on the outcome of the coup and what position India takes on it. The shadow of 1988, when India took an actively pro-democracy and pro-people position but the Tatmadaw managed to crush the agitation, hangs heavily over India's decision-makers. A repeat of that appears unlikely, although it is difficult to predict a stable outcome either way.

Still, India will have to decide whether its Act East Policy should be built on the popular will of the people of Myanmar or that of its increasingly anti-people army. For a country that has a millennial civilizational and people-to-people relationship interrupted only by 48 years of military rule when Myanmar turned towards China and the East, the answer should be obvious.

8

SRI LANKA

Towards New Turbulence

INDRANI BAGCHI

In September 2014, Shinzo Abe became the first Japanese prime minister (PM) to visit Sri Lanka in 24 years to revitalize a relationship that seemed to be falling into China's lap.[1]

Barely a week later, a Chinese Song-class conventional submarine along with the *Changxing Island* submarine support ship of the North China Sea Fleet made a port call in Colombo.[2] This was the first time a Chinese submarine openly visited a foreign country or registered its presence in the Indian Ocean. The timing could not have been worse. Not only had the Japanese PM just visited, the Chinese president Xi Jinping was in India and Chinese troops had transgressed the Line of Actual Control in Chumar in eastern Ladakh, their second in as many years. Mahinda Rajapaksa, the then Sri Lanka president, had chosen a singular moment to play his China card.

Later that month, Rajapaksa caught up with PM Narendra Modi in New York on the sidelines of the United Nations (UN)

General Assembly. Modi and Rajapaksa had already met when the latter had been invited for Modi's swearing-in ceremony in May 2014. In their conversation, Modi conveyed India's opposition to having Chinese submarines popping up in India's neighbourhood in that fashion. National Security Advisor Ajit Doval had registered India's reservations at his level. In his response, Rajapaksa promised that Chinese submarines would not make port calls in Colombo, and gave reassurances of Sri Lanka's sensitivity to India's security concerns.

A few weeks later, on 31 October, the same submarine was back in Colombo port! Indian intelligence had picked up the fact that it was returning to Colombo. Frantic calls were made between Indian officials and their Sri Lankan counterparts. At every stage, the Sri Lankan side denied the presence of any Chinese submarine at their port. On the morning when the submarine was readily visible, Sri Lankan defence minister Gotabaya Rajapaksa's office took a call from the Indian High Commissioner, Yash K. Sinha. On hearing protestations of innocence, Sinha is known to have retorted sharply, 'You will see it if you look out of the window.'

The second instance was literally the last straw, so far as India and Rajapaksa were concerned.[3] The Indian government considered this an almost unacceptable breach of faith and confidence. Rajapaksa, who was only dimly coming to terms with the fact that the new government in New Delhi was different from the old, also realized that he may have crossed a red line.

Modi and Mahinda Rajapaksa spoke again on the phone on 9 November 2014. Modi did not raise the issue of the submarine visit. Instead, he spoke about the conviction of five Indian fishermen who had been caught, tried and convicted in a Sri Lankan court and sentenced to death. The five fishermen—Emerson, P. Augustus, R. Wilson, K. Prasath and J. Langlet, all from Tamil Nadu—were arrested by the Sri Lankan Navy in November 2011.[4]

Rajapaksa acted swiftly. He commuted the sentence and pardoned them on 19 November. They were handed over to the Indian High Commission, flown to Delhi and then to Chennai. When Modi and Rajapaksa met again in Kathmandu later that month for the SAARC summit, they showed cordiality.

For Rajapaksa and Sri Lanka, however, India had crossed their 'red line' twice—in 2012 and 2013 when India voted against Sri Lanka not once but twice at the UN Human Rights Council (UNHRC), rapping Sri Lanka for human rights violations during the last war against the Liberation Tigers of Tamil Eelam (LTTE). Sri Lanka constituted the Lessons Learnt and Reconciliation Commission in 2010 modelled after the South African Truth and Reconciliation Commission, but with a far limited mandate. The 2011 report made the right noises: it talked about demilitarization, devolution of powers and investigation of disappearances, etc. However, the Rajapaksa government put little heart into its implementation. It led to former national security advisor and former envoy to Sri Lanka, Shivshankar Menon, warning Colombo that there would be 'consequences'.

In March 2012, the United States (US) sponsored a resolution against Sri Lanka at the UNHRC. India's role, naturally, became critical. The then foreign minister, S.M. Krishna, told reporters, 'The Centre will take into account the overall relationship between India and Sri Lanka while deciding whether or not to back the resolution when it comes up for consideration at the ongoing UNHRC session in Geneva.'[5] As it turned out, India voted against Sri Lanka on a country-specific resolution—unusual for Indian diplomacy—pressured by its political ally Dravida Munnetra Kazhagam and other Tamil parties. India did not participate in the debate and Indian officials said that they had made two 'changes' to the final resolution that would make it less 'intrusive'.[6] A Ministry of External Affairs (MEA) statement said, 'India believes that the primary responsibility for the promotion and protection of human rights lies with the States. Consequently, resolutions of this nature should fully respect the sovereign rights of states and contribute to Sri Lanka's own efforts in this regard.'[7]

The first vote could have been weathered, but a second vote in March 2013, when India again voted against Sri Lanka at the same forum was too much to bear. The entire nation watched the proceedings on TV with bated breath, listening to India's UN envoy, Dilip Sinha, say, 'We note with concern the inadequate progress by Sri Lanka in fulfilling its commitment to this Council in 2009. Further, we call on Sri Lanka to move forward on its public commitments, including on the devolution of political authority through full implementation of the 13th Amendment and building upon it.'[8] That proved to be a breaking point for Rajapaksa with India.

It was only in March 2014 that the then foreign minister Salman Khurshid prevailed upon Manmohan Singh to abstain in the third vote against Sri Lanka at the UNHRC.[9] It was a much-needed reprieve, putting oxygen back in a relationship that has a long history, stretching back to antiquity and a more troubled recent one. In March 2021, India was back to facing the same choice as the seventh UNHRC resolution against Sri Lanka's human rights abuses came up for a vote. India abstained amid a clamour by Western nations for India's support, while China and Pakistan both promised to support Sri Lanka. The resolution 'Promoting Reconciliation, Accountability and Human Rights in Sri Lanka' was, however, adopted after 22 member states of the 47-member Council voted in its favour.

Back in 2014, before Rajapaksa could get the full measure of the Modi government, internal machinations within Sri Lanka were plotting to get rid of him and install Maithripala Sirisena, former health minister who had defected as president—a move led by no less than the grand dame of Sri Lankan politics, Chandrika Kumaratunga. There were several reasons to remove Rajapaksa; India was only one of them. Other factors included the near total capture of state power by the Rajapaksa family, majoritarian authoritarianism with scant regard for minorities, thumbing a nose at international opinion, family-led corruption and the growing inroads being made by China. Anybody could tell that the last would have implications for the India relationship, not to speak of pushing Sri Lanka into just the kind of debt trap that it has.

Mahinda Rajapaksa attributed his shock defeat to India's machinations. In an interview later, he was to say, 'The manipulative dimensions of foreign powers and domestic forces played a part in the change. Then, much water has flown under the bridge.'[10] India dismissed suggestions that the Research and Analysis Wing station chief travelled out soon after the elections. But India had reason to be temporarily satisfied with the election results. Sirisena won the elections with 51.3 per cent of the vote, a sliver of a victory, but with a resounding mandate from the Tamil and Muslim sections, neither of whom were on Rajapaksa's list of priorities. Like Rajapaksa, Sirisena had impeccable Sinhala credentials. The transfer was easy. The two persons most surprised in Colombo that day were Rajapaksa himself and the Chinese ambassador, who, according to those present, hastily abandoned a game of golf. He returned to Beijing at the end of January. In the months prior to the elections, China had reportedly sponsored a total of $5 million in campaign paraphernalia for Rajapaksa, including payments to supporters, among others. Sirisena promised to limit Chinese influence in Sri Lanka, as did his new-old PM, Ranil Wickremesinghe.

Modi made the most of the changed atmosphere in Sri Lanka with his first visit in March 2015, signalling a shift in India's policy towards its island neighbour. On the morning of 13 March that year, Modi landed in Colombo and over the next couple of days, the contours of his policy became clearer. 'My vision of an ideal neighbourhood is one in which trade, investments, technology, ideas and people flow easily across borders,' Modi declared, assuring India's 'full commitment and support' to a development partnership with Sri Lanka.[11] Modi visited Anuradhapura, where he offered prayers at the famous Temple of the Sacred Tooth Relic as well as Jaffna in the north. He expressed his government's 'strong desire to cooperate and develop a Ramayana trail in Sri Lanka and a Buddhist Circuit in India'. Buddhism was the new cultural-religious arm of Modi government's diplomatic outreach to Sri Lanka.

Geopolitically, India wanted to situate its Sri Lanka relationship within the growing focus on the Indian Ocean Region (IOR), hence, Modi's visit included IOR nations as well. Bilaterally, Modi was indicating that while India would not abandon its traditional Tamil interests in Sri Lanka, it would shift focus by balancing its attentions between Colombo and Jaffna, that it would be as respectful of Sinhala aspirations as Tamil aspirations. Modi also wanted to shift the centre of gravity of the bilateral relationship to connectivity, infrastructure and a robust development partnership. In his Tamil outreach, Modi reached out to not only the politically aware Sri Lankan Jaffna Tamils, but the really poor Indian Tamils, who are the plantation workers—this is a strategy the Bharatiya Janata Party has adopted quite successfully while trying to break into new states in Indian politics, say, in West Bengal.

To this, one has to add two new factors: China's presence in Sri Lanka and the rise of Sinhala nationalism. But there is a third factor too—domestic political vicissitudes in Sri Lanka could derail many well-laid plans. India's own politics can throw up their own pressures. The Bharatiya Janata Party is lucky to not have a Tamil regional party in their alliance who is as demanding as the Dravida Munnetra Kazhagam.

India's Policy Dilemma

The LTTE, which was initially supported by India, was a shameful blot on India's history for which India paid the highest price, the life of a PM. The 2009 final war against the terror group saw India having to play a delicate balancing act between the United Progressive Alliance government's Tamil allies and India's security interests. Shivshankar Menon, then foreign secretary, Defense Secretary Vijay Singh and National Security Advisor M.K. Narayanan formed a troika to talk directly with the Lankan leadership, Basil and Gotabaya Rajapaksa and Lalith Weeratunga, including a midnight visit to Colombo in the middle of the war. Mahinda Rajapaksa wants that mechanism revived to oversee economic ties with India. It's probably no longer necessary because the Sri Lanka relationship is dealt with at the highest levels.[12]

Shivshankar Menon encapsulated India's Sri Lanka policy dilemma: 'We must engage in order to defend our interest in keeping Sri Lanka free of antagonistic outside influences while also trying to prevent the growth of Tamil extremism and separatism that could affect Tamil Nadu. These twin objectives are not necessarily perfectly aligned.'[13]

India's policies towards Colombo have traditionally largely run through Tamil Nadu and, therefore, Jaffna. Successive Indian governments have made the bottom line of their policies to Sri Lanka the welfare, rights and devolution of powers to the Sri Lankan Tamil minority. Modi has tried to nuance that position by adding new facets to the relationship. In 2017, he was the chief guest at the all-important Vesak celebrations in Sri Lanka, indicating that at least the cultural connect was working well. Interestingly, that visit was important for two other political signals that were sent.

For possibly the first time, Modi did not visit Jaffna, which had become customary for visiting Indian dignitaries. Instead, he travelled to Dickoya in the central hills to meet the impoverished and unempowered Indian Tamils who live and work in the tea plantations. These Tamils, originally from Trichy, Madurai and Tanjore, were sent to work in tea and rubber plantations in Sri Lanka by the British in the nineteenth century. They had a rotten deal—ignored even by the Sri Lankan Tamils of the North—which continued after Sri Lanka gained independence. Modi's focus on them highlighted the neglect of even Indian Tamils to the plight of their own people in Sri Lanka, preferring to fight for the Sri Lankan Tamils. With a newly formed Tamil Progressive Alliance, India was looking to reintroduce them into the Lankan political mainstream. India has built houses for them under a scheme that was used in the North. Speaking to them, Modi said, 'You kept your bonds with India alive, [I] assure you that India will support Sri Lanka's efforts towards your socio-economic development.'[14] In August 2018, Modi presided over a virtual ceremony to hand over the first 404 houses to the Indian Tamils at the central district of Nuwara Eliya. The $350 million grant to build houses was one of the largest grants by India in any country, adding another 10,000 houses to the project.

The move had another intention of putting pressure on the Sri Lankan Tamil parties as well. After supporting Sirisena in the 2015 elections, the Tamil parties that collectively form the

Tamil National Alliance barely managed to hold it together. They supported Rajapaksa in the 2019 presidential election, and have suffered several protests pointing to a lack of political direction. There have been questions regarding the rise of other Tamil leaders such as the former chief minister of the Northern Province, C.V. Vigneswaran.[15] More recently, there have been rumblings about rise in conversions to Islam by Tamil Hindus.[16] Clearly, there are new forces at work there. The Muslims of the Eastern Province too are forming a more distinct political identity, even though a majority of them are Tamil speakers. After the Easter terror attacks of 21 April 2019, they have come under a different kind of scrutiny particularly from the more militant Buddhists in the island.

In 2016, Sirisena presented a new devolution plan, which promised to promote democratic rights, national reconciliation, and guarantee fundamental rights and freedoms. A constituent assembly was also set up under Wickremesinghe to draft a new constitution, but this ran aground, in the face of protests by Sinhalas and the clergy, as well as sticking issues by the Tamils.

Officially, India's position on the Tamil question has remained the same and unlikely to change: India is in favour of 'a politically negotiated settlement acceptable to all sections of Sri Lankan society within the framework of an undivided Sri Lanka and consistent with democracy, pluralism and respect for human rights'.[17] India remains committed to the 13th Amendment, which is reiterated at every summit. The 26 September 2020 virtual summit between Modi and Rajapaksa saw the former reminding 'the new Government in Sri Lanka to work towards realizing the expectations of Tamils for equality, justice, peace and dignity within a united Sri Lanka by achieving reconciliation nurtured by implementation of the Constitutional provisions'.[18] He emphasized that implementation of the 13th Amendment to the Sri Lankan Constitution is essential for carrying forward the process of peace and reconciliation.

Nevertheless, India has to be more realistic about its chances of effecting internal change inside Sri Lanka. Election time in Tamil Nadu will be particularly fraught. Every party running New Delhi will have to keep that pressure on, no matter how unpopular it makes India in Sri Lanka.

The post-war scenario in Sri Lanka has brought two forces to the fore: Sinhala nationalism and China. As New Delhi has acknowledged, both of them have to be accommodated and addressed, albeit in different ways. With his outreach on Buddhism, Modi indicated that he was ready to embrace the cultural connect between India and Sri Lanka that ran through the Buddhist faith and, therefore, with the majority Sinhalas. After all, Buddhism is a big diplomatic cache with countries such as Mongolia, Thailand, Vietnam and Japan, among others. In 2020, for instance, India earmarked an extra $15 million for the preservation of Buddhist heritage and will facilitate Lankan pilgrims to travel to Kushinagar.

In 2017, Modi held a quiet meeting with Mahinda Rajapaksa in the residence of the Indian High Commissioner, Taranjit Singh Sandhu. Rajapaksa was accompanied by his brother Gotabaya and G.L. Peiris. Sandhu later told reporters, 'Rajapaksa's talks with Modi were a very cordial discussion and he was happy with India-Lanka cooperation over the years.' Both India and the Rajapaksas had begun an outreach to each other. Despite Rajapaksa's China leanings and evident corruption, Modi recognized him as a formidable political force in Sri Lankan politics, and a Sinhala nationalist. He believed that Rajapaksa and the High Commissioner would come back to power sooner or later.

Mahinda Rajapaksa himself could also have been feeling a trifle under-appreciated after the war. As he told an interviewer, 'After all, defeating the LTTE, a terrorist organization, was not done only for us, no? It was not just for a community or for one country. They killed Rajiv Gandhi, they were operating with other organizations in other countries too. They introduced suicide jackets to the world. So, defeating them helped many other countries too.'[19]

It explained why, in 2018, when Sirisena underwent his own 'constitutional coup' as it was called, the MEA responded very gently: 'India is closely following the recent political developments in Sri Lanka. As a democracy and a close friendly neighbour, we hope that democratic values and the constitutional process will be respected.'[20] For comparison, one only needed to see Indian statements on Maldives. (In February 2018, Maldivian president Abdulla Yameen defied the ruling of the Supreme Court on detentions and imposed emergency. India's response was harsh: 'In the spirit of democracy and rule of law, it is imperative for all organs of the Government of Maldives to respect and abide by the order of the apex court.'[21])

India's Loss, China's Gain

Sirisena's election opened the possibility that India might be able to counter the pervasive Chinese influence in Sri Lanka. It was in 2006 that Mahinda Rajapaksa first approached the Indian government to develop the Hambantota port. A team was sent to assess both the port and the Mattala airport. India rejected both citing lack of economic/commercial viability.[22] India failed to recognize the strategic importance of both, and the importance of keeping powers such as China out of Sri Lanka, even at a cost. Rajapaksa went to China, and the rest has been well-documented. India has since veered from dismissing China's 'string of pearls' as a threat to scrambling for the past decade, trying to catch up or prevent China from expanding its influence.

Often the cost has been much higher: for instance, in Mattala, which India took on a 40-year lease in 2018.

Among Sirisena's first decisions was to suspend all Chinese projects for 'review', including the Colombo Port City project and the hugely expensive Hambantota project. After a few months, it became painfully clear to the Sirisena government that they could not break the shackles of Chinese debt, nor could they make any dent in their mountain of debt—$11 billion, of which $8 billion was Chinese debt. Sri Lanka had become the poster child of China's expansion-by-debt policy, targeting vulnerable countries and egotistic rulers.

The Colombo Port City project was restarted under Chinese pressure. Wickremesinghe, considered to be close to India, himself presided over the handing over of the Hambantota Port on a 99-year lease to China.[23] Sirisena, according to sources in Sri Lanka, even allowed China to finance projects in his constituency. At present, the big Chinese investments include Colombo International Financial City, Colombo International Container Terminals and Hambantota Port, while in recent years, China has diversified its investments in agriculture, plantations, food processing, etc. All of these went ahead without check during the Sirisena—Wickremesinghe years.

In contrast, almost none of India's big investments such as Sampur power project, Mattala airport, Trincomalee Oil Tank Farms or the Eastern Container Terminal (ECT) have yet seen the light of day. Soon after the 2015 election, Sirisena and Wickremesinghe found they just could not get along, and their government was inherently unstable. Wickremesinghe seemed more savvy, but Sirisena, who may have started as being slightly diffident, quickly figured out the reins of power lay with him. Wickremesinghe and Sirisena went out of their way to undermine each other. One of the top casualties of that was Indian investments. The Chinese did their bit to keep

Indians at bay, their influence worked. But in others, like the LNG project, the Sirisena family was keen to give it to a South Korean company, while the powerful diesel lobby in Sri Lanka also opposed the LNG project by India.

For instance, Rajapaksa's government has sat on the ECT project citing protests by labour unions of the Sri Lanka Port Authority, none of which affect Chinese projects. What was less evident was the pressure by China to stall or delay the India–Japan project. The Mattala airport, next to Hambantota, was never a viable project. But the Chinese quietly informed the Sri Lankans that India and the US would use it as a listening post to their activities in nearby Hambantota. The Indians suddenly found a series of obstacles in their way. When it seemed that things might fall in place, Sirisena sacked Wickremesinghe and re-installed Rajapaksa as PM in October 2018. Rajapaksa, in 2017, had already led a protest against the government giving out the Hambantota port on a 99-year lease to China or Mattala airport to India.

In February 2021, the Rajapaksa Cabinet formally terminated the 2019 agreement for India and Japan to develop the ECT of the Colombo Port. The ostensible reason was a protest by trade unions against giving it to a foreign entity. The fact that China is developing the Colombo Port City did not seem to pose a similar problem. From the Indian point of view, this was a setback and an embarrassment. The Sri Lankan government instead offered the Western Container Terminal (WCT), a greenfield project, sweetening it by offering 85 per cent ownership to the India–Japan consortium as against 49 per cent in the ECT. Rajapaksa cited trade union pressure when Sri Lanka had 51 per cent ownership of ECT, but there appears to be little opposition to only 15 per cent Sri Lanka ownership in the WCT.

The thing is, India and other Western agencies make a lot

of noise over Sri Lanka's 'debt trap' to China. Neither Sri Lanka nor China sees it in that light. Sri Lanka generally has a higher tolerance for debt. Besides, China has already changed the nature of its assistance/loans to Sri Lanka. Earlier, China would advance loans as project loans, which could not be used to take care of balance of payments (BOP) crises. From 2020, China is moving towards what are called 'syndicated' loans where Sri Lanka is free to use as it sees fit. China gave $500 million to Sri Lanka in March 2020. Senior Chinese diplomat Yang Jiechi visited Colombo in October and advanced $90 million. The Chinese embassy in Colombo then tweeted that both countries were looking at another $500 million in syndicated loans. That would take China's loans to Sri Lanka to over $1 billion in just 2020. Meanwhile, Sri Lanka remains 'in discussions' with India on a loan deferment request.[24]

India has done much better with its development assistance programme. The *British Medical Journal* has lauded the national ambulance service in Sri Lanka, 1990 Suwa Seriya, which is now something of a national treasure. In 2016, the Indian government funded the introduction of these ambulances in nine provinces of Sri Lanka, and even trained the staff in Hyderabad. Between 2016 and 2019, India supplied over 300 ambulances, which now operate in 25 provinces in Sri Lanka. India's ongoing development projects cover fields as diverse as education, healthcare, transportation, agriculture, fisheries, handicraft and culture. While a large number of its grant assistance projects are located in the Northern Province, India has in the past five years diversified into high-impact development projects in the central and southern provinces, in keeping with the new policy of spreading out beyond the Tamil areas. One of the big projects is the housing project where India has built over 60,000 houses including 14,000 houses in the plantation areas. India's development assistance under the lines of credit are still works in progress—these include railway coaches, railway tracks, etc. It's fair to say that the Indian assistance programme touches the lives of ordinary Sri Lankan citizens across the country, even if they don't always bring commensurate political influence.

Sustained Hand-Holding

Strategically, Sri Lanka is crucial for India's Indian Ocean and Indo-Pacific policies, occupying vital real estate in the middle of the Indian Ocean. Shivshankar Menon described Sri Lanka as 'an aircraft carrier parked 14 miles off the Indian coast'. With more than 90 per cent of India's trade and energy supplies coming down sea lanes which has Sri Lanka sitting in the middle, one of India's biggest security and defence activities is to keep Sri Lanka away from hostile influences, and contain China's influence as much as possible.

In August, the Sri Lankan foreign secretary, Jayanath Colombage declared on a TV channel that was widely circulated that Sri Lanka wants to pursue a 'neutral' foreign policy, but will retain an 'India First' in strategic and security matters. Colombage said, 'President [Gotabaya Rajapaksa] has stated that in terms of strategic security, we will follow an "India first" policy. We cannot afford to be a strategic security threat to India and we don't have to be. We need to benefit from India.' Stressing what he called a 'neutral' foreign policy, the Lankan foreign secretary said that while Sri Lanka would engage with other powers for economic reasons, India would be their primary strategic partner.

On 28 November 2020, Doval met with his counterparts from Maldives and Sri Lanka in Colombo to restart a trilateral security dialogue after six years. The dialogue, which earlier had Mauritius and Seychelles as observers, will focus on

Indian Ocean security and defence cooperation between these three countries. The India–Maldives relationship has been transformed, which has made security and intelligence-sharing conversations much easier. With Sri Lanka, there has been a slight difference in approach between Gotabaya Rajapaksa and his brother and PM Mahinda Rajapaksa. Increased defence cooperation between these three countries will give them the comfort of not having to deal one-on-one with 'big brother' India. For its part, India will be looking to draw both the Maldives and Sri Lanka into a closer knit web of security cooperation.

The India–Sri Lanka relationship is in many ways too close for comfort. It has the potential of achieving great heights, and on the other hand, it could end up as a train wreck. In the short and medium term, at least three emerging challenges stand out for attention. The first is the growing threat of terrorism. India had, in an unprecedented exchange of information given advance warning on a terror strike which rocked Sri Lanka on Easter Sunday in April 2019. The incident, which highlighted the presence of ISIS (Islamic State of Iraq and the Levant)-inspired local groups in Sri Lanka with links to similar groups in Tamil Nadu, brought home the necessity of closer cooperation and intelligence-sharing between the two countries. Sri Lanka has to worry about religious conversions in the northern and eastern provinces, as well as a growing backlash against Muslims by militant Buddhist groups. This could lead to the kind of instability that is better pre-empted.

Second, India would be reluctant to review a free-trade agreement with Sri Lanka if the island country goes ahead with its plans to set up a free-trade zone with China. That could impact not only India–Sri Lanka trade linkages, it could push Sri Lanka deeper into Chinese clutches. At present, about 70 per cent of trans-shipment handled by the Colombo port is Indian cargo. But India is building trans-shipment ports on both seaboards. Sooner or later, Indian companies would be able to use Indian ports and cut costs rather than go to Colombo. It would make sense for Sri Lanka to tie India to itself by giving India a greater stake in the port, like with the ECT, to delay the inevitable. This links to the third emerging challenge—Sri Lanka wants to keep China's economic assistance while giving India primacy in security and strategic spheres. These cannot remain mutually exclusive, and Sri Lanka may not have the ability to play both games especially in a post-pandemic world, where divisions have only sharpened. Already, Lankan officials have objected to the Quad and big power 'games' in the Indian Ocean. It will require India to play a much deeper game with Sri Lanka, keeping it on India's side. India will have to involve Sri Lanka much more in its security sphere, but Sri Lanka's closer relationship with China could have different consequences.

India needs to resolve the fishermen's issue as neatly as possible. It is an Indian problem because Indian fishermen use practices that are environmentally unsustainable. On the other hand, India needs to keep the pressure on Colombo to deal more fairly with Tamil rights, even if there are realistic limits to how far India can go. This relationship needs sustained hand-holding by India.

9

THE MALDIVES

The Island of Hope

N. SATHIYA MOORTHY AND VINITHA REVI

At the advent of the Narendra Modi government in May 2014, the Maldives was next only to Pakistan as far as Indian strains, concerns and apprehensions were concerned. Thankfully, there still existed a very wide gap between the two neighbours in New Delhi's perspective, a gap that could be bridged in the case of the Maldives relations. Six years down the line, the Indian Ocean archipelago has become the greatest success of Modi's 'Neighbourhood First' policy, unveiled at his maiden inauguration in end of May 2014, and has the potential to be made New Delhi's model for bilateral South Asian relations, with a touch here, a change there. On the foreign policy front, especially on the neighbourhood, successive governments in India have established and demonstrated a certain continuity with changes, if any. However, New Delhi still has to make it an all-weather relationship on the Maldivian front, sustainable at the current pace, through the complexities of domestic politics that gets India-centric in terms of foreign policy priorities of individual parties and political regimes in the other country.

Standing shoulder to shoulder with leaders from India's neighbourhood, the then Maldivian president Abdulla Yameen was a seemingly enthusiastic participant at Prime Minister (PM) Modi's swearing-in ceremony in May 2014. Though high on political symbolism, this visit barely hid the strains in bilateral relations that Modi had inherited from his predecessor, Manmohan Singh and Yameen, in turn, from Mohammed Waheed Hassan Manik. Barring a short interlude, in which Yameen too professed an 'India First' Policy, throughout his time in office (2013–18), there were several low points. The Yameen government declined the invitation for India's multination 'Milan' Naval Exercises in March 2018—the Waheed regime had participated in the earlier edition in 2014—pressing India to take back two helicopters—one each of the Indian Navy and the Coast Guard that had been gifted in previous years for humanitarian missions under the command of the Maldives National Defence Force. They also declined to extend the visas for Indian military personnel flying and attending on them.

All this, even while the Yameen government was reaching out to China through repeated high-level visits, huge China-funded infrastructure projects and trade promotion in the form of a hurriedly signed Free Trade Agreement (FTA) that caused much controversy inside the Maldives and created further strains in bilateral relations with India. This fraying of bilateral ties is acknowledged in sobering terms by the High Commission of India in Male, which describes it as 'a brief period during former President Waheed's administration and to some extent during former President Yameen's regime, when there was a change in approach towards India'.[1] The period was 'between February 2012 and November 2018',[2] this time-frame pointedly corresponding to the terms of presidents Waheed and Yameen.

India and the Maldives have always had warm and strong bilateral ties going back decades. In 2012, former Indian minister of state for external affairs Shashi Tharoor wrote: 'The Maldives, where India enjoys relations that are comparable to those with Bhutan—intimate and trouble-free.'[3] The positive reference, which was also genuine, coming out of the Maldives, which India had found reassuring and which had been conspicuously absent under Yameen's presidency, finally returned when the incumbent government of President Ibrahim Mohamed Solih took office in November 2018. On his first official visit, Solih stated unequivocally that 'India is the closest friend of the Maldives.'[4]

What led to the strain in relations between February 2012 and November 2018? Under the Solih government, has a new chapter in bilateral relations opened up or have relations simply gone back to normalcy? Has Modi's 'Neighbourhood First' policy been a success in the Maldives? What is likely to impede India–Maldives relations in the future?

Tryst with Democracy

Before Yameen in 2013, Mohammed Nasheed of the Maldivian Democratic Party (MDP) became the first president in the Maldives's history to be elected through a multiparty election in 2008. Nasheed defeated incumbent Maumoon Abdul Gayoom, who had been president from 1978 to 2008. Nasheed is also better known for drawing global attention to climate change—a cause originally flagged by Gayoom since the late 1970s—when he held an underwater Cabinet meeting to highlight the dangers of sea-level rise on his archipelago nation, in the run-up to the Copenhagen Conference on climate change (2009).

Nasheed quit on 7 February 2012, one-and-a-half years before completing his term, amidst Opposition protests, climaxing with the participation of some policemen and policewomen in uniform. Though Nasheed later claimed his resignation was coerced, a Commonwealth-backed investigation found the power transfer to be 'legal and constitutional'[5] and the succession by his vice president, Mohammed Waheed Hassan Manik, for the rest of the five-year term was also as per the constitutional provision, akin to the US scheme. It is with the outgoing Waheed regime that India–Maldives relations started to strain, hitting a low-point when the Indian infrastructure GMR group was asked to pack up and leave.

Prior to Waheed's time, the Nasheed dispensation had signed a construction-cum-concession contract with GMR for the modernization of the nation's only international airport at its capital Male, as he had big plans for international tourism, the nation's economic mainstay, which in turn required the capacity and ability for the airport to receive more tourists. Citing procedural irregularities and improprieties on the part of the Nasheed government in granting the airport contract and alleging violations of some key contractual commitments by GMR, the political opposition took their earlier parliamentary reservations to the streets through a massive campaign, demanding the president's resignation.

In the forefront of what was otherwise a political protest were some 'religious NGOs' that were peeved by the Nasheed administration's perceived diplomatic softness towards the US and Israel, despite the America-led 'War on Terror' in Afghanistan and Iraq, two other Islamic nations like the Maldives. Apart from seeking Nasheed's exit, the protestors also demanded GMR's ouster, with a visible tinge of anti-India sloganeering filling Male's air from 23 December 2011 to 7 February 2012, when Nasheed stepped down. The protests are since referred to as the 'December 23rd Movement'. The political opposition attributed GMR-centric motives behind

New Delhi halting visa-on-arrival facility for Maldivians travelling to pursue education or for urgent medical care. They also refused to acknowledge that the Indian ban on export of river sand to the Maldives for massive construction works was based on court orders against sand mining, which caused ecological degradation in India.

During his one-and-half-year rule, President Waheed ordered the closure of GMR operations in Male airport. It had the backing of his successor, Yameen, who was seen as the brain behind the 'December 23rd Movement', which in turn was the brainchild of President Gayoom, his half-brother. After Yameen came to power through the controversial presidential poll of 2013, in which the Maldivian Supreme Court was seen taking sides, an arbitration court in Singapore ordered the Maldivian government to pay huge compensation and damages to GMR. Though the Government of India was not a party to the GMR contract, it was hoping that a successful conclusion of the same could create a model for cooperation, applicable to other neighbouring nations too, in which the Indian private sector could be encouraged to participate in a big way. The failure to resolve it, likewise, New Delhi feared would have a cascading effect, and therefore wanted to avert such a course.

The Yameen Years

Like Nasheed and even Waheed before him, for his first official overseas visit, President Yameen chose India, spending his 2014 New Year's Day in the Indian capital. His discussions with PM Manmohan Singh were focussed not on GMR's continuance but on its exit. So, when he came again only months later for PM Modi's swearing-in, the GMR deal, for all practical purposes, was behind both nations, giving the two leaders an occasion and opportunity to try and revive bilateral relations, as if on a clean slate, considering that 'Neighbourhood First' had become the early articulation and demonstration of PM Modi's foreign policy priorities.

Inviting all South Asian leaders, including that of Pakistan, New Delhi's on-again-off-again adversary, for Modi's swearing-in was a decidedly dramatic move, designed to signal to India's neighbours, its desire, mood and temperament for a new start. A commitment to regional integration at the SAARC Summit in Kathmandu, later in 2014, formed a part of this. While India's relations with some of its neighbours visibly improved with this targeted policy, the Maldives unfortunately was not one of them. In the Yameen years, bilateral relations only went from bad to worse, opening for the first time a new chapter of bilateral animosity as never before.

During this time, India's worst fears came true, with the Maldives leaning far towards China. These fears flowed from the new 'Foreign Policy' for the Maldives, which Yameen unveiled on 20 January 2014, not long after his India visit, though it was in the works even under the Waheed regime. The new policy underscored the need for the nation to grow economically strong and self-reliant, to be able to have a 'foreign policy that is independent' (read: of India).

Earlier, President Nasheed had inaugurated the Chinese embassy in Male on 9 November 2011, the day PM Manmohan Singh was landing at the Male airport for an onward journey to southern Addu City, where the Maldives was hosting the 17th SAARC Summit. If the coincidence seemed ominous, China's role in the Maldives's political economy expanded indelibly (only) under Yameen, through mega-infrastructure projects, the most visible of them being the 2.1-km Sinamale sea bridge—originally named 'China–Maldives Friendship Bridge'—connecting capital Male and the airport island of Hulhule.

From an Indian perspective, the divergences during the Yameen presidency became identifiable with two major concerns: one, viz., China and the other relating to his democratic credentials or lack of it. Yameen's closeness to China has been widely discussed, with many in the international community referring to him as 'China-backed Maldives President'. During Yameen's time, President Xi Jinping became the first Chinese leader to visit the Maldives since it gained independence from the British in 1965.

Interestingly, this was the second meeting between Xi and Yameen in a matter of weeks. Back-to-back reciprocal presidential visits seldom happen other than to avoid or defuse wars. Hence, the peace-time quick exchanges reflected a level of rare closeness between nations and also bonhomie between leaders, all compounding India's discomfort with China's pervasive presence in the nation's 'traditional sphere of influence', particularly the Indian Ocean Region (IOR).

Yameen further surprised both the international community and his domestic opposition by concluding a Free Trade Agreement (FTA) with China, for which he rushed through parliamentary authorization after it had supposedly recessed, in a short-notice special session. New Delhi was purportedly surprised as less than a year earlier, Yameen had declared that the Maldives's first FTA, when signed would be with India, but later blamed it on slow progress in negotiations.

As reported by the Chinese Ministry of Commerce, the two countries would reduce tariffs for over 95 per cent of goods to zero and commit 'to opening the service market such as finance, healthcare and tourism and agreed to cooperate practically in key areas'.[6] Criticizing the FTA on grounds that it could push the Maldives into a Chinese debt trap, Nasheed said, 'The free trade agreement is very one-sided...the numbers don't match.'[7]

Ambassador Rajiv Bhatia, a veteran Indian diplomat, pointed out that 'Maldives's exports to China are less than one per cent of China's to Maldives. Tariff-free entry of Chinese goods will thus be a huge one-sided advantage for Beijing while imposing a significant revenue-loss on the Maldives.'[8] He further noted, 'Domestic critics have also argued that with the services thrown open to large Chinese companies, the growth, the very existence, of the Maldives-owned enterprises may be jeopardised.'[9] In huge infrastructure projects, it translated as no role for the nation's burgeoning construction industry and also local labour.

Just as with India's other smaller neighbours, in the case of the Maldives, too, their appetite for growth and attraction to China for funds was understandable. New Delhi's concerns related to the host nation's ability to make full repayment on China's usury-like terms and the consequences for the nation's sovereignty and territorial integrity, to which India's larger security concerns too were tied. India's fears came true, though later, when common neighbour Sri Lanka had to agree to a debt-equity swap deal over the southern-most Hambantota Port, facing straight into the Indian Ocean sea lanes of communication. India was apprehensive about a similar situation emerging in the case of the Maldives, too. China also obtained a 99-year lease of the Hambantota property, call it Sri Lankan real estate, or 'territory'. In the case of the Maldives, as the MDP (at the time in Opposition) warned, 'Further entrapment of the country into a Chinese debt-trap will result in additional stress on strategic national assets and increasing instability in the Indian Ocean region.'[10]

New Delhi was all the more uncomfortable with Yameen's increasingly defensive and secretive conduct when it came to dealings with China, including the legislative secrecy conferred on the allocation of Maldivian islands for resort development and a constitutional amendment allowing foreign ownership of freehold land. As India's former National Security Advisor, Shiv Shankar Menon argues, 'We should get used to the idea that all our smaller neighbours, if they see India–China rivalry, will find it useful to deal with us in order to get things from the Chinese and deal with the Chinese in order to get things from us.'[11]

Foreign Minister Abdulla Shahid explained Yameen's strategy, thus: 'The previous government tried to play India and China against each other, which is a childish policy. In international relations, you don't play your friends against each other. You establish principled relationships.'[12] Yet, Yameen's drift away from India was deliberate and indicative of his inexplicable preference for China from the start—and simultaneous inexplicable antagonism towards New Delhi.

India's Response

Perhaps as a reaction to the Opposition staging three monthly rallies in the first half of 2015, the Yameen government revived a pending criminal case against Nasheed, which had been shelved ahead of the 2013 presidential polls to facilitate his participating in it. India had played a role in the long adjournment of the ongoing criminal trial, which involved Nasheed as the president ordering the midnight arrest of Criminal Court Chief Judge, Abdulla Mohamed, at the height of the 'December 23rd Movement' protest.

The trial, which could have been put on hold, was seemingly fast-tracked, and was also converted into an 'anti-terror' case under a rarely used 1989 law. It came at a time when the two governments were discussing dates for PM Modi's maiden visit to the Maldives, as part of the first-ever four-nation Indian Ocean trip by any Indian leader, covering also Mauritius,

Seychelles and Sri Lanka. Given the sensitivity of the issue and the tension it foretold, New Delhi dropped the Maldives leg of the tour. The Yameen government's 'regret' over the Indian decision was perfunctory at best.

When the trial court hurriedly sentenced Nasheed to 13 years of imprisonment, the spokesperson of India's external affairs ministry said in an official statement, 'We are deeply concerned over the developments in the Maldives. We are monitoring the situation there.'[13] Later, Nasheed was reluctantly granted 'prison-leave' to have spinal surgery in the United Kingdom (UK). Then Indian foreign secretary S. Jaishankar, now minister of external affairs, undertook a special trip to Male for the purpose. In the UK after the surgery, Nasheed sought and obtained 'political asylum' from the host nation, the second for him after the earlier one obtained in the 1990s when Gayoom was the president.

On 2 February 2018, the Maldivian Supreme Court ordered the release of political prisoners, including Nasheed, and also the reinstatement of 12 opposition MPs who had been stripped of their membership, through an order posted only on its website. India's external affairs ministry said, 'In the spirit of democracy and rule of law, it is imperative for all organs of the government of Maldives to respect and abide by the order.' Only a couple of days later, India condemned President Yameen's declaration of emergency in the aftermath of the Supreme Court's order. He also had one of the judges arrested on corruption charges and got the truncated Bench to reverse the original order.

In yet another unprecedented decision of the kind, India declared Yameen's ruling majority group leader in Parliament, Ahmed Nihan, *persona non grata* on arrival at the Chennai airport and sent him back in June 2018, reflecting New Delhi's greater unhappiness with the Yameen government's democracy credentials, or rather, the lack of it. However, Nasheed's call at this stage, from his self-exile, for India to intervene militarily in the Maldives did not have supporters in India.

The Indian reaction to Yameen's decisions, on what would otherwise typically be seen as 'internal affairs' of the Maldives, needs to be contextualized. Never before in recent years had India reacted thus to domestic developments in a neighbouring country. Though India has largely avoided explicit democracy-promotion work in the neighbourhood, its engagement of the kind can be seen as pioneering the dictum, 'Responsibility to Protect' (R2P), long before the international community recognized it.

Though not acknowledged as such, New Delhi's need for intervention in the Bangladesh Liberation War (1971) owed to humanitarian considerations flowing from massive refugee relief operations it had to undertake. This was also among the earliest of R2P initiatives of the size and quantum in the world after the Second World War. So was the case when India was forced to intervene and facilitate talks between Sri Lankan stakeholders in the aftermath of the anti-Tamil 'Pogrom-1983' (also known as Black July), in which hundreds of Tamils were killed in cold blood, their women ravaged and their property destroyed, thus forcing 3,50,000 of the victim community to risk unsure sea-travel and reach the safety and security of the Indian shores as refugees.

But the Maldives's was the first case, notably in the post-Cold War era, when India indicated a willingness at playing an 'R2P' role, that too after the term had acquired international currency, if circumstances so demanded—and in the background of PM Modi's 'Neighbourhood First' policy. New Delhi was sending out the message that India's commitment to the neighbourhood was multifaceted.

A New Beginning

Appraising decades of India–Maldives bilateral relations, it appears that the current Solih–Modi time is witnessing an unprecedented boost of positivity, underlined by a strong sense of partnership and mutual respect for each other. Solih, a democracy activist for many years and government leader in Parliament during Nasheed's presidency, was the latter's choice for presidential candidate, when it became clear that the Yameen administration was determined not to let him enter the country and contest the 2018 elections. Solih later won the party nomination in an open ballot, which is a requirement under the 2008 democracy constitution, of which other political parties have often made a sham.

Under the Modi–Solih leaderships, India–Maldives relations have become even more close and multidimensional than any time in the past, with their interests converging on a range of issues such as maritime domain awareness, peace and stability in the IOR, democratic institutions and the rule of law, climate change, terrorism and responding to the global COVID-19 pandemic. Diplomatic engagement has been at its highest and among the best. Modi being the only foreign dignitary invited to Solih's inauguration, followed by Solih's early official visit to New Delhi signalled a sure, constructive change in relations—and in an open, transparent manner. This contrasted with the secrecy surrounding Xi–Yameen engagement in the previous years.

Several senior ministers of Solih's government, including those of defence, finance and economic development have visited India for official discussions, some of them more than once. The Maldivian foreign minister Abdulla Shahid, who has visited India several times, once declared relations between the two nations to be 'rock solid'.[14]

During Solih's maiden visit, India announced a financial assistance package of $1.4 billion, of which the Government of India provided $50 million as budgetary support in two equal instalments in December 2018 and January 2019. In 2020, when the Maldivian economy took a bigger beating, owing to the global COVID-19 pandemic, India extended a further $250 million in budgetary support. The new Indian initiatives under 'Neighbourhood First' contrasts with past practices of decades, when New Delhi primarily restricted assistance to budgetary support, without much direct development funding—the kind that would be visible, but more importantly would touch the daily lives of the average Maldivian.

The Indian High Commission in Male explained that the grant was in response to President Solih's request to PM Modi to help overcome the difficult economic situation caused by the pandemic. It added that 'Maldives is the only country to which India has provided such assistance,'[15] explaining that it was being provided under the most favourable terms. In his address to the United Nations General Assembly, Foreign Minister Shahid, while thanking all those who extended their support to the Maldives during the pandemic, specifically mentioned India and its financial assistance of $250 million, calling it the 'single largest financial assistance from a donor.'[16]

At the commencement of New Delhi's COVID-management initiatives in the neighbourhood, in March 2020, India sent a team of doctors and specialists to assist in the pandemic preparedness in the Maldives. India also sent two consignments of essential medicines and 580 tonnes of food-aid, particularly ahead of the annual Ramadan festival season. Further, New Delhi lifted export restrictions on medical consumables, respiratory apparatus, testing kits and reagents during this time. Given the existing ban on civilian flights, New Delhi pressed into service a transport aircraft of the Indian Air Force. India has further agreed to a request by the Maldives to send doctors and nurses on short-term contracts to reinforce and support the Maldives's health system in its fight against COVID-19.

Overcoming the pandemic-induced travel ban, the foreign ministers of both countries have held virtual conferences, and the two sides have signed multiple agreements during this time, possibly with greater seriousness and urgency than under normal circumstances. Prime Minister Modi and External Affairs Minister Jaishankar have been in constant touch with their counterparts in Male, assuring and reassuring them of India's continued commitment and prioritized approach to assisting the Maldives in these most difficult of times. This sentiment was captured in a recent tweet by Modi in September 2020 when he stated, 'As close friends and neighbours, India and Maldives will continue to support each other in our fight against the health and economic impact of COVID-19.'[17]

This is, however, not the first time that India has rushed assistance to the Maldives, as and when sought, prioritizing Maldivian needs at times to those nearer home. In substance, it began with India rushing military aid through 'Operation Cactus' (1988) after a Sri Lankan Tamil mercenary group attempted a coup against President Gayoom's decade-old regime. Civilian aid was similarly rushed through military means, first at the time of 'Asian tsunami' (2004) and later to meet capital Male's drinking water crisis (December 2014), after the city's only desalination plant was destroyed in fire.

Development Funding

Independent of pandemic-related aid and assistance, under the 'Neighbourhood First' policy, India's approach towards the Maldives involves development-based assistance and development-led infrastructure. While frequent diplomatic contacts are reflective of a healthy bilateral equation, real progress comes from impacting positively on the lives of the Maldivian people. Apart from the existing ones, an additional 1,000 educational scholarships, 2,500 LED streetlights and 2.5 million LED bulbs to Male City Council are all a part of India's High Impact Community Development Projects (HICDP) programme under the 'Neighbourhood First' policy.

The HICDP concept is aimed at reaching out to the local population at their level, not limited to larger infrastructure projects and assistance for the nation as a whole. Such schemes thus include assistance at the level of the local bodies, for school buildings and civic amenities in different islands. As with Male, India has funded similar projects with other islands, both big and small, including the local council of southern Addu City, the Maldives's second-largest 'population centre' after Male.

Infrastructure Projects

On big-ticket schemes, India has signed a $500-million agreement to fund the largest infrastructure project in the Maldives, through the Greater Male Connectivity Project (GMCP). Named 'Thilamale' sea bridge, it will connect the Maldavian capital Male with the neighbouring islands of Villingili, Gulhifahu and Thilafushi, thus helping also to decongest the national capital. For a South Asian capital, Male has the highest density of population. Given the huge housing crisis and also the consequent high cost of living, rentals and also attendant social problems such as high drug abuse among the nation's youth, the MDP had made GMCP a key election promise.

India hopes that the Thilamale Bridge will help revitalize and transform the Maldivian economy. Maldivian Foreign Minister Shahid said, 'Once completed, the project will be the single largest infrastructure project in the Maldives.'[18] Unavoidable comparisons with Sinamale Bridge completed with Chinese loans bring to notice that the India-aided bridge, 6.7 km long, will be more than three times the length of the other.

The Thilamale Bridge is in the news for another reason as well. Along with other projects funded by India under 'Neighbourhood First', India is adopting a transparent tender policy to be handled by the Maldivian government. This is also true of the India-funded 100-bed cancer hospital in the reclamation island of Hulhumale, in Male's Ocean suburb. As is the Indian practice, local entrepreneurs are able to participate in those projects and local youth can aspire for jobs and thus substantial additions to family incomes—both unavailable under China-funded projects in the Maldives and elsewhere.

The Maldives is a football-crazy nation. Given, however, Solih's interest in cricket, India has extended a line of credit for the Maldives to build the nation's first cricket stadium at Hulhumale. In February 2019, India sent former national cricketers Yuvraj Singh and Harbhajan Singh, as part of an Air India team, to take part in the India–Maldives Cricket Friendship Series. The series was supported by the Ministry for Youth, Sports and Community Empowerment, and momentously saw the participation of Solih, who also captained the team. So much so that when they met, Modi gifted Solih a cricket bat with signatures of India's national team. At the invitation of India, Solih made an unofficial visit to Bengaluru in April 2019 to watch a cricket match and also to discuss ways to take cricket in the Maldives forward through capacity-building and training.

A significant goal within the 'Neighbourhood First' policy has been an emphasis on connectivity. This is particularly crucial for 'Small Island Developing States' such as the Maldives. To this end, India has taken up the construction of a $800 million airport modernization work in the northern island of Kulhudhuffushi, the largest population centre after Male and Addu. Despite the global pandemic, India launched the first-ever cargo ferry service between the two nations, connecting the south Indian ports of Thoothukudi and Kochi with Kulhudhuffushi and Male ports.

Kulhudhuffushi is the third-largest 'population centre' in the country after Male and Addu, and is the closest to the Indian coast, with familial connections to people in north Kerala and Minicoy. Improved connectivity to the island strengthens a larger development goal of the Maldivian government, which has been focused on the economic development of North, especially under President Nasheed earlier. For a beginning, India will subsidize the service at approximately $3 million.

Cargo transportation between the two countries thus far was handled by relatively smaller dhows, with all inherent limitations. By providing direct connectivity between the two countries on a predictable and affordable basis, India is hoping to improve trade prospects by lowering transportation costs for traders and hence Maldivian consumers, who depend on exports from India and Sri Lanka for their daily living needs and even basic medicines. Considering the Maldivian resource crunch, starting with human resources, and thus limited to a small market, cargo transportation of the kind will directly benefit the Maldivian people more than can be understood. Equally important from a Maldivian perspective is the fact that the service will provide refrigerated transportation for Maldivian exporters of tuna and other marine products to target the Indian market.

Navigating the Future

Looking ahead, though bilateral relations are perhaps at their peak, there remain certain potential challenges that New Delhi will need to navigate with creativity and dexterity. Some of these issues are structural while others relate to Maldivian domestic politics. As far as challenges for India are concerned, China remains a formidable one. The ways to respond to China in the Maldives will need to be creative, development-led and urgent in its implementation. It is notable that unlike in the era before 'Neighbourhood First', there is a greater sense of purpose in India's decision-making and speed in implementation, thus addressing an eternal complaint from the neighbourhood as a whole. The traditional Indian practice of engaging the host nation in deciding their priorities and involving local talent and entrepreneurship, especially in infrastructure projects, big and small, can go a long way in cementing relations with the local population, going beyond ties with their elected governments.

In this context, more recent Indian initiatives deserve mention. During his Maldives visit in February 2021, India's external affairs minister S. Jaishankar publicly reiterated New Delhi's support for Foreign Minister Abdulla Shahid's candidacy for the UN General Assembly presidency.[19] The election is due in the UN General Assembly annual session in October 2021. News reports have since indicated that former Afghan foreign minister Dr Zalmai Rassoul is also in the fray. Considering that both Afghanistan and the Maldives are preferred friends, and given PM Modi's 'Neighbourhood First' policy, New Delhi's decision in this regard is significant even from an Indian point of view.

Apart from taking forward the work on other India-funded development projects, the visit was marked by the signing of bilateral agreements for India to build a harbour and dockyard for the Maldives National Defense in Uthuru Thila Falhu island, through a $50 million line of credit.[20] Both sides have since denied suggestions that the agreement provided for Indian defence forces to access the harbour and dockyard facilities.

The request for Indian assistance in this regard was originally made by the Yameen dispensation in 2013. However, when it was finally signed during Jaishankar's visit, supporters of Yameen protested both inside and outside Parliament.[21] It did not have much public impact, as foreseeing trouble, the two governments decided to sign the agreement in the view of television cameras, unlike various secret deals that the Yameen government had signed with China.

At the same time, both Jaishankar (and Foreign Secretary Harsh V. Shringla before him) made it a point to meet with a cross-section of political party leaders, including those representing Yameen's interests, during their respective visits. This is expected to assuage at least some of their anti-India sentiments flowing from such misconception and miscommunication, and also open up a line of communication to New Delhi, more than at the level of the Indian High Commission in Male.

Traditionally, the Maldives and Sri Lanka have been India's first line of defence in geostrategic and neighbourhood security matters when looked at from the sea. This is where greater Chinese activity in the IOR is of real and realistic concern for India, going beyond the theoretical construct of the kind for nations like the US. In the midst of the COVID-19 pandemic management, the Solih government took the initiative of signing a 'Framework Agreement' with the US for bilateral military cooperation. The US statement in this regard mentioned a 'rules-based maritime order' and military training as among the outcomes from the agreement. After James Baker in 1992, Mike Pompeo became the first US Secretary of State to visit the Maldives on an official visit, in October-end 2020.

Before the 'Framework Agreement', the US and the Maldives signed Washington's standard 'Acquisition and Cross-Servicing Agreement' in a low-key affair under Nasheed's presidency in 2010. Later, under the Waheed regime, the US had reportedly proposed that the two nations sign the Status of Forces Agreement, whose standard format, when leaked, stalled its progress. When questioned by the media, the US State Department claimed that they had kept India informed. New Delhi did not react. Nor has it formally acknowledged the 2020 'Framework Agreement' between the Maldives and the US, as may have been inferred by a section of the media. Given India's own increasing defence and security ties with the US, New Delhi seems to have taken a benign view of the Maldives's Framework Agreement with the US.

Finally, India needs to pay attention to the Maldives's internal politics, whose landscape is perpetually changing as coalitions break up, re-arrange themselves or fade into irrelevance. In the 2018 presidential polls, the MDP joined hands with other opposition parties, including the Jumhooree Party of billionaire-businessman Qasim Ibrahim, whose support alone had helped Nasheed (2008) and Yameen (2013) to win the presidency. The religion-centric Adhaalath Party, which partnered in the anti-Nasheed protests of 2011–12, and even President Gayoom's hurriedly formed 'Maumoon Reform Movement' backed MDP's Solih in the presidential polls.

The unilateral decision of Nasheed as MDP president to snap alliance ties ahead of the parliamentary polls in 2019, despite incumbent Solih's open efforts to continue the same, follows the pattern set by him during the 2009 parliamentary polls after he had been elected president. This may have consequences for the MDP in the 2023 presidential polls as the MDP party is seen as being increasingly untrustworthy for future poll alliances of the kind.

This is more so in the context of Yameen, who had seemingly hijacked Gayoom's conservative, non-fundamentalist vote share, wholesale, polling a respectable 42 per cent vote share against Solih's 58 per cent in the 2018 polls. In the case of the MDP, the figure fell to 46 per cent in the 2019 parliamentary polls despite the party winning more than two-thirds of seats, 65 of 87. This means that in a polarized presidential poll in 2023, as in 2008 and 2018, the MDP may have a tough time.

Against this background, the Progressive Party of Maldives and the People's National Congress, both identified with Yameen, have launched rallies across the country, strikingly in the midst of a pandemic, demanding his release from prison. They reiterated their claims that the ruling MDP government was selling the Maldives to foreign powers and launched an 'India Out' campaign, in reference to the continued stationing of Indian military pilots and technicians. Despite a two-thirds majority in Parliament for the ruling MDP, people can be persuaded to think afresh in the next presidential polls. Should the Yameen camp capture electoral power, India-funded projects and bilateral relations as a whole can run into rough weather. This does not look probable at the moment, but India needs to be guarded about the possibility, all the same.

If at the start of 2014, the Maldives was not in the purview of India's 'Neighbourhood First' policy, straggling just behind Pakistan in terms of a strained and difficult bilateral equation, by 2021, under the ruling MDP and President Solih, the nation has become one of the biggest success stories of 'Neighbourhood First', indeed worthy of closer study for possible modification and adaptation by New Delhi for similarly strengthening relations with other friendly nations in South Asia.

NOTES

Introduction

1. Praveen Swami, 'In a First, Modi Invites SAARC Leaders for His Swearing-In,' *The Hindu*, 23 May 2016, https://www.thehindu.com/news/national/in-a-first-modi-invites-saarc-leaders-for-his-swearingin/article6033710.ece, accessed 24 March 2021.
2. Breakthrough Diplomacy, 'Neighbourhood First Initiative,' Ministry of External Affairs, India, 2014, https://www.mea.gov.in/Images/pdf/Breakthroughdiplomacy.pdf, accessed 24 March 2021.
3. 'Three Years of Modi Government: Where India's Relations with Its Neighbours Stand,' *The Indian Express*, 27 May 2017, https://indianexpress.com/article/india/three-years-of-modi-government-where-indias-relations-with-its-neighbours-stand-4673042/, accessed 24 March 2021.
4. Sachin Parashar/TNN, 'Border Row with India Worsens, Nepal to Release New Map,' *The Times of India*, 20 May 2020, https://timesofindia.indiatimes.com/india/border-row-with-india-worsens-nepal-to-release-new-map/articleshow/75837113.cms, accessed 24 March 2021.
5. Daniel Balazs, 'The China-India Standoff in Ladakh: A Relook,' *The Diplomat*, 9 December 2020, https://thediplomat.com/2020/12/the-china-india-standoff-in-ladakh-a-relook/, accessed 24 March 2021.
6. 'Agreement Between the Government of the Republic of India and the Government of the People's Republic of China on Confidence-Building Measures in the Military Field Along the Line of Actual Control in the India-China Border Areas,' UN Peacemaker, 29 November 1996, https://peacemaker.un.org/sites/peacemaker.un.org/files/CN%20IN_961129_Agreement%20between%20China%20and%20India.pdf, accessed 25 March 2021.
7. 'Doklam to Galwan: Have Modi-Xi Informal Summits Been More about Optics than Border Peace?' *The Print*, 25 May 2020, https://theprint.in/

190 ▪ Politics and Geopolitics

8   talk-point/doklam-to-galwan-have-modi-xi-informal-summits-been-more-about-optics-than-border-peace/428998/, accessed 25 March 2021.
8   Rahul Tripathi and Hakeem Irfan Rashid, 'India Set to Ramp up Infrastructure along China's Border,' *The Economic Times*, 26 June 2020, https://economictimes.indiatimes.com/news/defence/india-set-to-ramp-up-infrastructure-along-china-border/articleshow/76631962.cms?from=mdr, accessed 25 March 2021.
9   'Why China Is Making Belligerent Moves to Rattle India: The Cause of Concern,' *The Economic Times*, 29 May 2020, https://economictimes.indiatimes.com/news/defence/why-china-is-making-belligerent-moves-to-rattle-india/darbuk-shyok-daulat-beg-oldie-road/slideshow/76086428.cms, accessed 25 March 2021.
10 'Quad Member States Review Connectivity Cooperation, Security in Indo-Pacific,' *Hindustan Times*, 18 December 2020, https://www.hindustantimes.com/india-news/quad-member-states-review-connectivity-cooperation-security-in-indo-pacific/story-KV486oPljPW11u9i7vQ1PK.html, accessed 25 March 2021.
11 C.K. Lal, 'KP Oli Rode on Anti-India Wave. He Is Now Looking at Delhi for a Diplomatic Lifeline,' *The Print*, 12 January 2021, https://theprint.in/opinion/kp-oli-rode-on-anti-india-wave-he-is-now-looking-at-delhi-for-a-diplomatic-lifeline/583672/, accessed 25 March 2021.
12 Shishir Gupta, '10 Chinese Spies Caught in Kabul Get a Quiet Pardon, Fly Home in Chartered Aircraft,' *Hindustan Times*, 4 January 2021, https://www.hindustantimes.com/world-news/10-chinese-spies-caught-in-kabul-get-a-quiet-pardon-fly-home-in-chartered-aircraft/story-YhNI0zjmClMcj6T7TCCwVM.html, accessed 25 March 2021.
13 ANI, 'China Backing Away from Its Initial Financial Promises to Pakistan under CPEC: Report,' *The Economic Times*, 25 December 2020, https://economictimes.indiatimes.com/news/international/world-news/china-backing-away-from-its-initial-financial-promises-to-pakistan-under-cpec-report/articleshow/79950928.cms?from=mdr, accessed 25 March 2021.
14 'China's Role in SAARC,' The Brookings Institution, 20 November 2014, https://www.brookings.edu/research/chinas-role-in-saarc/, accessed 25 March 2021.
15 Harsh V. Pant, 'From Turmoil to Clarity: International Relations in the New Decade,' Observer Research Foundation (ORF), 4 January 2021, https://www.orfonline.org/expert-speak/turmoil-clarity-international-relations-new-decade/, accessed 25 March 2021.
16 'MEA: Statements: Speeches & Statements,' Ministry of External Affairs, Government of India, 12 January 2021, https://www.mea.gov.in/Speeches-Statements.htm?dtl%2F24321%2FPrime%2BMinisters%2Bspeech%2Bat%2Bthe%2B18th%2BSAARC%2BSummit, accessed 25 March 2021.
17 Ananth Krishnan, 'India, China Should Create "Enabling Conditions" to

Settle Border Dispute, Says Wang Yi,' *The Hindu*, 7 March 2021, https://www.thehindu.com/news/international/india-china-should-create-enabling-conditions-to-settle-border-dispute-says-wang-yi/article34012426.ece, accessed 25 March 2021.

Chapter 1: Afghanistan

1. Conversation with Abdullah Abdullah, 24 March 2019. Much the same way, Karzai, as chairman of the Afghan Interim Administration, told Prime Minister Atal Bihari Vajpayee in February 2002 that India and Afghanistan should have tactical relations.
2. A Conversation with H.E. Mohammad Ashraf Ghani, President of the Islamic Republic of Afghanistan, United States Institute of Peace (USIP) 25 March 2015, https://www.usip.org/events/conversation-he-mohammad-ashraf-ghani, accessed 31 March 2021.
3. 'US Admiral: "Haqqani Is Veritable Arm of Pakistan's ISI",' *BBC News*, 22 September 2011, https://www.bbc.com/news/av/world-us-canada-15026909, accessed 31 March 2021.
4. Steve Coll, *Directorate S: The C.I.A. and America's Secret Wars in Afghanistan and Pakistan*, Allen Lane, London, 2018, pp. 156–7.
5. Paragraph 5 of the Agreement states that 'India agrees to assist, as mutually determined, in the training, equipping and capacity building programmes for Afghan National Security Forces.' See https://mea.gov.in/ bilateral-documents.htm?dtl/c5383/Text+of+Agreement+on+Strategic+Partnership+ between+the+Republic+ of+India+and+the+Islamic+Republic+of+Afghanistan, accessed 31 March 2021.
6. As briefed by Umer Daudzai at the Indian Council for World Affairs, 17 May 2019.
7. This is an idea not just confined to the time when the Taliban ruled Afghanistan, but has been a continuing preoccupation of the deep Pakistani state. For example, the former chief of the Pakistani Army, General Kayani, affirmed that 'we want strategic depth in Afghanistan'. See quoted in Robert B. Oakley and T.X. Hammes, 'Prioritizing Strategic Interests in South Asia,' Strategic Forum, US Institute for National Strategic Studies, National Defense University, no. 256 (June 2010).
8. Statement by the Spokesperson of the Iranian Foreign Office, Saeed Khatibzadeh, 'Iran Calls for Immediate US Withdrawal from Afghanistan,' *Tehran Times*, 27 November 2020, https://www.tehrantimes.com/news/455143/Iran-calls-for-immediate-U-S-withdrawal-from-Afghanistan, accessed 31 March 2021.
9. Ryan Crocker, 'I Was Ambassador to Afghanistan. This Deal is a Surrender,' *The Washington Post*, 30 January 2019, https://www.washingtonpost.com/opinions/i-was-ambassador-to-afghanistan-this-deal-

is-a-surrender/2019/01/29/8700ed68-2409-11e9-ad53-824486280311_story.html, accessed 31 March 2021.

10 Letter dated 16 July 2020 from the Chair of the Security Council Committee pursuant to resolutions 1267 (1999), 1989 (2011) and 2253 (2015) concerning Islamic State in Iraq and the Levant (Da'esh), Al-Qaida and associated individuals, groups, undertakings and entities addressed to the President of the Security Council, 23 July 2020, UNSC, https://www.ecoi.net/en/file/local/2036549/S_2020_717_E.pdf, accessed 31 March 2021.

11 Tweet by Javid Faisal of the Afghan National Security Council, 5 April 2020, https://twitter.com/Javidfaisal, retrieved on 27 November 2020.

12 Mark Hosenball, 'War on Terror: The Road to September 11,' *Newsweek*, 30 September 2001, https://www.newsweek.com/war-terror-road-september-11-151771, accessed 31 March 2021. Also see Jeffrey Goldberg and Mark Ambinder, 'Ally from Hell,' *Atlantic*, December 2011, https://www.theatlantic.com/magazine/archive/2011/12/the-ally-from-hell/308730, accessed 31 March 2021.

13 Henry Kissinger, 'How to Exit Afghanistan,' *The Washington Post*, 7 June 2011, https://www.washingtonpost.com/opinions/how-to-exit-afghanistan-without-creating-wider-conflict/2011/06/06/AG9ydPLH_story.html, accessed 31 March 2021.

Chapter 2: Pakistan

1 For more about Pakistan's foreign policy, please read the author's *Explaining Pakistan's Foreign Policy: Escaping India*, Routledge, New York, 2011.

2 Text of the Simla Agreement, 2 July 1971, Ministry of External Affairs, Government of India, https://mea.gov.in/in-focus-article.htm?19005/Simla+Agreement+July+2+1972, accessed 26 March 2021.

3 Text of the Lahore Declaration, February 1999, Ministry of External Affairs, Government of India, https://mea.gov.in/in-focus-article.htm?18997/Lahore+Declaration+February+1999, accessed 26 March 2021.

4 Suhasini Haidar, 'Modi Stuns All with Surprise Stopover in Lahore,' *The Hindu*, 25 December 2015, https://www.thehindu.com/news/modi-stuns-all-with-surprise-stopover-in-lahore-following-unannounced-stop-in-kabul/article8029007.ece, accessed 26 March 2021.

5 Nida Najar, 'Gunmen Killed in Pathankot, India, Air Base Attack,' *New York Times*, 2 January 2016, https://www.nytimes.com/2016/01/03/world/asia/india-air-base-attack-pathankot.html, accessed 26 March 2021; Mukhtar Ahmad, Rich Philips and Joshua Berlinger, 'Soldiers Killed in Army Base Attack in Indian-administered Kashmir,' CNN, 19 September 2016 https://www.cnn.com/2016/09/18/asia/india-kashmir-attack/index.html, accessed 26 March 2021.

6 'Kashmir Attack: Tracing the Path that Led to Pulwama,' *BBC News*, 30 April

2019, https://www.bbc.com/news/world-asia-india-47302467, accessed 26 March 2021.

7   Jeffrey Gettleman, Suhasini Raj, Kai Szhultz and Hari Kumar, 'India Revokes Kashmir's Special Status, Raising Fears of Unrest,' *New York Times*, 5 August 2019 https://www.nytimes.com/2019/08/05/world/asia/india-pakistan-kashmir-jammu.html, accessed 26 March 2021.

8   'Modi Blames Pakistan for Mumbai Terror Attack,' *The Economic Times*, 28 November 2008, https://economictimes.indiatimes.com/modi-blames-pakistan-for-mumbai-terror-attack/articleshow/3769298.cms, accessed 26 March 2021.

9   Shivam Vij, 'Why Modi's Invitation to Nawaz Sharif Could Backfire,' *Scroll.in*, 26 May 2014, scroll.in/article/665323/why-modis., accessed 26 March 2021.

10 Prashant Jha, 'Modi, Sharif Had Hour-Long "Secret" Meeting during Saarc 2014,' *Hindustan Times*, 30 November 2015, www.hindustantimes.com/india/modi-sharif-had-hour-long-secret-meeting-during-saarc-2014/story-oaPYNkJI2sUS09cdHjWnCL.html., accessed 26 March 2021.

11 Elizabeth Roche, 'Narendra Modi Sends Ramzan Greetings to Nawaz Sharif,' *Mint*, 16 June 2015, www.livemint.com/Politics/RHUOnybnhZw8XaSUd7EiDO/Narendra-Modi-sends-Ramzan-greetings-to-Nawaz-Sharif.html, accessed 26 March 2021.

12 Nidhi Razdan, 'India, Pakistan Hold Secret NSA-Level Talks in Bangkok, Issue Statement,' *NDTV.com*, 6 December 2015, www.ndtv.com/india-news/national-security-advisors-of-india-and-pakistan-meet-in-bangkok-issue-joint-statement-1251656, accessed 26 March 2021.

13 'India, Pakistan to Hold "Comprehensive" Talks, Discuss Terror, Kashmir,' *Hindustan Times*, 10 December 2015, www.hindustantimes.com/india/india-pakistan-will-start-comprehensive-dialogue-says-sushma-swaraj/story-FYBmEgQF7jXGeHzcmHsCbJ.html, accessed 26 March 2021.

14 ' Narendra Modi Holds Impromptu Talks with Nawaz Sharif in Lahore,' *Scroll.in*, 25 December 2015, scroll.in/latest/801024/narendra-modi-reaches-lahore-to-meet-pakistan-prime-minister, accessed 26 March 2021.

15 Rohan Venkataramakrishnan, 'Pathankot Terror Attack: Eight Crucial Unanswered Questions,' *Scroll.in*, 4 January 2016, scroll.in/article/801374/pathankot-terror-attack-eight-crucial-unanswered-questions, accessed 26 March 2021.

16 'Pathankot Attacks: Joint Investigation Team from Pakistan Arrives in Delhi,' *Scroll.in*, 27 March 2016, scroll.in/latest/805753/pathankot-attacks-joint-investigation-team-from-pakistan-arrives-in-delhi, accessed 26 March 2021.

17 'NIA Rebuts Claim That It Did Not Give Pakistan's Investigation Team Enough Evidence on Pathankot,' *Scroll.in*, 5 April 2016, scroll.in/latest/806188/pakistan-investigative-team-says-india-staged-pathankot-attack-pakistan-media-report, accessed 26 March 2021.

194 ▪ Politics and Geopolitics

18 'Pakistan, India Peace Talks "Suspended", *BBC News*, 8 April 2016, www.bbc.com/news/world-asia-india-35994599, accessed 26 March 2021.

19 'Uri Base Attack: 17 Soldiers and Four Militants Have Been Killed, Army Chief to Visit Site,' *Scroll.in*, 18 September 2016, scroll.in/latest/816817/militants-strike-army-headquarters-in-uri-kashmir-no-casualties-reported, accessed 26 March 2021.

20 Manjeet Singh Negi, 'Surgical Strikes in PoK: How Indian Para Commandos Killed 50 Terrorists, Hit 7 Camps,' *India Today*, 2 October 2016, www.indiatoday.in/india/story/uri-avenged-inside-story-indian-army-surgical-strikes-pok-343995-2016-09-29, accessed 26 March 2021.

21 Sanjeev Miglani and Asad Hashim, 'India Says Hits Pakistan-Based Militants, Escalating Tensions,' *Reuters*, Thomson Reuters, 29 September 2016, www.reuters.com/article/us-pakistan-india-kashmir-idUSKCN11Z0IJ, accessed 26 March 2021.

22 Tanvi Kulkarni and Sylvia Mishra, 'The Pulwama Aftermath: Making Sense of India's Response,' *South Asian Voices*, 6 March 2019, https://southasianvoices.org/the-pulwama-aftermath-making-sense-of-indias-response-%EF%BB%BF/, accessed 26 March 2021.

23 Maria Abi-Habib and Hari Kumar, 'Pakistani Military Says It Downed Two Indian Warplanes, Capturing Pilot,' *The New York Times*, 27 February 2019, www.nytimes.com/2019/02/27/world/asia/kashmir-india-pakistan-aircraft.html, accessed 26 March 2021.

24 PTI, 'Pak. Formally Suspends Trade Ties,' *The Hindu*, 10 August 2019, www.thehindu.com/news/national/pak-formally-suspends-trade-ties/article28977922.ece, accessed 26 March 2021.

25 'Balakot Air Strikes Impact: Pakistan Suffers over USD 50 Mn Losses Due to Airspace Closure,' *The Hindu BusinessLine*, 19 July 2019, www.thehindubusinessline.com/news/world/balakot-air-strikes-impact-pakistan-suffers-over-usd-50-mn-losses-due-to-airspace-closur, accessed 26 March 2021.

26 Rajendra Jadhav, 'Anti-Pakistan Wave Helps Modi Salvage Some Votes from India's Unhappy Farms,' *Reuters*, Thomson Reuters, 8 March 2019, www.reuters.com/article/us-india-election-kashmir-farmers-analys/anti-pakistan-wave-helps-modi-salvage-some-votes-from, accessed 26 March 2021.

27 India Today Web Desk, 'Our Nuclear Weapons Are Not for Diwali: PM Modi on Pak's Nuclear Button Threat,' *India Today*, 21 April 2019, www.indiatoday.in/elections/lok-sabha-2019/story/our-nuclear-weapons-are-not-for-diwali-pm-modi-on-pak-nuclear-button-1506893-2019-04-21, accessed 26 March 2021.

28 Stela Dey, 'Imran Khan Dials PM Modi, Congratulates Him on Election Victory,' *NDTV.com*, 26 May 2019, www.ndtv.com/india-news/imran-khan-congratulates-pm-narendra-modi-on-election-victory-on-phone-call-2043238, accessed 26 March 2021.

29　Jawed Naqvi, 'Modi Reminds Imran of Promise to Fight Poverty with India', *DAWN*, 24 February 2019, www.dawn.com/news/1465696, accessed 26 March 2021.

30　'Kartarpur Corridor: India Pilgrims in Historic Visit to Pakistan Temple', *BBC News*, 9 November 2019, www.bbc.com/news/world-asia-india-50342319, accessed 26 March 2021.

31　Salman Masood, Mujib Mashal and Hari Kumar, 'Pakistan and India Renew Pledge on Cease-Fire at Troubled Border', *New York Times*, 25 February 2021, https://www.nytimes.com/2021/02/25/world/asia/pakistan-india-ceasefire.html, accessed 26 March 2021.

32　Ankit Panda, 'India, Pakistan Exchange Lists of Nuclear Sites Pursuant to Their Non-Attack Agreement', *The Diplomat*, 6 January 2020, thediplomat.com/2020/01/india-pakistan-exchange-lists-of-nuclear-sites-pursuant-to-their-non-attack-agreement/, accessed 26 March 2021.

33　Hakeem Irfan Rashid, 'Terror and Talks Cannot Go Together, Says Rajnath Singh', *The Economic Times*, 23 October 2018, economictimes.indiatimes.com/news/defence/home-minister-rajnath-singh-appeals-to-kashmiris-not-to-visit-gunfight-sites/articleshow, accessed 26 March 2021.

34　Shahid Amin, 'Need For New Thinking in Indo-Pak Ties', *The CSS Point*, https://thecsspoint.com/need-for-new-thinking-in-indo-pak-ties-by-shahid-m-amin/, accessed 26 March 2021.

Chapter 3: China

1　Ashley J. Tellis, 'Hustling in the Himalayas: The Sino-Indian Border Confrontation', Carnegie Endowment for International Peace, Washington D.C., June 2020.

2　Jayadeva Ranade, 'Implications of the Ongoing Tension with China along the LAC', Issue Brief Centre for China Analysis & Strategy, New Delhi, May 2020.

3　Sino-Indian Joint Press Communique, 23 December 1988, Beijing, www.fmprc.gov.cn, accessed 1 April 2021.

4　Joint statement between the Republic of India and the People's Republic of China on Building a Closer Developmental Partnership, 19 September 2014, www.mea.gov.in.

5　Joint statement between India and China during Prime Minister's visit to China, 15 May 2015, www.mea.gov.in.

6　Zhexin Zhang, 'The Belt and Road Initiative: China's New Geopolitical Strategy?' Stiftung Wissenschaft und Politik, Berlin, October 2018, www.swp-berlin.org.

7　Ministry of External Affairs, Official Spokesperson's response to a query on participation of India in OBOR/BRI Forum, New Delhi, 13 May 2017, www.mea.gov.in.

8   Ministry of External Affairs, Recent Developments in Doklam Area, New Delhi, 30 June 2017, www.mea.gov.in.
9   M. Taylor Fravel, 'China's Sovereignty Obsession,' *Foreign Affairs*, New York, June 2020.
10 Jeff M. Smith, 'The Simmering Boundary: A "New Normal" at the India–China Border?' Strategic Studies, ORF, New Delhi, June 2020.
11 Gautam Bambawale, 'To Send a Message, It Is Time to Ban Chinese Firms from India's 5G Trials,' *Hindustan Times*, New Delhi, 24 August 2020.
12 Gautam Bambawale, 'It Can No Longer be Business-as-Usual,' *Hindustan Times*, New Delhi, 1 July 2020.
13 This is being pursued by the other three Quad nations. India's joining the network will make it part of the Quad's economic outreach to the Indo-Pacific region.

Chapter 4: Nepal

1   'Bound Together by "Roti-Beti": Rajnath Singh on India–Nepal Ties,' *The Quint*, 15 June 2020, https://www.thequint.com/news/india/defence-minister-rajnath-singh-on-india-nepal-border-tensions-new-map-bill, accessed 26 March 2021.
2   Aniket Singh and Arnav Singh, 'Why India's "Big Brother" Attitude towards Nepal May Benefit China,' *The Quint*, 17 September 2020, https://www.thequint.com/voices/opinion/india-nepal-trade-economy-historical-ties-closeness-to-china-border-conflict-modi-govt-foreign-policy, accessed 26 March 2021.
3   IANS, 'PM Narendra Modi to be First Indian PM to Visit Nepal in 17 years,' *India Today*, 1 August 2014, https://www.indiatoday.in/india/story/narendra-modi-to-visit-nepal-after-17-years-first-prime-minister-202543-2014-08-01, accessed 26 March 2021.
4   Manjeev S. Puri, 'Nepal Ties and the Benaras to Bengaluru Spectrum,' *The Hindu*, 17 June 2020, https://www.thehindu.com/opinion/lead/nepal-ties-and-the-benaras-to-bengaluru-spectrum/article31845772.ece, accessed 26 March 2021.

Chapter 5: Bhutan

1   Aby Tharakan, 'Too Much Dragon, Too Little Kingdom,' *The Hindu*, 12 July 2016, https://www.thehindu.com/opinion/op-ed/too-much-dragon-too-little-kingdom/article4918267.ece, accessed 30 March 2021.
2   Suhasini Haider, 'Hydropower Debt, Delays Biggest Challenge in Ties with India, say Bhutan Officials,' *The Hindu*, 26 September 2017, https://www.thehindu.com/news/national/hydropower-debt-delays-biggest-challenge-in-

ties-with-india-say-bhutan-officials/article19630701.ece, accessed 30 March 2021.
3   Article 2 of the 1949 Treaty of Perpetual Peace and Friendship provided, 'Bhutan agrees to be guided by the advice of the Government of India in regard to external relations.' In the 2007 Treaty, this was amended to, 'The Government of the Kingdom of Bhutan and the Government of the Republic of India shall cooperate closely with each other on issues relating to their national interests.'
4   PTI, 'President Pranab Mukherjee Hails "Most Memorable" Bhutan Visit,' *The Economic Times*, 8 November 2014, https://economictimes.indiatimes.com/news/politics-and-nation/president-pranab-mukherjee-hails-most-memorable-bhutan-visit/articleshow/45080847.cms?from=mdr, accessed 30 March 2021.
5   'Bhutanese PM in India: Tshering Tobgay Meets Narendra Modi, Agrees to Enhance India-Bhutan Ties in Areas of "mutual interest", *First Post*, 7 July 2018, https://www.firstpost.com/photos/india-gallery/bhutanese-pm-in-india-tshering-tobgay-meets-narendra-modi-agrees-to-enhance-india-bhutan-ties-in-areas-of-mutual-interest-4688361.html, accessed 30 March 2021.
6   Shubhajit Roy, 'China Makes New Claim in Eastern Border with Bhutan,' *Indian Express*, 6 July 2020, https://indianexpress.com/article/world/china-makes-new-claim-in-eastern-border-with-bhutan-6491875/, accessed 30 March 2021.
7   Shubhajit Roy, 'China Makes New Claim in Eastern Border with Bhutan,' *Indian Express*, 6 July 2020, https://indianexpress.com/article/world/chinamakes-new-claim-in-eastern-border-with-bhutan-6491875/, accessed 30 March 2021.
8   All trade and investment data have been derived from the following sources: irectorate General of Foreign Trade (DGFT) and ICRIER study on India-Bhutan economic relations, published in August 2019. Nisha Taneja, Samridhi Bimal, Taher Nadeem and Riya Roy, Working Paper 384, India-Bhutan Economic Relations, 2019, Indian Council for Research on International Economic Relations, doi:https://icrier.org/pdf/Working_Paper_384.pdf, accessed 30 March 2021.
9   'Changing Profile of India's Hydro Power Import from Bhutan,' SANDRP (South Asia Network on Dams, Rivers and People), 20 April 2015, https://sandrp.in/2015/04/20/changing-profile-of-indias-hydro-power-import-from-bhutan/#more-4954, accessed 30 March 2021.
10 The 12th Five-year Plan 2018–23 of Gross National Happiness Commission, Bhutan https://www.gnhc.gov.bt/en/wp-content/uploads/2017/05/Finalized-Guideline.pdf, accessed 30 March 2021.

Chapter 6: Bangladesh

1. 'English Rendering of the PM's Statement at the General Debate of the 69th Session of the United Nations General Assembly (UNGA),' https://www.pmindia.gov.in/en/news_updates/english-rendering-of-the-pms-statement-at-the-general-debate-of-the-69th-session-of-the-united-nations-general-assembly-unga/, accessed 1 April 2021.
2. "DOCUMENTS," *Pakistan Horizon*, Vol. 24, no. 2 (1971): 98–170, http://www.jstor.org/stable/41393075, accessed 1 April 2021.
3. Angana Das, 'India's Neighbourhood Policy: Challenges and Prospects,' *Jindal Journal of International Affairs*, Vol. 4, no. 1.
4. Imtiaz Ahmed, 'Future Directions of Bangladesh Foreign Policy: Dreams or Nightmares?' in *Changing Global Dynamics: Bangladesh Foreign Policy*, Ed. AKM Abdur Rahman, Dhaka, Bangladesh International Institute of International & Strategic Studies, 2018, p. 7–8.
5. Pranab Mukherjee, *The Coalition Years:1996–2012*, Rupa Publications, New Delhi, 2017, p. 113–15
6. 'MEA: Statements: Bilateral/Multilateral Documents,' Ministry of External Affairs, Government of India, https://www.mea.gov.in/bilateral-documents.htm?dtl%2F5147%2FJoint+Statement+ on+the+ occassion+of+the+visit+of +the+PM+of+India+to+Bangladesh, accessed 1 April 2021.
7. 'Bay of Bengal Maritime Boundary Arbitration between Bangladesh and India (Bangladesh v. India),' PCA, https://pca-cpa.org/en/news/bay-of-bengal-maritime-boundary-arbitration-between-bangladesh-and-india-bangladesh-v-india/, accessed 1 April 2021.
8. 'Bay of Bengal Maritime Boundary Arbitration between Bangladesh andIndia Bangladesh v. India),' PCA, https://pca-cpa.org/en/news/bay-ofbengal-maritime-boundary-arbitration-between-bangladesh-and-indiabangladesh-v-india/, accessed 1 April 2021.
9. 'Annex VII Arbitral Tribunal Delimits Maritime Boundary Between Bangladesh and India in the Bay of Bengal,' American Society of International Law (ASIL), https://www.asil.org/insights/volume/18/issue/20/annex-vii-arbitral-tribunal-delimits-maritime-boundary-between, accessed 1 April 2021.
10. Sanjay Bharadwaj, 'India–Bangladesh Land Boundary Agreement: Ramifications for India's Security,' *CLAWS Journal*, 2015, https://archive.claws.in/images/journals_doc/28433813_sanjaybhardwaj.pdf, accessed 1 April 2021.
11. 'Modi and Hasina Have the Opportunity to Strengthen Bilateral Ties,' *The Hindustan Times*, 8 June 2015, https://www.hindustantimes.com/ht-view/modi-and-hasina-have-the-opportunity-to-strengthen-bilateral-ties/story-YzlmvUt3K5lnn4EBufrWaP.html, accessed 1 April 2021.
12. 'MEA: Statements: Bilateral/Multilateral Documents,' Ministry of External

Notes ▪ 199

Affairs, Government of India, Joint Declaration between Bangladesh and India during Visit of Prime Minister of India to Bangladesh, https://mea.gov.in/bilateraldocuments.htm?dtl%2F25346%2FJoint_Declaration_between_Bangladesh_and_India_during_Visit_of_Prime_Minister_of_India_to_Bangladesh_quot_Notun_Projonmo_Nayi_Dishaquot, accessed 1 April 2021.

13 'MEA: Statements: Bilateral/Multilateral Documents', Ministry of External Affairs, Government of India. 'India-Bangladesh joint statement during the State Visit of Prime Minister of Bangladesh to India, April 2017. https://www.mea.gov.in/bilateral-documents.htm?dtl%2F28362%2FIndia++Bangladesh+Joint+Statement+during+the+State+Visit+of+Prime+Minister+of+Bangladesh+to+India+April+8+2017, accessed 1 April 2021.

14 'India-Bangladesh joint statement during Official Visit of Bangladesh PM to India', Ministry of External Affairs, India, https://mea.gov.in/bilateral, accessed 1 April 2021.

15 'Bangladesh Exports to India Cross $1bn Mark', *Dhaka Tribune*, 10 July 2019, https://www.dhakatribune.com/business/economy/2019/07/10/bangladesh-exports-to-india-cross-1bn-mark, accessed 1 April 2021.

16 'The Constitution of the People's Republic of Bangladesh (ACT NO. OF 1972)', bdlaws.minlaw.gov.bd, http://bdlaws.minlaw.gov.bd/act-367.html accessed 1 April 2021.

17 'GDP per Capita (Current US$) - Bangladesh.' Data, The World Bank, https://data.worldbank.org/indicator/NY.GDP.PCAP.CD?locations=BD, accessed 1 April 2021.

18 'Bangladesh - Foreign Direct Investment, Net Outflows (% of GDP).' Trading Economics, https://tradingeconomics.com/bangladesh/foreign-direct-investment-net-outflows-percent-of-gdp-wb-data.html, accessed 1 April 2021.

19 Dipanjan Roy Chaudhury, 'India, Bangladesh Explore Expansion of Development & Eco Partnership as Hasina Meets Foreign Secy', *The Economic Times*, 18 August 2020, https://economictimes.indiatimes.com/news/politics-and-nation/india-bangladesh-explore-expansion-of-development-eco-partnership-as-hasina-meets-foreign-secy/articleshow/77618800.cms, accessed 1 April 2021.

20 Joyeeta Bhattacharjee, 'Role of Border Haat in Management of India-Bangladesh Border', Cuts International, 2020, https://cuts-crc.org/pdf/briefing-paper-role-of-border-haat-in-management-of-india-bangladesh-border.pdf. accessed 1 April 2021.

21 Senior Correspondent, 'Bangladesh Is India's "Foremost" Partner in ITEC Programme, Says Riva Das,' bdnews24.com, https://bdnews24.com/economy/2019/09/20/bangladesh-is-indias-foremost-partner-in-itec-programme-says-riva-das, accessed 1 April 2021.

22 'International Water Law Project,' International Water Law Project | Statute of the Indo-Bangladesh Joint Rivers Commission, https://www.internationalwaterlaw.org/documents/regionaldocs/indo-bangladesh.html,

accessed 1 April 2021.
23   Jayanta Basu, 'Teesta Has One-Sixteenth of Water Needed,' *The Third Pole*, 28 February 2018, https://www.thethirdpole.net/2017/04/14/teesta-has-one-sixteenth-of-water-needed/, accessed 1 April 2021.
24   Nilanjan Ghosh, 'Why India Has Not Been Able to Resolve the Teesta Stalemate,' ORF, 25 November 2019, https://www.orfonline.org/research/why-india-has-not-been-able-to-resolve-the-teesta-stalemate-58093/, accessed 1 April 2021.
25   Pinaki Roy, 'To India's Chagrin, Bangladesh Turns to China to Transform Teesta River,' *The Third Pole*, 15 August 2012, https://www.thethirdpole.net/2020/09/28/to-indias-chagrin-bangladesh-turns-to-china-to-transform-teesta-river/, accessed 1 April 2021.
26   'No Hindus Will Be Left after 30 Years,' *Dhaka Tribune*, 21 November 2016, https://www.dhakatribune.com/bangladesh/2016/11/20/abul-barkat-632-hindus-left-country-day/, accessed 1 April 2021.
27   Shelley Feldman, 'The Hindu as Other: State, Law, and Land Relations in Contemporary Bangladesh,' *South Asia Multidisciplinary Academic Journal* (Association pour la Recherche sur l'Asie du Sud, 22 April 2016), https://journals.openedition.org/samaj/4111, accessed 1 April 2021.
28   Imtiaz Ahmed, Paper, 'Changing Global Dynamics: Bangladesh Foreign Policy,' Ed. AKM Abdur Rahman, Dhaka, Bangladesh International Institute of International & Strategic Studies, 2018, p. 7.
29   PTI, 'Citizenship (Amendment) Bill: Bangladesh Faults India,' *The Hindu*, 11 December 2019), https://www.thehindu.com/news/national/bangladesh-faults-india-on-cab/article30279413.ece, accessed 1 April 2021.
30   'Cow Slaughter in India,' *Indian Journal of Law and Public Policy*, 21 March 2019, https://ijlpp.com/cow-slaughter-in-india/, accessed 1 April 2021.
31   Joyeeta Bhattacharjee, 'Locking Horns at the Border,' *The Indian Express*, 20 July 2020, https://indianexpress.com/article/opinion/columns/india-bangladesh-cattle-smuggling-border-west-bengal-6515253/, accessed 1 April 2021.
32   PTI, 'Exim Bank Provides USD 500 Mn Credit to Bangladesh for Defence Procurement,' *The Economic Times*, 6 December 2019, https://economictimes.indiatimes.com/news/defence/exim-bank-provides-usd-500-mn-credit-to-bangladesh-for-defence-procurement/articleshow/72401580.cms?from=mdr, accessed 1 April 2021.
33   Wang Yamei, 'Huawei All Set for 5G Technical Support in Bangladesh,' *Xinhua*, 9 November 2019, http://www.xinhuanet.com/english/2019-11/09/c_138541799.htm, accessed 1 April 2021.
34   Pinak Ranjan Chakravarty, 'Bangladesh and the Art of Balancing,' *New Indian Express*, 26 September 2019, https://www.newindianexpress.com/opinions/2019/sep/26/bangladesh-and-the-art-of balancing-2039192.amp, accessed 1 April 2021.

35 Soumya Bhowmick and Syed Mafiz Kamal, 'India–Bangladesh Partnership in Post-Pandemic Economic Recovery,' Observer Researcher Foundation (ORF), 5 October 2020, https://www.orfonline.org/research/india-bangladesh-partnership-in-post-pandemic-economic-recovery-2/, accessed 1 April 2021.

Chapter 7: Myanmar

1 The prime minister of the Tibetan government in exile based in India was also invited.
2 More recently in 2021, with a fresh ceasefire between the two armies, there are signs of a thaw in relations that had taken for the worse since then over multiple terrorist attacks against Indian military targets.
3 Bay of Bengal Initiative for Multi-Sectoral Technical and Economic Cooperation
4 'India's Duty Free Tariff Preference for LDCs: A Business Guide,' https://www.intracen.org/uploadedFiles/intracenorg/IndiaDutyFreeTariff.pdf, accessed 13 April 2021.
5 Short for the Ayeyawady-Chao Phraya-Mekong Economic Cooperation Strategy.
6 For example: MoS Murlidharan, MEA: Statements: Speeches & Statements. (n.d.), retrieved 23 December 2020, https://mea.gov.in/Speeches-Statements.htm?dtl%2F33258%2FSpeech_by_Minister_of_State_for_External_Affairs_on_Building_Bridges_for_Constructive_Development_at_the_6th_IndiaCLMV_Cambodia_Lao_PDR_Myanmar_and_Vietnam, accessed 13 April 2021.
7 The Ayeyawady, Salween, Mekong and Chao Phraya, amongst others.
8 Election results in 1990 won by the NLD were annulled.
9 Partly because India is not a traditional 'donor,' nor a participant in donor coordination meetings on the grounds that India's is not a donor relationship but a development partnership.
10 'Supporting the Transition: Understanding Aid to Myanmar since 2011,' The Asia Foundation, February 2018, https://asiafoundation.org/wp-content/uploads/2018/03/Supporting-the-Transition-Understanding-Aid-to-Myanmar-since-2011_ENG.pdf. Where 2 Indian projects worth approx. $ 750 million receive only passing mention, assessed 13 April 2021.
11 'Visit of Chief of Army Staff and Foreign Secretary to Myanmar,' https://mea.gov.in/pressreleases.htm?dtl%2F33092%2F, accessed 13 April 2021.
12 In tandem with the initial increase in exports to the ASEAN with the coming into force of the India–ASEAN Free Trade Agreements in Goods, Services and Investments.
13 Notably the Shwe gas field and the gas pipeline to Yunnan in which OVL (ONGC Videsh Limited) and GAIL have stakes.
14 It is uncertain if this has been fulfilled in the post-coup context.

202 ▪ Politics and Geopolitics

15 Such as construction materials, automobiles and auto parts, textile fibres and fabrics, agricultural machinery and inputs, petroleum and petroleum products, etc. and also ways to stabilize and diversify exports of beans and pulses and agricultural products from Myanmar.
16 For a more detailed examination of the status and role of the North-east in India's Look and Act East policies, please refer to Gautam Mukhopadhaya, 'North East, Act East', Occasional Publication 80, India International Centre, 2017.
17 Ministry of External Affairs, joint statement during State Visit of the President of Myanmar to India, February 2020, https://mea.gov.in/bilateraldocuments.htm?dtl/32435IndiaMyanmar+Joint+Statement+during+the+State+Visit+of+the+President+of+Myanmar+to+India+February+2629+2020 (para 6), accessed 13 April 2021.
18 Ministry of External Affairs, joint statement during State Visit of the President of Myanmar to India, August 2016, https://www.mea.gov.in/bilateraldocuments.htm?dtl/27343/India+Myanmar+Joint+Statement+during+the+visit+of+the+President+of+Myanmar+to+India+29+August+2016 (para 12), accessed 13 April 2021.
19 Land Ports Authority of India: ICP Moreh, http://lpai.gov.in/content/innerpage/icp-moreh.php, accessed 13 April 2021.
20 For example, the Ministry of External Affairs leads connectivity projects in Myanmar as a diplomatic, good will, development and strategic tool of its Look East, Neighborhood First and Act East policies. The Inner Line Permit, Protected Area Permit, the ICP, the Assam Rifles, Intelligence Bureau and the Armed Forces Special Powers Act, and even the National Executive Committee, fall under the Ministry of Home Affairs. Trade decisions lie with the Ministry of Commerce with no presence in the North-east. Customs and banking come under different branches in the Ministry of Finance. Roads, railways, inland waterways, ports and shipping fall under their respective line ministries. Development bodies report to different regional bodies and central ministries with the NITI Aayog providing advice. The Ministry of Development of North Eastern Region is expected to play a coordinating, funding and developmental role, but it has no authority coordinating overall policy.
21 Meticulously researched and compiled by Col. Jaideep Chanda, 'Irrawaddy Initiatives: Reviewing India's Engagement with Myanmar,' Research Paper, Vivekanada International Foundation.
22 Muse, Chinshehaw in the Kokang Autonomous Region and Kampetki in Kachin state.
23 Col. Jaideep Chanda, 'Irrawaddy Initiatives: Reviewing India's Engagement with Myanmar,' Research Paper, Vivekanada International Foundation.
24 'Commerce and Conflict: Navigating Myanmar's China Relationship,' Crisis Group, 2 April 2020, https://www.crisisgroup.org/asia/south-east-

asia/myanmar/305-commerce-and-conflict-navigating-myanmars-china-relationship, accessed 13 April 2021.

Chapter 8: Sri Lanka

1. Ranga Sirilal and Serajul Quadir, 'Abe Becomes First Japanese PM to Visit Sri Lanka in 24 Years,' Reuters, Thomson Reuters, 7 September 2014, https://in.reuters.com/article/us-southasia-japan/abe-becomes-first-japanese-pm-to-visit-sri-lanka-in-24-years-idUSKBN0H20HW20140907, accessed 14 April 2021.
2. Vijay Sakhuja, 'Chinese Submarines in Sri Lanka Unnerve India: Next Stop Pakistan?' *China Brief*, Vol. 15, no. 11, The Jamestown Foundation, 29 May 2015, https://jamestown.org/program/chinese-submarines-in-sri-lanka-unnerve-india-next-stop-pakistan/, accessed 14 April 2021.
3. Sachin Parashar/TNN, 'Chinese Submarine Docking in Lanka "inimical" to India's Interests: Govt,' *The Times of India*, https://timesofindia.indiatimes.com/india/Chinese-submarine-docking-in-Lanka-inimical-to-Indias-interests-Govt/articleshow/45025487.cms, accessed 14 April 2021.
4. M. Srinivasan, 'Fishermen on Death Row Freed,' *The Hindu*, 14 April 2016, https://www.thehindu.com/news/national/sri-lanka-releases-indian-fishermen/article6614883.ece, accessed 14 April 2021.
5. N. Sathiya Moorthy, 'India, Sri Lanka and the UNHRC,' Observer Research Foundation (ORF), 8 March 2012, https://www.orfonline.org/research/india-sri-lanka-and-the-unhrc/, accessed 14 April 2021.
6. PTI, 'India Votes for Resolution against Sri Lanka,' *The Hindu*, 20 July 2016, https://www.thehindu.com/news/international/india-votes-for-resolution-against-sri-lanka/article3150059.ece, accessed 14 April 2021.
7. 'Explanation of Vote at the UNHRC on Promotion, Reconciliation and Accountability in Sri Lanka,' Ministry of External Affairs, Government of India, 22 March 2012, https://www.mea.gov.in/Speeches-Statements.htm?dtl/19097/Explanation+of+vote+at+the+UNHRC+on+PromotionReconciliation+ and+Accountability+in+Sri+Lanka, accessed 14 April 2021.
8. PTI, 'UNHRC Adopts US-sponsored Resolution against Lanka,' *The Hindu BusinessLine*, 12 March 2018, https://www.thehindubusinessline.com/news/unhrc-adopts-us-sponsored-resolution-against-lanka/article20593540.ece1, accessed 14 April 2021.
9. Indrani Bagchi/TNN, 'India Abstains on Human Rights Vote on Sri Lanka, Rescues Foreign Policy,' *The Times of India*, 27 March 2014, https://timesofindia.indiatimes.com/world/south-asia/India-abstains-on-human-rights-vote-on-Sri-Lanka-rescues-foreign-policy/articleshow/32793377.cms, accessed 14 April 2021.
10. Debasish Roy Chowdhury, 'Sri Lanka Should Thank China, Not Attack It,

204 ▪ Politics and Geopolitics

Ex-president Rajapaksa Says,' 12 March 2015, *South China Morning Post*, https://www.scmp.com/news/asia/diplomacy/article/1735379/sri-lanka-should-thank-china-not-attack-it-ex-president, accessed 14 April 2021.

11 https://twitter.com/pmoindia/status/576323247697838080, accessed 14 April 2021.

12 Suhasini Haider and Amit Baruah, 'Release of Rajiv Gandhi Convicts: We Would've Had Different Line, Says Mahinda Rajapaksa,' *The Hindu*, 12 September 2018, https://www.thehindu.com/opinion/interview/for-the-security-of-india-stability-in-sri-lanka-is-very-important/article24929236.ece, accessed 14 April 2021.

13 Shivshankar Menon, *Choices: Inside the Making of Indian Foreign Policy*, Penguin Random House India, 15 November 2016 (loc 1774).

14 https://twitter.com/ani/status/862944575228264448, accessed 14 April 2021.

15 Suhasini Haider and Amit Baruah, 'Release of Rajiv Gandhi Convicts: We Would've Had Different Line, says Mahinda Rajapaksa,' *The Hindu*, 12 September 2018, https://www.thehindu.com/opinion/interview/for-the-security-of-india-stability-in-sri-lanka-is-very-important/article24929236.ece, accessed 14 April 2021.

16 Taylor Dibbert, 'Devolution the Only Solution: C.V. Wigneswaran on Tamil Ties with the Sri Lankan State,' *The Wire*, 11 August 2016, https://thewire.in/south-asia/devolution-the-only-solution-northern-provinces-vigneswaran-on-tamil-ties-with-the-sri-lankan-state, accessed 14 April 2021.

17 N. Manohoran, 'Pangs of Proximity,' *The Deccan Herald*, 3 November 2018, https://www.deccanherald.com/opinion/main-article/workers-woes-in-smart-cities-970813.html, accessed 14 April 2021.

18 Pushkar Banakar, 'Realise Ambitions of Tamils, Implement 13th Amendment Fully: PM Modi Tells Sri Lankan Counterpart,' *The New Indian Express*, 27 September 2020, https://www.newindianexpress.com/thesundaystandard/2020/sep/27/realise-ambitions-of-tamils-implement-13th-amendment-fully-pm-modi-tells-sri-lankan-counterpart-2202336.html, accessed 14 April 2021.

19 Suhasini Haider and Amit Baruah, 'Release of Rajiv Gandhi Convicts: We Would've Had Different Line, says Mahinda Rajapaksa,' *The Hindu*, 12 September 2018, https://www.thehindu.com/opinion/interview/for-the-security-of-india-stability-in-sri-lanka-is-very-important/article24929236.ece, accessed 14 April 2021.

20 'Closely Following Developments in Sri Lanka, Hope Democratic Values Will Be Respected, Says India,' *The Hindustan Times*, 28 October 2018, https://www.hindustantimes.com/india-news/hope-democratic-values-respected-says-india-on-sri-lanka-political-crisis/story-dkN5P0B6DWLFRrzrhj8OGP.html, accessed 14 April 2021.

21 'Press Release on India's Reaction over Evolving Situation in Maldives after Order of the Supreme Court of Maldives,' Ministry of External Affairs, https://

www.mea.gov.in/press-releases.htm?dtl/29409/Press_Release_on_Indias__over_evolving_situation_in_Maldives_after_order_of_the_Supreme_Court_of_Maldives, accessed 14 April 2021.
22 As told to the author by officials involved in the developments.
23 In December 2016, an agreement between Sri Lanka Ports Authority (SLPA) and CMPHCL stated that the government would sell 80 per cent shares of Hambantota port on a 99-year lease to the Chinese company.
24 M. Srinivasan, 'Sri Lanka in Talks to Secure $500 mn in Chinese Loans,' 13 October 2020, https://www.thehindu.com/news/international/sri-lanka-in-talks-to-secure-500-mn-in-chinese-loans/article32837581.ece, accessed 14 April 2021.

Chapter 9: The Maldives

1 High Commission of India, Male, 'India-Maldives Bilateral Relations,' Government of India, https://hci.gov.in/male/?pdf1185?000, accessed 2 April 2021.
2 High Commission of India, Male, 'India-Maldives Bilateral Relations,' Government of India, https://hci.gov.in/male/?pdf1185?000, accessed 2 April 2021.
3 Shashi Tharoor, *Pax Indica India and the World of the 21st Century*, Allen Lane, India, 2012, p.108.
4 Kallol Bhattacherjee, 'India Is the Closest Friend of the Maldives: President Solih,' *The Hindu*, 16 December 2018.
5 'Maldives Report Rejects Nasheed Coup Claims,' *BBC News*, 30 August 2012, https://www.bbc.com/news/world-asia-19417339, accessed 2 April 2021.
6 Ministry of Commerce, Republic of China, 'China and Maldives Sign the Free Trade Agreement, 8 December 2017, http://english.mofcom.gov.cn/article/newsrelease/significantnews/201712/20171202683630.shtml, accessed 2 April 2021.
7 Anbarasan Ethirajan, 'Maldives-China Deal "One-Sided", Says Ex-President Nasheed,' *BBC News*, 19 November 2001, https://www.bbc.com/news/world-asia-46269504, accessed 2 April 2021.
8 Rajiv Bhatia, 'For Maldives, It Is "China First" Now,' The Gateway House, 13 December 2017, https://www.gatewayhouse.in/maldives-china-first/, accessed 2 April 2021.
9 Rajiv Bhatia, 'For Maldives, It Is "China First" Now,' The Gateway House, 13 December 2017, https://www.gatewayhouse.in/maldives-china-first/, accessed 2 April 2021.
10 Yuji Kuronuma, 'China has India Surrounded in their New Game,' *Nikkei Asia*, 19 December 2017, https://asia.nikkei.com/Spotlight/Asia-Insight/China-has-India-surrounded-in-their-new-Great-Game2, accessed 2 April 2021.
11 Shiv Shankar Menon, 'It Is Natural that Smaller Neighbours like Lanka Will

Play India against China, Interview, *The Wire*, 29 December 2016, https://thewire.in/diplomacy/india-lanka-china-menon-ltte, accessed 2 April 2021.

12 Nayanima Basu, 'Relationship with India Outstanding, China Generous: Maldives FM Abdulla Shahid', *The Print*, 18 January 2020, https://theprint.in/diplomacy/relationship-with-india-Outstanding-china-is-generous-maldives-fm-abdulla-shahid/351444/, accessed 2 April 2021.

13 Press Trust India (PTI), 'India Concerned over Nasheed Jail Term in Maldives', *The Hindu*, 14 March 2015, https://www.thehindu.com/news/national/13year-imprisonment-for-mohamed-nasheed-in-maldives-india-expresses-concern/article6993366.ece, accessed 2 April 2021.

14 Narayan Lakshman, 'We Have Rock-Solid Ties, Says Maldivian Minister', *The Hindu*, 16 May 2018.

15 High Commission of India, Male, Press Release on Budgetary Support, 21 September 2020, https://hci.gov.in/male/?11516?000, accessed 2 April 2021.

16 Abdulla Shahid, Statement by His Excellency: Minister of Foreign Affairs at the General Debate of the 75th Session of the United Nations General Assembly, September 2020, https://estatements.unmeetings.org/estatements/10.0010/20200929/uvy65GbbAgSh/12mvW5Hvq1f6_en.pdf, accessed 2 April 2021.

17 PTI, 'India and Maldives Will Continue to Support Each Other: Modi', *The Hindu*, 21 September 2020, https://www.thehindu.com/news/national/india-and-maldives-will-continue-to-support-each-other-modi/article32657322.ece, accessed 2 April 2021.

18 'India Funds $500m Maldives Project to Counter China's Influence', *Aljazeera News*, 14 August 2020, https://www.aljazeera.com/news/2020/8/14/india-funds-500m-maldives-project-to-counter-chinas-influence, accessed 2 April 2021.

19 Ministry of External Affairs, Remarks by External Affairs Minister at the Joint Conference with Minister of Foreign Affairs of Maldives in Male, 20 February 2021.

20 Ministry of External Affairs, Joint Press Statement on Official Visit of External Affairs Minister of India to the Maldives, 21 February 2021.

21 Meera Srinivasan, 'Maldives Parliament Debates Defence Deal with India', *The Hindu*, 22 February 2021.

LIST OF CONTRIBUTORS

Indrani Bagchi is Diplomatic Editor of *The Times of India*.

Gautam Bambawale is a former Indian Ambassador to China.

Pinak Ranjan Chakravarty is a former Indian High Commissioner to Bangladesh.

V.P. Haran is a former Indian Ambassador to Bhutan.

N. Sathiya Moorthy is Distinguished Fellow and Head, Chennai Initiative, Observer Research Foundation, ORF.

Gautam Mukhopadhaya is a former Indian Ambassador to Myanmar.

Aparna Pande is Director of the Initiative on the Future of India and South Asia at the Hudson Institute, Washington D.C.

Jayant Prasad is a former Indian Ambassador to Afghanistan.

Manjeev Singh Puri is a former Indian Ambassador to Nepal.

Vinitha Revi (PhD) is a Chennai-based independent researcher.

INDEX

5G trials, 51
1816 Treaty of Sugauli, 68
1967 India-Myanmar Boundary
 Agreement, 130
1999 Kargil War, 22
2011 Strategic Partnership
 Agreement, 1

Acquisition and Cross-
 Servicing Agreement, 186
Act East Policy, 102, 124
Addu City, 173, 182
Adhaalath Party, 187
Advantage Assam Global
 Investor's Summit, 83
Afghan National Defense and
 Security Forces (ANDSF),
 5, 6, 16
Afghan policy, 2
Afghan State, 12, 14, 19
Aid to Nepal, 61
Akhaura-Agartala rail, 113
Aksai Chin, 48

Al-Qaeda (AQ), 2, 13, 14, 17
al-Zawahiri, Ayman, 14
anti-Pakistan sentiment, 22
articulation in Hindi, 73
Arun-III, 61
Asian Century, 49
Asian tsunami, 181
Assam, 83, 118, 144
Atmanirbhar Bharat, 52
Auto ancillary manufacturers,
 51
Awami League (AL), 102, 103,
 104, 106, 117
Azhar, Masood, 45

balance of power, xix
Banerjee, Mamata, 107
Bangladesh Nationalist Party
 (BNP), 102, 103, 104, 106,
 107, 117, 123
Bangladesh's Islamic identity, 102
Basic Exchange and
 Cooperation, 54

Batang La, 86
Bay of Bengal identity, xix
Bay of Bengal Initiative for Multi-Sectoral Technical and Economic Cooperation (BIMSTEC), xix, 58, 59, 64, 92, 102, 121, 124, 149
Belt and Road Initiative (BRI), ix, xiii, xviii, xx, 9, 43, 44, 45, 71, 122, 145, 146, 147, 148
Bengali nationalism, 102
Bhairahawa, 71
Bharatiya Janata Party, ix, 1, 26, 32, 57, 156, 157
Bhutan, ix, xi, xix, 46, 79, 80, 81, 82, 83, 84, 85, 86, 87, 88, 89, 90, 91, 92, 93, 94, 95, 96, 97, 98, 99, 100, 102, 122, 127, 170
Bhutto, Benazir, 22
'big brother attitude', 105
bilateral engagement, x, xi, xii, xxii, 82, 102, 125
Bilateral grid connectivity, 114
bin Laden, Osama, 14, 17
Biratnagar, 62
Birgunj, 62
Bollywood, 73
Border Haats, 111
border killings, 118
BRICS-BIMSTEC, 132
Buddhism, 129, 156, 160

Caretaker Government, 105
cattle smuggling, 120
Chabahar Port, 8
China–Pakistan Economic Corridor (CPEC), xvi, 9, 44, 148
China policy, xxi
Chiphen Rigpel, 97
Christian missionaries, 74
Chumar, 38, 42, 151
Citizenship Amendment Act (CAA), 117, 118
Climate-smart agricultural technologies, 125
Cold War, 126, 178
Colombage, Jayanath, 165
Consulate General of Bhutan, 83
Coronavirus pandemic, 75
creation of Bangladesh, 21, 24
currency swap, 82
cyberspace, 105

Da'esh, 5, 13, 14, 15, 16
Dantak, 84
Darbuk-Shyok-Daulat Beg Oldie Road, xiii
Daudzai, Umer, 7
'decoupling', xiii
de-escalation process, xi
disengagement process, xi
Doha Agreement, 11, 12, 13, 16

Doka La, 46, 85, 86
Doklam crisis, xi, 80
Doval, Ajit, 128, 132, 152, 165
Druk Green Power Corporation, 93, 94
Druk Research and Education Network, 83

Easter terror attacks, 159
Economic Stimulus Plan, 88
E-library, 81
Ethnic Armed Organizations (EAOs), 128, 132, 133, 145

Farakka Barrage, 115
Financial Action Task Force, 32, 45
Foreign Minister Shah Mehmood Qureshi, 31

Galwan Valley, xii
Gandhi, Rajiv, 39, 40, 50, 161
Ganges Water Sharing Treaty, 105
Ghani, Ashraf, 1
Global Environment Facility (GEF), 85, 87
global lockdown, 75
Golden Jubilee Railway Line, 95
Greater Male Connectivity Project (GMCP), 182
Ground Earth Station, 82

Gyemochen, 86

Hambantota port, 161, 163
Haqqani, xv, 4, 5, 6, 14, 36
Haqqani, Sirajuddin, 5
Harakat-ul Jihad Islami, 104
Hasina, Sheikh, 105, 106, 107, 108, 122
Hekmatyar, Gulbuddin, 19
High Impact Community Development Projects (HICDP), 182
Himalayan borders, xx
Hinduism, 57
Hindu Rashtra, 67
Hindustan Antibiotics Limited, 52
Hizb-e-Islami, 18, 19, 20
Hizbul Mujahideen terrorists, 31
Huawei, 51, 122
Hulhumale, 183
Hydroelectric power, 61

illegal migration, 117
India-Afghanistan air-freight corridor, 8
India-Maldives Cricket Friendship Series, 183
India-Myanmar-Thailand Trilateral Highway, 121
Indian Army, 38, 46, 49, 57, 72, 76, 78, 84, 128

Indian Council for Research on International Economic Relations (ICRIER), 90
Indian Drugs and Pharmaceuticals Limited, 52
India-Nepal Treaty of Peace and Friendship, 57
Indian Military Training Team (IMTRAT), 84
Indian Ocean Naval Symposium, 113
Indian Ocean Region (IOR), x, xv, xvii, xviii, xxi, 156, 174, 179, 186
Indian Railways, 62, 65
Indian Tamils, 156, 158
'India Out', 188
India–Pakistan dyad, xvii
India's surgical strike, 25
Indo-Bhutan Friendship Treaty, 80
Indo-Pacific maritime geography, xiii
Infrastructure Leasing & Financial Services (IL&FS), 66
Instrument of Accession, 23
Integrated Check Post (ICP), 61, 62, 142, 144
Intel sharing, 54
International Security Assistance Force (ISAF), 5, 6, 14, 15

Inter-Services Intelligence (ISI), 4, 5, 15
Islamic Emirate of Afghanistan, 7, 17
Islamization, 102, 104

Jaffna, 156, 157, 158
Jaish-e-Mohammed (JeM), 25, 31
Jamaat-ul-Mujahideen, 104
Jampheri ridge, 86, 87
Jatiyo Party, 102
Jayanagar-Janakpur stretch, 62
Jinping, Xi, xi, 40, 41, 72, 147, 151, 174
Joe Biden administration, 55
Joint Coordinated Patrols, 113
Jumhooree Party, 187

Kailash Manasarovar, 41, 68
Kaladan Corridor, 121
Kalapani, 68
Karakoram Pass, xiii
Kartarpur Corridor, 33
Karzai, Hamid, 1
Kashmir, xi, 11, 17, 21, 23, 24, 25, 26, 27, 29, 31, 32, 35, 36, 44, 45, 48
'Kashmir first' policy, 36
Kataiya-Kusaha, 61
Keqiang, Li, 43
Kholongchhu hydro project, 81

Khurshid, Salman, 154
Koirala era, 69
Kosi, 65
Krishna, S.M., 153
K. Sinha, Yash, 152
Kulhudhuffushi, 184
Kumaratunga, Chandrika, 155
Kyaukpyu Deep Sea Port, 147

Lahore Declaration of 1999, 24
Land Boundary Agreement (LBA), 108
Lashkar-e-Taiba, 15, 17
Leh, xiii
Lessons Learnt and Reconciliation Commission, 153
Liberation Tigers of Tamil Eelam (LTTE), 153, 157, 160
Limpiyadhura, 68, 76
Line of Actual Control (LAC), xi, xii, xx, xxi
Line of Control (LoC), xi, 29
Lipulekh, 68
Lumbini, 71

Madhesis, 63, 66
Maharaja of Kashmir, Hari Singh, 23, 25
Maitree Express, 105
Make in India, 53
Maldivian Democratic Party (MDP), 170, 175, 182, 187, 188
Mangdechhu project, 93
Maoist insurgency, 73, 74
Maritime Boundary dispute, 107, 108
Menon, Shivshankar, 153, 157, 165
Millennium Challenge Corporation, 75
Modi government, vii, ix, xxii, 29, 31, 32, 34, 35, 131, 132, 140, 143, 155, 156, 168
Modi, Narendra, vii, ix, x, xi, xix, xxii, 1, 2, 3, 7, 10, 18, 19, 22, 25, 26, 27, 28, 29, 30, 31, 32, 33, 34, 35, 39, 40, 41, 42, 43, 47, 57, 58, 59, 63, 64, 65, 79, 80, 81, 82, 83, 92, 93, 100, 101, 108, 124, 126, 127, 128, 129, 131, 132, 134, 140, 141, 143, 151, 152, 153, 155, 156, 158, 159, 160, 168, 169, 170, 172, 173, 176, 178, 179, 180, 181, 183, 185
Muhammad Ershad, Gen. Hussain, 103
Mujibur Rehman, Sheikh, 102, 103, 124
Mukherjee, Pranab, 59, 82, 105
Musa Qala, 15
Muzaffarpur-Dhalkebar, 61

MW Budhi Gandaki hydro
  project, 66
Nabil, Rahmatullah, 4
Narayanan, M.K., 157
National Knowledge Network,
  83, 109, 135
National League for
  Democracy (NLD), 126, 132,
  137, 146
National Police Academy, 65
National Register of Citizens
  (NRC), 118
National Security Advisor
  (NSA), 27
National Socialist Council
  of Nagaland-Khaplang
  (NSCN-K), 128
Nationwide Ceasefire
  Agreement, 128
Nay Pyi Taw, 147, 148
Nehru, Jawaharlal, 22, 79, 95
'Neighbourhood First'
  initiative, ix
Nepal Army, 72
Nepal–China ties, 72
Nepal Communist Party
  (NCP), 75, 76, 77
Nepalese Gorkhas, 78
'new' South Asia, xxi
Nijgadh, 66
North Atlantic Treaty
  Organization, 5

North China Sea Fleet, 151
nuclear tests, 126
Nuwara Eliya, 158

One Belt, One Road, 43, 44
open border, 56, 57
Operation Azm, 4
Operation Cactus, 181
Oversight Mechanism, 60

Padmasambhava, 98
Pahari community, 75
Paharis, 66
Pakistani Army, 3, 4, 5, 6, 17,
  103
Pakistani military-intelligence
  establishment, 37
Pakistan policy, xxi
Pancheshwar Multipurpose
  Project, 65
Pangda village, 85
Pangong Tso, xi
Pashupatinath Temple, 64
Pathankot terrorist attack, 25
People's Liberation Army
  (PLA), 38, 42, 46, 49, 52, 85,
  86, 123
People's Republic of
  Bangladesh, 102
People's Republic of China
  (PRC), xvii, 39
Permanent Court of
  Arbitration (PCA), 107, 108

pharmaceutical industry, 52
Pokhara, 71
Pompeo, Mike, 186
pre-COVID, 110
Pulwama, 25, 31, 32, 35, 64

Qaumi Madrassa, 104
Quadrilateral Security
  Dialogue, xiv
Quetta Shura, 4, 13

Rahman, Gen. Ziaur,, 103
Rajapaksa, Gotabaya, 152, 157
Rajapaksa, Mahinda, 151, 152,
  155, 157, 160, 161, 166
Rauf Aliza, Abdul, 14
Rawalpindi, 3
Raxaul-Parwanipur, 61
Red Lines, 68
Renewable energy, 99
Republic of India, 102
Resolute Support Mission, 5
'Responsibility to Protect'
  (R2P), 178
reverse migration, 118
Rinpoche, Guru, 98
Rohingya crisis, 133
Rohingya refugees, 109, 114,
  118
Rooppur nuclear power plant,
  111
Royal Bhutan Army, 46, 84
RuPay card, 135

SAARC Motor Vehicle
  Agreement, 91
Sabroom, 109, 114
Sakteng wildlife sanctuary, 85,
  87
SATCOM, 82
scorched-earth response, 134
Shah Massoud, Ahmad, 17
Shanghai Cooperation
  Organization (SCO), 27
Sheikh Hasina, 102, 103, 104,
  105, 106, 124
Shouhardya, 105
Shura, 2, 4, 13
Siachen, 21, 24
Siliguri corridor, 84, 86
Simla Agreement, 24
Sinche La, 85
Singh, Harbhajan, 183
Singh Manmohan, 22, 26, 40,
  93, 95, 107, 154, 169, 172,
  173
Singh, Manmohan, 22, 26, 40,
  93, 95, 107, 169, 172, 173
Singh, Vijay, 157
Singh, Yuvraj, 183
Sinha, Dilip, 154
Sinhala nationalism, 157, 160
Sino-Indian Contestation, xi
Sino-Indian ties, xi
Sir Creek, 21
Sirisena, Maithripala, 155, 158,
  159, 161, 162, 163

social media, 81, 134
Sonowal, Sarbananda, 83
South Asian Association for Regional Cooperation (SAARC), ix, xvii, xix, 27, 58, 63, 81, 91, 127, 153, 173
South Asian Free Trade Area, 110
South Asian geography, xiv
State identity in South Asia, xv
Status of Forces Agreement, 187
Sunkosh storage dam, 94
Swaraj, Sushma, 7, 27

Tamil extremism, 157
Tamil Nadu, 153, 157, 160, 166
Tamil Progressive Alliance, 158
Tatmadaw, 126, 131, 132, 133, 137, 145, 148, 149
Tehreek-e-Taliban Pakistan, 4
Terai region, 63
terrain mapping, 123
Tharoor, Shashi, 170
The Nehru-Wangchuck Cultural Centre, 98
the Quad, xiv, 45, 46, 53, 54, 167
Thilamale Bridge, 182, 183
Thoothukudi, 184
TikTok, 50
Tobgay, Tshering, 81, 83
Torsa Nala, 85, 86

Treaty of Perpetual Peace and Friendship, 79
Tshering, Dr Lotay, 83, 88

Unified Marxist Leninist (UML), 69, 75, 76, 77
Union Solidarity and Development Party (USDP), 131, 137, 146
Uri terror attack, 25
Uthuru Thila Falhu, 185

Vajpayee, Atal Bihari, 22, 40, 82, 105
Varthaman, Abhinandan, 31
Vigneswaran, C.V., 159
V. Shringla, Harsh, 186

War of Liberation, 102, 105, 118
Weeratunga, Lalith, 157
Wickremesinghe, Ranil, 156
Wilayat Khorasan, 14, 15
Wuhan, 47, 48

Yameen, Abdulla, 161, 169, 170, 172, 173, 174, 175, 176, 177, 178, 179, 186, 187, 188

Zaranj-Delaram Road, 8
Zia, Khaleda, 104, 106